Deregulation and the Future of Intercity Passenger Travel

MIT Press Series on the Regulation of Economic Activity

General Editor
Richard Schmalensee, MIT Sloan School of Management

1 *Freight Transport Regulation*, Ann F. Friedlaender and Richard H. Spady, 1981
2 *The SEC and the Public Interest*, Susan M. Phillips and J. Richard Zecher, 1981
3 *The Economics and Politics of Oil Price Regulation*, Joseph P. Kalt, 1981
4 *Studies in Public Regulation*, Gary Fromm, editor, 1981
5 *Incentives for Environmental Protection*, Thomas C. Schelling, editor, 1983
6 *United States Oil Pipeline Markets: Structure, Pricing, and Public Policy*, John A. Hansen, 1983
7 *Folded, Spindled, and Mutilated: Economic Analysis and* U.S. *v.* IBM, Franklin M. Fisher, John J. McGowan, and Joen E. Greenwood, 1983
8 *Targeting Economic Incentives for Environmental Protection*, Albert L. Nichols, 1984
9 *Deregulation and the New Airline Entrepreneurs*, John R. Meyer and Clinton V. Oster, Jr., with Marni Clippinger, Andrew McKey, Don H. Pickrell, John S. Strong, and C. Kurt Zorn, 1984
10 *Deregulating the Airlines*, Elizabeth E. Bailey, David R. Graham, and Daniel P. Kaplan, 1985
11 *The Gathering Crisis in Federal Deposit Insurance*, Edward J. Kane, 1985
12 *Perspectives on Safe and Sound Banking: Past, Present, and Future*, George J. Benston, Robert A. Eisenbeis, Paul M. Horvitz, Edward J. Kane, and George G. Kaufman, 1986
13 *The Economics of Public Utility Regulation*, Michael A. Crew and Paul R. Kleindorfer, 1987
14 *Public Regulation: New Perspectives on Institutions and Policies*, Elizabeth E. Bailey, editor, 1987
15 *Deregulation and the Future of Intercity Passenger Travel*, John R. Meyer and Clinton V. Oster, Jr., with John S. Strong, José A. Gómez-Ibáñez, Don H. Pickrell, Marni Clippinger, and Ivor P. Morgan, 1987

Deregulation and the Future of Intercity Passenger Travel

John R. Meyer and Clinton V. Oster, Jr.

with

John S. Strong, José A. Gómez-Ibáñez,
Don H. Pickrell, Marni Clippinger, Ivor P. Morgan

The MIT Press
Cambridge, Massachusetts
London, England

This book was set in Times New Roman by Asco Trade Typesetting Ltd., Hong Kong and printed and bound by Halliday Lithograph in the United States of America.

Library of Congress Cataloging-in-Publication Data

Deregulation and the future of intercity passenger travel.

(MIT Press series on the regulation of economic activity; 15)
Bibliography: p.
Includes index.
1. Aeronautics, Commercial—United States—Deregulation. 2. Transportation—United States—Passenger traffic. I. Meyer, John Robert. II. Series.
HE9803.A35D46 1987 387.7′42′0973 86-27308
ISBN 0-262-13225-7

Contents

List of Contributors

Marni Clippinger, Center for Business and Government, Harvard University

José A. Gómez-Ibáñez, Graduate School of Design and Kennedy School of Government, Harvard University

John R. Meyer, Center for Business and Government, Harvard University

Ivor P. Morgan, School of Management, Boston University

Clinton V. Oster, Jr., Transportation Research Center, Indiana University

Don H. Pickrell, Transportation Systems Center, U.S. Department of Transportation

John S. Strong, School of Business Administration, College of William and Mary

List of Tables and Figures

Tables

Figures

Series Foreword

Government regulation of economic activity in the United States has grown dramatically in this century, radically transforming government-business relations. Economic regulation of prices and conditions of service was first applied to transportation and public utilities and was later extended to energy, health care, banking, and other sectors. In the early 1970s explosive growth occurred in social regulation, focusing on workplace safety and health, environmental preservation, consumer protection, and related goals. Regulatory reform has occupied a prominent place on the agendas of recent administrations, and considerable economic deregulation has occurred, but the aims, methods, and results of many regulatory programs remain controversial.

The purpose of the MIT Press series, Regulation of Economic Activity, is to inform the ongoing debate on regulatory policy by making significant and relevant research available to both scholars and decision makers. Books in this series present new insights into individual agencies, programs, and regulated sectors, as well as the important economic, political, and administrative aspects of the regulatory process that cut across these boundaries.

In this book, their second in this series, John Meyer and Clinton Oster study airline deregulation and its consequences in the context of the fundamental and roughly contemporaneous changes that occurred in intercity bus, rail, and auto travel. They present a good deal of new evidence on the U.S. experience with airline deregulation, going well beyond its effects on domestic fares and schedules. They then build on this work to study the emerging multisector economics of deregulated intercity passenger transportation. This study should thus be of interest to anyone concerned with transportation and transportation policy broadly defined, as well as to students of the airlines or of economic regulation.

Richard Schmalensee

Preface

In the spring of 1979 the Harvard Airline Deregulation Study, under the auspices of the Harvard Faculty Project on Regulation, began a multiyear study of the effects of airline deregulation. What was originally intended as a three- or four-year study was extended to nearly eight years as unanticipated events such as dramatic fuel price increases, back-to-back recessions, and the PATCO strike complicated and extended the airlines' adjustment to deregulation. During these years, too, there were other distractions from the research: at least three of the study team were married (to others outside the project) and four children were born to members of the group.

The first report of this effort, *Airline Deregulation: The Early Experience*[1], was published in 1981 and examined the airline industry's initial adaptations to deregulation. The second report, *Deregulation and the New Airline Entrepreneurs*,[2] published in 1984, focused on one of the major postderegulation trends, the rapid growth of entrepreneurial low-cost jet carriers and commuter airlines and their effects on the airline industry. As we continued our work, unexpected events again intervened with our original plan as it became clear that airline deregulation marked the beginning of a trend of extending more competition throughout the intercity passenger transportation market. This book, the project's third and final report, examines both the airline deregulation experience and the broader topic of the likely implications of bringing the entire intercity passenger transportation industry more in line with free-market principles.

This study, and indeed the entire eight-year effort, owes considerable debt to several institutions and many individuals. The Harvard Business School's Division of Research and the United Parcel Service Foundation provided both the initial support that launched the effort in 1979 and subsequent funding as well. The John A. Olin Foundation provided funds needed to undertake a major expansion of the scope of the study. The John F. Kennedy School of Government and the Center for Business and Government at Harvard provided physical homes for the study team as well as the administrative and logistical support that has been essential for our efforts. The Transportation Research Center at Indiana University has also provided support for the later stages of this study. The U.S. Department of Transportation provided funding for three research projects that have made important contributions to this book: one on the effects on service levels of the Bus Regulatory Reform Act of 1982, a second study on the impacts of airline deregulation on airline employment levels, and a third study of commuter airline marketing alliances.

This study has benefited from many capable research assistants, four of whom deserve special mention. Ben Berman made major contributions to both the productivity analysis in chapter 6 and the cost analysis in appendix A, Patty Muldowney contributed to the cost analysis in appendix A and to the simulations of chapter 11, Alan Grayson contributed to the demand analysis in appendix B, and Jane Cetlin contributed to the analysis of the terms of employment in chapter 6.

We owe special debts to Eleanor Lintner and Jane Wilson, who have managed with unfailing grace and good humor to keep track of innumerable drafts and have kept the production of the manuscript running smoothly despite our best efforts to create confusion. They have also checked sources, corrected spelling and grammar, and otherwise helped with editing. Without their help, the project would never have been completed. Perhaps, too, they feel a greater sense of satisfaction and relief than the rest of us that the undertaking is now finally finished.

In a project of this scope and complexity, questions of authorship are often difficult and can rarely be resolved with precision. From its inception, the Harvard Airline Deregulation Study has been continually marked with an uncommon degree of interaction among all involved. All of the chapters have benefited from inputs of many members of the group. Indeed, it is this spirit of cooperation and open interchange that has made the entire project such an enjoyable experience. We have tried to indicate major authorship contributions by designating the chapters that were written "with" other people. Perhaps the term "with" understates their contribution since they typically both conducted much of the specific research reported in the chapters and wrote the initial drafts. Nevertheless, it is our judgment that this term most accurately reflects the high degree of cooperation and interchange that characterized this study. In the case of two chapters and the appendixes, we have recognized an even greater contribution and designated authorship as "by" particular study members, even though these portions of the book also benefited from the contributions of others. Those chapters not otherwise designated were written by ourselves with, of course, help from the others on the project.

Finally, of course, the conclusions and opinions are those of the authors and do not necessarily reflect those of individuals or institutions that have provided us with support or assistance.

John R. Meyer
Clinton V. Oster, Jr.

Deregulation and the Future of Intercity Passenger Travel

1

A Turning Point in Transportation Policy

In the 1950s economists and others studying the U.S. transportation scene began to consider the possibility that the regulatory institutions then surrounding the industry had perhaps outlived their usefulness. One such study published in 1959[1] arrived at three major and interrelated conclusions:

1. Transportation activities of all kinds were becoming increasingly competitive because of technological, demographic, and other structural changes.
2. Competition made government regulation of the industry increasingly cumbersome and outdated so that regulation impeded rational allocation of resources in the industry.
3. Regulatory insistence on a continuation of highly uneconomic cross subsidies, whereby income from profitable services was used to make up losses elsewhere, had become untenable; specifically, losses from rail passenger services imposed burdens on rail finances that were so great that the survival of important, and otherwise economically justifiable, rail freight services were endangered.

On the basis of these findings the basic policy recommendation was to deregulate much, or all, of transport operations. As summarized in the preface to that earlier study:

> Still, the basic message would be ... simply, that the major reason the transportation industries have not grown and prospered as much as most industries is that transportation has been overregulated. Furthermore, the solution to excessive regulation is not to increase but to decrease the scope of government controls. This may seem obvious, but it departs sufficiently from the emphasis of the solutions usually suggested as to be heretical.[2]

Times, and circumstances, have obviously changed. Certainly it would no longer be deemed heretical to advocate less regulation. Indeed, domestic transportation has been largely deregulated in the United States in the years since that study was published in 1959. Yesterday's heresy has become today's conventional wisdom, for better or worse.

Change, however, did not occur overnight. Fundamentally important changes really didn't happen until 1971 when intercity rail passenger service became almost totally dependent on direct public subsidies (in lieu of the private cross subsidies that preceded). A government-sponsored "for profit" corporation, Amtrak, was created to operate such services. After the fact, and perhaps not totally unexpectedly, Amtrak has proved quite unprofitable, with over 50 percent of its funding coming from government.

Established practices and patterns in intercity passenger travel were further altered, even briefly traumatized, by the energy crises of the middle and late 1970's. Gasoline became much more expensive and sometimes was simply not available due to so-called supply disruptions. Government responded with dramatic and important changes in public policy, such as the imposition of a 55 mile per hour speed limit on the nation's highways and mandating that new U.S. automobiles achieve an average of 27.5 miles per gallon on a fleet wide basis by the 1985 model year.[3] All these changes meant that American automobiles became smaller, lighter, and slower so that intercity automobile travel was at least somewhat less attractive than previously.

By far the most significant change, however, was the Airline Deregulation Act of 1978. That act clearly had an impact not only on established players within the U.S. industry but also on those outside as well. Indeed, the U.S. airline deregulation experience has been so pervasive that it is not unfair to say that the market for intercity passenger travel in the United States, and probably abroad as well, will never be the same as a consequence.

But the changes did not end there. The airline deregulation of 1978 was followed in 1980 by substantial deregulation of both trucks and railroads. Among other reasons for rail deregulation, there was no longer any need for regulation to create or protect rail monopolies so as to generate passenger subsidies, since these were now funded directly by government. For trucking, as well as railroads and many other industries, the early favorable experiences with airline deregulation provided a model of what might be achieved through deregulation. Finally, again drawing on the airline role model, in 1982 most intercity bus operations in the United States were deregulated. As the airlines and buses became increasingly free-market oriented, and the deficits for Amtrak services increased in the early 1980s, congressional pressures also mounted to subject remaining rail passenger services to commercial market tests of revenue adequacy and cost efficiency.

Indeed, most public policy changes occurring since 1970 in intercity travel have led to increased reliance on the marketplace to identify the role that each mode should play. Thus the Bus Regulatory Reform Act of 1982 not only permitted bus lines to escape most government regulation, much in the fashion of the airlines, but also explicitly stated as a regulatory objective "to recognize and preserve the inherent advantage of each mode of transportation."[4] By contrast, government policies prior to the 1970s often acted to protect relative modal positions regardless of changes in cost or demand.

Public policy changes are carried out, of course, against a background of continuous change in the underlying fundamentals, such as demographics and available technologies. A crucial question for determining the relative importance of the different intercity passenger modes is the relative rate at which they experience technological change. A common fallacy in intercity passenger analyses is to presume substantial changes in one mode, accompanied by substantial stagnation in another, and from this to proceed to very optimistic projections about traffic growth for the mode presumed to enjoy the singular advantage of technological advancement. Sunday supplements to major metropolitan newspapers have been particularly prone to this error when reporting the reputed advantages of some new development in high-speed rail transport, but the confusion has hardly been confined to the Sunday media.

Therefore it is significant that during the 1970s there was little evidence to suggest that one or a few modes enjoyed substantially more technological advances than the others. This contrasts with the 1960s, when both the airlines and the highway modes improved substantially relative to the railroads (due to the introduction of jets and creation of the interstate highway system). However, though intercity rail passenger performance almost certainly did not decay in absolute terms during the 1970s, the railroads did not much improve their standing relative to their major competitors. Furthermore intercity rail passenger travel at the end of the 1970s was not as fast, convenient, and perhaps comfortable as it was in the 1930s and was even more inferior relative to its major highway and aviation competition than it had been four or five decades previously. In short, technological change over the past 40 or 50 years has clearly worked to the relative advantage of both the aviation and highway modes. This change in the relative performance and efficiency of the various intercity modes, incidentally, is one of the most undeniable and obvious of all basic trends in transportation during the twentieth century.

A clear implication of that trend, of course, is that one would expect, as has happened, that the highway and aviation modes would grow at the expense of rail. Although rail was the dominant mode at the turn of the century, since the 1930s the automobile has not only dominated but its share of the total intercity travel market has hovered between 80 and 90 percent (except for a brief period during World War II when wartime controls and conditions sharply curtailed auto use and boosted that of the public modes).[5] The only really major change to occur in the intercity travel market since the end of World War II is that the shares of both rail and bus have declined steadily while that of air has increased. By 1983 the bus' share of passenger miles had fallen below 2 percent and rail's share had dropped below 1 percent, while air's share had grown to just over 14 percent.[6] Of course few trends are immutable, so a natural question is whether these tendencies, so pronounced during the middle part of the twentieth century, will persist. Furthermore, if public policy becomes as involved in promoting rail transport as in developing aviation and highway travel, will some of these trends at least be somewhat attenuated or allayed?

These are essentially the issues with which this book is concerned: to determine the relative roles that the different intercity passenger modes might be expected to play in the future under different assumptions about developments in public policy, technology, demographic patterns, and consumer preferences. The book also provides an opportunity to revisit some of the older public policy issues and forecasts concerning intercity passenger transportation. As noted, transportation has been largely deregulated in the United States. Rail passenger service is now largely a subsidized ward of government, with cross subsidies almost entirely eliminated. The jet engine is a proven and dominant technology in commercial aviation. Have these technological developments and policy changes worked as expected? Do relative costs now determine modal shares? Are these modal shares as expected? Are they in keeping with earlier trends? How will they affect the future development of intercity passenger travel in the United States?

All these issues are obviously quite interdependent. Indeed, the striking thing about all of transportation policy is how interdependent it is—how different modes and activities can be seriously affected by changes in other modes and attendant public policies. In the present context, for example, withdrawal of railroads from most of their uneconomic passenger services was a prerequisite to surface freight deregulation, and a full delineation of the economic viability and limits of commercial air and bus travel. That delineation in turn greatly simplified airline and bus deregulation for a variety of reasons, not the least of which was providing a potential solution to the so-called "small town service problem."

In general, the road to rationalization of intercity passenger travel in the United States has involved four major and sequential steps: (1) elimination of the railroad cross subsidy, (2) deregulation of the major public mode, the airlines, (3) elimination of most regulations applying to the other public modes, bus and rail, and (4) increased pressure on government passenger transport activities—Amtrak, highways, airports, airways, and so on—

to adhere, at least roughly, to commercial principles. In large measure all of these have been done. This is the story of what that might mean for future intercity travel in the United States.

The story is presented in two parts. First, in part I, chapters 2 through 9, the U.S. experience with airline deregulation is summarized and evaluated. A survey is made of the financial impacts of deregulation on the airline industry, the various strategic responses to deregulation undertaken by both the old and new airlines, and the effects these have had on employees in the industry and on domestic and international travelers. The possible impact of airline deregulation on the marketing and distribution of reservations and tickets is also examined.

Part II is concerned with the emerging economics of a competitive, almost totally deregulated intercity passenger transportation industry. In chapters 10 and 11 the economic implications of enhanced competition in intercity travel, as unleashed by deregulation and technological change, are analyzed. In doing this, broad developments in intercity bus, rail, and auto travel are reported and analyzed; also the underlying cost and demand structures for intercity passenger travel are explored so as to determine the relative roles that the different modes might be expected to play in intercity travel under different assumptions about energy, public policy, technology, and demographic developments.

Finally, in chapter 12, the implications of these various analyses are developed in terms of what they might mean for public policy and the future. This concluding chapter is especially concerned with what various basic economic and technological trends, interacting with different public policy options, might mean for the structure of the industry.

I

THE U.S. EXPERIENCE WITH AIRLINE DEREGULATION

2

Antecedents and Consequences

Regulatory Antecedents

Regulation of airline passenger service formally began in the United States with the creation of the Civil Aeronautics Authority (CAA) in 1938, which was reorganized into the Civil Aeronautics Board (CAB) in 1940. The CAB exercised complete control over entry, exit, routes, and fares from regulation's inception until 1976, when the move toward less regulation began.

Under CAB regulation an airline was required to have a Certificate of Public Convenience and Necessity before offering scheduled airline service on any route. When economic regulation began in 1938, 16 carriers were granted grandfather certificates to continue their existing operations. Through mergers, these 16 carriers had evolved into 10 domestic trunk airlines by the mid-1970s. Although many applications and attempts were made over the years, no new trunk carriers (with the partial exception of Northeast Airlines) were allowed to enter the industry under CAB regulation.

Even though new trunk carriers were not permitted, the CAB, under prodding from Congress, did grudgingly allow some new entrants into the industry. These included so-called local service carriers and supplemental carriers (charter operators). The local service carriers were originally formed (mainly just after World War II) to provide regional "feeder" services for the trunk airlines, but over the years many came to resemble small trunk airlines in their operations. The supplemental carriers were permitted to offer only nonscheduled charter flights to groups of travelers. While most of the trunk airlines conducted some charter operations, the supplemental carriers' applications to become scheduled carriers were always denied.

The CAB was only slightly more permissive about the entry of existing carriers into new city-pair markets than of new carriers into the industry. When a route was already served by an incumbent carrier, the CAB was reluctant to allow new entry if the incumbent objected on the grounds that such entry would divert existing traffic and cause financial hardship. As a further restriction, route awards necessitated an application procedure and hearings that were very lengthy and often expensive.

The CAB used route awards to pursue diverse policy objectives. Monopoly routes were sometimes given to carriers in a weak financial position in an attempt to maintain stability in the industry. Attempts were also made through route awards to reduce the subsidies needed by local service carriers for service to small communites.

Another critical aspect of CAB regulation was its authority over fares. Fare offerings generally were limited to coach and first-class fares based on the mileage traveled. Although the CAB allowed limited experimentation with discount or promotional fares at various times (e.g., standby discount fares in the late 1960s), these could be eliminated by the CAB at virtually a moment's notice. Fares generally were revised upward, though, to reflect increases in costs, thus allowing the airlines to pass on most or all cost increases to passengers. Perhaps, more important, the CAB set the fare taper with respect to length of flight to be less steep than the cost taper. This relationship between fares and costs created losses and disincentives for short-haul/small town service, while creating intense service rivalry and incentives to acquire wide-bodied aircraft for long hauls. In general, by suppressing virtually all fare competition, prederegulation CAB procedures encouraged competition based on service rather than price. When combined with relatively rapid industry growth, such an environment did not breed an intense preoccupation with cost controls. For example, when faced with a labor dispute the conventional managerial wisdom in the industry under regulation was to settle a strike quickly rather than lose market share and growth by taking a prolonged shut down. Furthermore excessively generous labor settlements, or other managerial ineptitude for that matter, could usually be absorbed by some combination of market growth and technologically induced gains in productivity without asking the regulators for a fare increase; a major consequence was that consumers reaped fewer benefits from technological gains than they otherwise would. In essence, the substantial productivity improvements generated by rapid technological change in the industry (by many measures the highest of any U.S. industry in the immediate post-World War II decades) were substantially absorbed in rising labor and other costs.

CAB approval was also necessary for airline companies to merge. In general, the CAB took a restrictive view of mergers, granting approval only to maintain industry stability when one of the merger candidates was in serious financial trouble. Merger thus served mainly as a tool for averting bankruptcies.

Overall, the basic guiding principles of the CAB seemed to be equalizing the size of companies and avoiding bankruptcies so as to maintain stability in the industry. The CAB used its authority over entry, exit, route awards, and fares to maintain the financial viability of even the weakest carriers. Consequently new route awards rarely went to the "big four" trunk lines

(United, American, TWA, and Eastern). As a last resort to avoid an imminent bankruptcy, the CAB would also force mergers, often sweetened by access to new routes. As a reflection of these tendencies in CAB policies, regulation encouraged development and recruitment of management with legal and political skills, somewhat to the exclusion of skills in marketing and cost control.

In 1976 the CAB undertook significant departures from its previous restrictive policies by allowing discount fares and advocating airline deregulation. By 1977 the Board had accelerated this move toward less regulation by giving airlines even wider latitude to experiment with discount fares and stressing fare reductions as an important factor in the selection of applicants for new routes. In essence, this administrative deregulation came very close to complete deregulation except that entry was restricted; that is, participation was limited to the same closed set of participants that had populated the industry for several decades.

As shown in chapter 3, the airlines experienced an unprecedented boom under the administrative deregulation of 1976 to 1978. The industry not only made record profits in 1977 and 1978 ($700 million of net income in 1977 and $1.2 billion in 1978) but came close to achieving returns on investment comparable to other U.S. industries, something that the industry had seldom achieved previously under regulation. Of course these years also coincided with a strong business cycle recovery and stable to declining energy prices. Nevertheless, deregulation was also given much credit. The fact that intrastate carriers, never under CAB regulation, almost always achieved higher rates of return than the major airlines while charging lower fares was also cited as strong evidence in favor of deregulation.[1] As a consequence legislation formally eliminating domestic airline regulation was enacted, with the U.S. Senate voting 85–0 in favor and the U.S. House of Representatives affirming by a 363–8 vote. The final legislation was signed into law by President Carter on October 24, 1978.

Industry Performance after Formal Deregulation

The Airline Deregulation Act of 1978 removed all remaining major obstacles to route entry by established carriers, opened up entry to entirely new carriers ("fit, willing and able" criteria replacing "public convenience and necessity"), and phased out all fare regulations. In addition the act scheduled the disbanding of the CAB thereby eliminating most lingering doubts or uncertainties about the limited future of regulation in the airline industry. A significant difference between administrative deregulation, or even previous cycles of "enlightened" regulation, and formal deregulation was thus the apparent permanence of the reforms.

The early and highly favorable experience with administrative deregulation generally helped to increase support for deregulation in the industry. However, administrative deregulation coincided with an expanding U.S. economy and declining energy prices. In addition there were few or no problems in the years 1976 through 1978 with airport capacity or organized labor, and competition still was among a closed set of companies.

By contrast, formal deregulation in October 1978 was followed by a great deal of economic turbulence. The fall of the Shah of Iran and the attendant rise in energy prices significantly increased airline operating costs and resulted in unexpectedly early obsolescence of fuel-inefficient aircraft. Back-to-back U.S. recessions in 1980 and then again in 1981–82 stultified growth in air traffic, just as previous recessions had done. Also, the shift in U.S. monetary policy that induced historic highs in interest rates in the early 1980s occurred at a time when many airline companies were purchasing new fuel-efficient aircraft. Finally, the PATCO strike in August 1981 resulted in capacity limitations at some major airports.

In general, virtually all the industry's problems up until late 1982 are easily accounted for by recession or fuel and interest cost effects external to the industry and little affected by deregulation. By late 1982 and early 1983, in contrast, fare wars permitted by deregulation may have added to the industry's difficulties.

Indeed, under deregulation, airline bankruptcy became a reality as the CAB no longer acted to prevent such occurrences. Route access was also no longer an incentive for a financially strong carrier to take on the problems of a weak one through merger. Routes could now be easily acquired through straightforward entry. The reality of bankruptcy also meant that unrestricted credit, always scarce to airlines, became virtually nonexistent, and airlines became increasingly reliant on equipment trusts and leases.

Even with all this economic and financial turbulence, the industry continued to improve its productivity. As reported in chapter 6, deregulation has permitted much better matching of aircraft to markets resulting in better aircraft utilization and improved load factors. In addition the more complete development of hubs after deregulation (as described in chapter 5) has improved operations.

The evidence on costs since deregulation is even more unequivocally favorable than that on productivity. Specifically, since deregulation costs per available seat mile (ASM) have not escalated as fast as factor input prices. Costs per revenue passenger mile (RPM) have generally come down even faster as load factors have improved under deregulation (especially after controlling for recession effects).

As one major consequence of these lower costs, passenger airfares unquestionably have been lower on average because of deregulation than they otherwise would have been, particularly for the longer hauls of over 500 miles. Even on the shorter hauls, fares as a percentage of costs were roughly the same after as before deregulation despite the reduction of short-haul government subsidy and the elimination of cross subsidies. As documented in chapter 7, average fares (or yields) have mainly been reduced by the extension of discount fares to over 80 percent of all markets and ready acceptance of these fares by travelers, so that over 60 percent of all passengers were flying on discount fares by 1984 and over 70 percent by 1986.

Service, for reasons also explained in chapter 7, has probably improved on balance under deregulation, but the record is mixed.[2] Full fare business travelers may be worse off where load factors have increased under deregulation, resulting in more crowded planes (less space in which to work or sit comfortably) and less availability of last minute reservations. In addition there may be somewhat less clustering of big city departures during the hours most desired by business travelers because the airlines under deregulation are permitted to compete on fares as well as on service. On the other hand, many smaller towns and cities now receive more direct nonstop service to their nearest hub, especially during business hours. Service to small towns that was provided by government subsidized local service carriers prior to deregulation has been largely replaced by unsubsidized commuter carriers.[3] In only a few cases has replacement service required some continued subsidy, so government subsidy costs have dropped substantially. Since deregulation, however, small town service is likely to be in a somewhat less comfortable commuter turboprop plane than the subsidized jet that it replaced.

Flight frequencies have increased in most markets under deregulation, especially after correcting for recession effects. Service frequency has improved in all sizes of markets. New entrant jet carriers have opened up markets not previously served, as well as "upgrading" many travelers from slower surface modes.

One consequence of this expanded service and opening of new markets is that total employment in the airline industry has almost certainly been greater under deregulation than it would have been under continued regulation. New entrant carriers obviously have created jobs that would not otherwise have been available. But, as shown in chapter 6, even the old established carriers seemingly have employed more than they otherwise would, apparently because of increased traffic volumes caused by promotional and discount fares.

New employees in the industry, however, have received less pay on average than the established employees. The new entrant jet carriers generally have had lower (and nonunion) pay scales than the older airlines. A strong trend has also emerged toward dual wage structures with newly hired employees, even at the most established and unionized airlines, earning less than older workers.

Other groups dependent on the airlines for employment or business have also been affected by deregulation. The CAB, as one of its final acts, lifted the exclusivity clause on which the travel agent business was built, making this part of the airline market the last to be deregulated. In the aftermath, as described in chapter 8, the two dominant computer reservation systems on which travel agents rely have been brought under antitrust challenge. Large business clients have also found more and more ways to circumvent payment of full agency fees (thus lowering travel agent profit margins) and seem impatient to hasten the day when fees are largely eliminated. Nonbusiness travelers, by contrast, have seemingly become more reliant on travel agents due to the increased complexity of fares and service offerings created by deregulation.

Domestic deregulation has also spurred the U.S. government to renew its historic, though intermittent, desire for an international "open skies" policy. U.S. negotiators have been particularly receptive to trading access to U.S. gateways for permitting enhanced numbers of U.S. carriers on international routes. The CAB, in its final years, also gave great credence to promotional fares in making international route awards to U.S. carriers. In general (as shown in chapter 9), the opening up of gateways, the increasing number of carriers per international route, and the emphasis on fare promotions in picking entrants have increased competitive pressures in international markets that have a U.S. base.

Summary: Assessing the Airline Deregulation Experience

Airline deregulation, as with other major public regulatory changes, has resulted in some having gained while others have lost.[4] Overall, airline fares are lower than had regulation continued, with the drop largely due to discount fares. Service has also probably improved for the majority of travelers with typically more flights on each route and more airlines serving each city. The airlines have also become more productive and cut costs, largely because of the added incentives for low costs in an openly competitive environment and the removal of regulatory incentives and restrictions that hampered efficient use of airlines' resources.

Set against these cost and productivity gains are the losses experienced by unionized labor. Since deregulation, wage increases have been much more modest than previously, and in some instances there have been actual wage reductions. Employment in the industry, however, is higher due to deregulation, not only in total but even among the established unionized carriers.

Most prederegulation concerns about possible adverse social impacts also do not seem to have materialized. By most measures service to small communities is now at least as good, and probably better, than under regulation and the subsidy cost to the government is dramatically lower. But a few communities have lost service, and in some instances all service.

Airline safety has also apparently not been degraded; indeed, the industry has amassed a slightly better safety record since deregulation (in scheduled domestic service) than in the comparable period before.[5] This has happened, moreover, despite the air traffic controllers' strike of 1981, more commuter service, new entrant carriers, and low profitability in the recession years of 1980 and 1982. By most measures the commercial airliner is still a much safer way to travel than the private auto or private airplane, but certain services, in particular where new commuters have replaced jet carriers, may be slightly less safe than before.[6]

Deregulation may also have intensified congestion at some airports by permitting more rapid and intensive development of hub and spoke networks. On the other hand, deregulation probably helped to reduce some airport congestion by allowing and encouraging the use of secondary airports and off-peak promotional fares, so that the net effect is difficult to determine. There is also some evidence that airport congestion has thwarted some of the goals of deregulation as the fares to and from congestion-restricted airports tend to be higher, all else equal. In general, not everyone has participated equally in lower fares created by deregulation; for example, those flying between major cities have probably benefited more than those with small town origins or destinations

The evidence is also mixed on the effect that deregulation might eventually have on industry structure and performance. The apparent consensus prior to the fact was that deregulation would lead to a substantial consolidation of the industry. However, a most striking early aspect of deregulation (as discussed in chapter 4) has been the emergence of new set of competitive jet carriers, either entirely new creations or emergent from embryonic roots as intrastate carriers (and therefore not subject to prior CAB regulation). Deregulation has also been marked by considerable growth of small commuter carriers specializing in short-haul service to small communities. The trunk carriers' market share therefore declined by about 10 percentage points during the first four years of deregulation.

Nevertheless, the future structure of the U.S. airline industry may be more concentrated than it was in the immediate aftermath of deregulation. Whether any such increased concentration, if it comes, will have adverse effects on consumers remains to be established. Much may depend on what application is, or is not, made of antitrust policies in the future.

In sum, the experience with deregulation has been largely, though not totally, favorable. Most outcomes, as detailed in the next seven chapters, have been more or less as predicted by deregulation's proponents. Furthermore few, if any, of the disasters predicted by opponents have occurred. There have also been some unexpected developments, some favorable and some unfavorable, as documented in the chapters that follow.

3

Airline Financial Performance since Deregulation

with John S. Strong

Airline financial performance has fluctuated sharply, experiencing several distinct phases since deregulation formally began in late 1978. Record traffic volumes and profits were achieved in 1978 and early 1979. But this unprecedented performance deteriorated steadily over the next four years. Battered by fuel price increases, recession, and air traffic control restrictions, the industry barely broke even in 1980 and then realized unprecedented losses of $236 million in 1981 and over $880 million in 1982.[1] In 1982 Braniff International became the first major carrier to file for bankruptcy in the history of the industry, followed subsequently by Continental, and several bankruptcies of smaller airlines.

Beginning in 1983, the industry recovered somewhat, aided by economic expansion and continued moderation in factor costs, notably fuel and labor. Even then, the industry's 1983 operating profit of $240 million was more than offset by interest expense, resulting in a 1983 net loss of almost $120 million. In large measure this erratic performance simply reflected the fact that the airline industry has always been one of the most heavily leveraged in the United States: in 1983 airline equity represented only 32 percent of total invested capital while the all-industry average was 59 percent.[2]

Conditions improved dramatically for the industry in 1984, as carriers benefited from the strong domestic economy and international travel was spurred by a strong dollar. Operating income exceeded $2 billion, with net income soaring to over $800 million. Despite this overall picture of industry recovery, however, financial difficulties continued for several major carriers. By 1985 the industry appeared to be moving toward one group of very profitable carriers and a second group of airlines whose financial performance in 1984 appeared very fragile. The diverse sources of these financial difficulties ranged from high operating costs to severe debt burdens. One result of these disparities was the 1986 announcement of various merger plans involving nine of the larger carriers, as well as the acquisition of Pan Am's Pacific routes and fleet by United Air Lines.

As in the past and under regulation, airline financial performance continued to be conditioned by the general economic and operating environment. But in the early years of deregulation that external environment was arguably the most difficult in the industry's history. Problems created by the sharp increase in the price of jet fuel in 1979–1980 were compounded by the economic recessions of 1980 and 1981–1982. Many older planes in commercial airline fleets became unprofitable to operate at the fuel, labor, and other factor costs of the 1980s.[3] Declining cash flows led to a growing reliance on debt finance during a period of record high interest rates. Finally, the air traffic controllers' strike in August 1981 led to capacity restrictions at many of the nation's major airports. Each of these factors clearly had serious consequences for industry profitability and potentially important longer-term implications for investment capabilities and equipment replacement. In the early 1980s a growing percentage of U.S. commercial airplanes were nearing the end of their physical asset lives, with estimates being made that U.S. airlines would need a total of $30 to $49 billion for replacement and expansion from 1981 through 1991.[4]

Airline Financial Performance, 1972–1983

Although the first five years of deregulation saw the airlines go from record profits to record losses, it must be recognized that the air carrier industry has never been a strong financial performer.

In Figure 3.1 the pretax return on investment of the airline industry is compared with that of all U.S. nonfinancial corporations. The earnings performance of the industry historically not only has been lackluster, but also earnings have been relatively erratic and closely linked to the business cycle, even under regulation. From 1978 to 1982, though, the gap between the performance of the airlines and other industries widened substantially. Then, in 1983, it was almost eliminated, and in 1984 the airline industry's pretax return on investment was actually better than that for nonfinancial corporations.

Nonoperating revenues were used extensively to improve reported financial results from 1979 to 1983, as many carriers sold equipment and other assets.[5] The most publicized transactions were Pan Am's sale of its New York office building and its Intercontinental Hotels subsidiary. In fact, the sale of almost $500 million in assets was the only reason the industry was able to report positive net income in 1980.[6] As the economy reentered recession in late 1981, the market for used aircraft fell sharply, primarily because the formation of new airlines virtually stopped. Depressed prices for older planes and a lack of other assets that could be easily sold caused nonoperating revenues to fall from $166 million in 1981 to $131 million in 1983.[7] However, the situation would have been much worse except for "safe harbor" leasing, briefly permitted under a 1981 change in

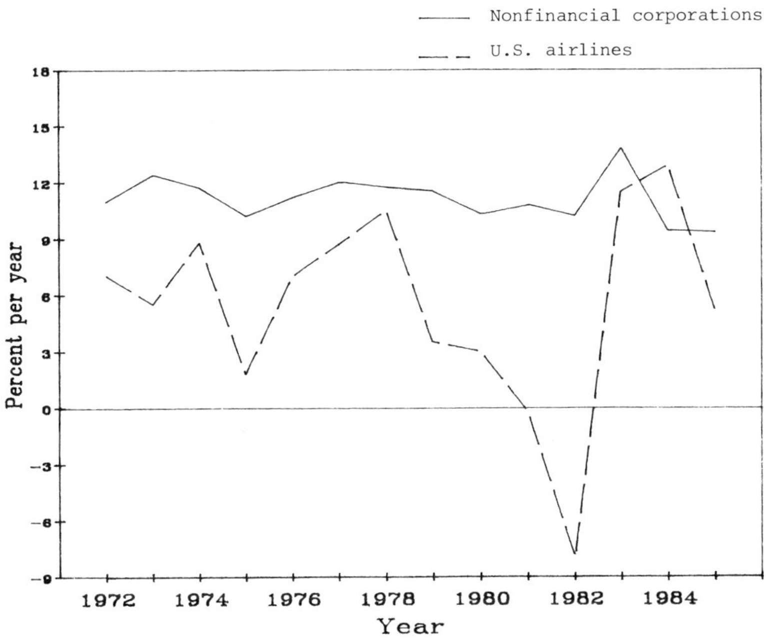

Figure 3.1 Pretax return on investment: airlines vs. nonfinancial corporations, 1972–1985. (Source: Federal Reserve Board, *Flow of Funds Accounts*, various years. *Moody's Transportation Manual*, various years.)

the tax laws that allowed the airlines to sell $261 million in depreciation and investment tax credits to other companies in 1981, $402 million in 1982, and $386 million in 1983[8]

Overall, nonoperating revenues from the sale of assets and tax benefits reduced airline losses by over $2 billion between 1980 and 1983. But such relief was limited and temporary. As already noted, a surplus of used planes ultimately resulted in a depressed secondary aircraft market. And by 1984 airline balance sheets had been largely "stripped," with few assets remaining that could be easily liquidated to generate cash. Finally, revisions in tax leasing laws enacted in 1982 sharply restricted the use of safe harbor provisions.[9]

By contrast, the postderegulation rise in nonoperating expenses proved much more durable, potentially representing a critical long-term problem for the industry. The largest nonoperating expense, interest, was stable throughout the mid-1970s at an annual level of about $400 million for the industry. Between 1977 and 1979 annual industry interest expense rose from $400 million to $705 million and then more than doubled between

1979 and 1982, reaching a level of $1,512 million. Roughly half of this was due to rate increases on old debt, with the other half representing interest on new borrowings undertaken to meet various reequipment and financing needs.[10] Moreover much of this long-term debt was borrowed at fixed rates with limitations on early redemption.

Variations in Industry Financial Performance

Substantial differences in the financial performances of different types of carriers and individual airlines are hidden in the industrywide aggregates. As shown in table 3.1, even in the depressed years of 1982 and 1983 roughly half of the industry was able to make both an operating profit and a net profit. Actually, in 1982 Pan Am alone accounted for 47 percent of the industry's operating loss and 55 percent of the net loss.[11] Table 3.1 also shows that in 1982 operating and net income were only loosely related: in ten cases operating results were better than net income, while for the other

Table 3.1 Financial results by airline, 1982–1983 (millions)

	1982		1983	
Airline	Operating income	Net income	Operating income	Net income
Air Florida	−33.5	−93.4	−11.0	−39.2
American	9.1	−19.6	281.5	227.9
Delta	−8.2	20.8	−207.3	−86.7
Eastern	−18.8	−74.9	−100.1	−183.7
Frontier	9.0	17.2	−18.8	−13.8
Northwest	−8.4	5.0	68.9	50.1
Ozark	18.1	7.5	2.4	2.0
PSA	−7.1	19.5	−1.3	−15.8
Pan Am	−314.5	−485.3	51.1	−51.0
People Express	10.5	1.0	20.4	10.5
Piedmont	23.8	30.5	60.5	25.5
Republic	37.2	−39.9	−31.0	−111.0
Southwest	39.2	34.0	68.5	40.9
Texas Air/ New York Air/ Continental	−46.0	−49.0	−150.3	−218.4
TWA	−101.3	−44.5	−65.8	−12.4
United	−9.4	30.8	216.3	142.0
USAir	79.3	59.1	128.0	80.6
Western	−30.8	−16.8	−56.4	54.5

Source: Airline annual reports.

eight airlines the opposite was true. However, by 1983 operating and net income had become more closely linked as financial difficulties came to reflect operating problems while nonoperating revenues declined.

Industry losses immediately after deregulation were also largely concentrated among the long-haul major airlines, as shown in table 3.2. Long-haul carriers have always experienced more volatile earnings, even under regulation. However, their post-1978 losses were aggravated by excess wide-body capacity and aggressive price competition, mainly among the established carriers who had been in the industry prior to deregulation.[12] In contrast, short-haul carriers as a group remained profitable (except for the short-haul majors in 1983).[13]

Causes of Airline Losses in the Early 1980s

By 1983 the finances of much of the U.S. airline industry were obviously in poor condition. It was not obvious, though, just how much of the red ink and weakening of balance sheets was attributable to deregulation and how much to the two economic recessions of 1980 and 1981–1982, the sharp fuel price increase in 1979, and the air traffic control restrictions imposed after the PATCO strike of August 1981.

Isolating the financial effects of deregulation requires projecting what might have happened to airline profits had deregulation not occurred. To make this distinction, an air travel demand model was estimated (a detailed description of which is presented in appendix B) which included variables measuring how recession, rising fuel costs, and deregulation separately contributed to the airline industry's earnings performance. These traffic demand estimates were then combined with empirically based assumptions about yields, unit costs, and capacity management to simulate how industry earnings might have fared under different economic and regulatory conditions.

Specifically, in the demand model, variations in total domestic revenue passenger miles (RPMs) were related to measures of standard airline fares and the extent of discounting; the level of economic activity, as indicated by real (inflation-adjusted) national personal disposable income; the real price of gasoline (a measure of the cost of alternative transportation); and dummy variables to measure the effects of seasonal fluctuations, the air traffic controllers' strike, and the route entry and exit freedoms given to airlines after deregulation. The model was estimated using quarterly data for the years 1970 through 1982. The model closely tracked actual RPMs

Table 3.2 Traffic and earnings variations, by carrier groups within the U.S. airline industry, 1973–1984

Carrier group	1973	1974	1975	1976	1977	1978	1979	1980	1981	1982	1983	1984
Short-haul majors[a]												
RPMs (billions)	34.1	33.1	33.9	36.4	39.1	47.3	53.6	53.3	52.4	53.6	62.3	63.9
Operating income ($ millions)	151.2	262.0	82.6	210.7	232.8	328.1	287.6	276.6	182.8	52.3	−179.4	673.0
Long-haul majors[b]												
RPMs (billions)	82.6	83.4	83.9	92.9	99.9	113.8	122.5	114.0	107.1	116.1	123.2	169.5
Operating income ($ millions)	297.9	363.1	−35.0	236.1	255.7	507.9	−277.6	−364.7	−627.6	−675.5	345.3	1089.4
Other short-haul carriers[c]												
RPMs (billions)	6.6	7.3	7.4	8.7	9.9	12.4	13.0	16.1	18.4	20.8	25.4	24.0
Operating income ($ millions)	43.7	81.8	28.0	72.3	103.3	110.8	72.4	75.5	92.4	74.3	13.1	243.6

Sources: *Air Carrier Traffic Statistics*, Civil Aeronautics Board, various years. *Air Carrier Financial Statistics*, Civil Aeronautics Board, various years. Air carrier annual reports, 1982, 1983, 1984.

Note: Traffic and earnings data reflect domestic operations only. Republic Airlines includes consolidation of AirWest, North Central, and Southern Airlines.

a. Delta, Eastern, USAir.

b. American, Continental, National, Northwest, Pan Am, TWA, United, Western.

c. Frontier, Ozark, Piedmont, Texas Air, Republic.

for the major airlines, with the independent variables explaining over 98 percent of the variation in RPMs over the period.

Deregulation allowed the airlines more freedom to offer excursion and other discount fares targeted at price-sensitive travelers; the percentage of travelers paying regular coach fares declined from almost 70 percent in 1977 to roughly 30 percent in 1982 (see chapter 7). The aggregate sensitivity of air travelers to reductions in the average fare paid, which includes both discount and coach fares, might therefore have increased after deregulation to the extent that airlines were able selectively to offer discount fares to discretionary travelers. To reflect this possibility, the model incorporated separate estimates of the response of air travel to changes in both standard and discount fares in the periods before and after deregulation (for the methodology, see the appendix). As expected, the results showed that reductions in the average fare brought about substantially greater increases in air travel after deregulation than prior to 1978.

Recession and Airline Industry Profitability

To estimate how the industry might have fared in the absence of the 1980 and 1981 to 1982 recessions, passenger traffic volumes were predicted assuming that real disposable personal income would have risen at its historic trend of 2.5 percent annually beyond 1978, rather than at the 1 percent annual rate actually observed. With fares remaining at their observed levels, this higher rate of income growth would have produced traffic volumes about 6 percent above their actual levels in 1980, 8 percent higher in 1981, and as much as 10 percent higher by 1982. These higher RPM levels should translate, of course, into increased revenues, assuming that fare levels would be unchanged. Of course, higher traffic might have increased revenues even more if the added demand permitted airlines to raise fares.

The increase in operating costs from carrying these higher passenger volumes was estimated by assuming that available seat-miles (ASMs) would have been increased by 5.2 percent in 1980, 7.4 percent in 1981, and by 9.4 percent in 1982, which represents the addition of 20 percent more capacity than required to accommodate the added traffic.[14] Under these assumptions systemwide load factors would have risen only from 58.0 to 58.4 percent in 1980, from 57.4 to 58.0 percent in 1981, and from 59.2 to 59.9 percent during 1982. With operating expenses per ASM remaining at their actual levels, total operating expenditures would have increased by the same percentages as ASMs.

Table 3.3 Effect of recession on operating revenue, expense, and income of the U.S. domestic airline industry, 1980–1983

Item	1980 Actual	1980 Without recession[a]	1981 Actual	1981 Without recession[a]	1982 Actual	1982 Without recession[a]	1983 Actual	1983 Without recession[a]
RPMs (billions)	235.9	249.8	221.8	240.6	231.0	254.5	250.5	269.8
Systemwide load factor (percent)	58.0	58.4	57.4	58.0	59.2	59.9	60.7	60.9
Total operating revenue ($ millions)	30,549.1	32,346.6	32,360.6	35,103.5	32,247.6	35,528.2	35,174.3	38,068.8
Total operating expense ($ millions)	30,778.1	32,379.9	32,882.2	35,301.8	32,868.2	35,944.4	34,831.4	37,701.1
Net operating income	−229.0	−32.8	−521.6	−198.3	−620.6	−416.2	342.9	367.7

a. The "without recession" effects were simulated by estimating industry RPMs, etc., using a regression model with income as an explanatory variable and predicting results with income at nonrecession levels. For further details on the methodology, see J. A. Gómez-Ibáñez, C. V. Oster, Jr., and D. H. Pickrell, "Airline Deregulation: What's Behind the Recent Losses?" *Journal of Policy Analysis and Management* 3 (Fall 1983).

Table 3.3 summarizes the implications of this no-recession scenario for passenger traffic, carrier load factors, and industrywide operating income.[15] Although load factors would not have remained at the high levels attained in 1979 (averaging 60 percent), they would have been (under the assumptions made) very slightly higher than those actually observed between 1980 and 1983. Revenues would have increased commensurately with the higher RPM levels generated by faster economic growth. After adjusting for the additional operating expense entailed in carrying these higher traffic volumes, the major airlines' net operating income might have been improved by as much as $196 million in 1980, $323 million in 1981, $204 million in 1982, and just under $25 million in 1983. The 1982 and 1983 differentials are less than in 1981 because revenue yields in 1982 and 1983 were only slightly above operating costs per ASM; in effect, under the assumptions employed, additional fare income barely covered the additional expense in the simulations for those years.

Forecasting Errors and Resulting Overcapacity

With the benefit of hindsight it seems apparent that the effect of the 1980 and 1981–1982 recession on earnings was compounded by traffic forecasting errors that led to provision of costly overcapacity. Airline capacity planning is generally done roughly two quarters in advance (e.g., airlines plan summer capacity during the preceding winter). This lead time is required to revise, publish, and disseminate schedules, to reposition equipment, and to restructure operations.

To assess the possible effect of forecasting errors on airline profits, actual capacity provided by the airlines was compared with what would have occurred had airlines been able to tailor capacity to achieve a target load factor of 60 percent, given actual traffic volumes.[16] The results are shown in table 3.4. Actual capacity exceeded the "target" capacity by 3.4 percent in 1980, 4.5 percent in 1981, and 1.4 percent in 1982. If capacity had been reduced by these amounts, operating expenses might have declined by as much as 1.2 percent in 1980, 1.6 percent in 1981, and 0.5 percent in 1982. (The cost savings are only about one-third the capacity reductions because labor and equipment costs are assumed to be largely fixed in the short run.) These estimated savings total approximately $370 million in 1980, $520 million in 1981, and $150 million in 1982. With such capacity tailoring, the industry might have earned $140 million in 1980, more or less broken even in 1981, and reduced operating losses by one-quarter in 1982.

Table 3.4 Effect of traffic forecasting and capacity errors on operating revenue, expense, and income of the U.S. airline industry, 1980–1982

	1980		1981		1982	
	Actual	With capacity adjustment[a]	Actual	With capacity adjustment[a]	Actual	With capacity adjustment[a]
RPMs (billions)	235.9	235.9	221.8	221.8	231.0	231.0
ASMs (billions)	406.7	393.2	386.4	369.7	390.2	385.0
Actual ASMs as percentage of target ASMs	103.4		104.5		101.4	
Total operating revenue ($ millions)	30,549.2	30,549.1	32,360.6	32,360.6	32,247.6	32,247.6
Total operating expense ($ millions)	30,778.1	30,408.8	32,882.2	32,362.7	32,868.2	32,713.7
Net operating income ($ millions)	−229.0	140.3	−521.6	−2.1	−620.6	−466.1

Source: Data obtained from carrier annual reports.
a. Capacity was assumed to be at a level that achieved a 60 percent load factor while costs were adjusted downward less than proportionately to reflect nonvariable or fixed elements in airline cost structures.

The Effect of Rising Fuel Prices

From 1978 through the end of 1981, the average price paid by domestic air carriers for fuel rose from less than 40 cents to over $1.05 per gallon.[17] Some of this increase was absorbed by substituting other inputs to reduce fuel consumption (e.g., by flying aircraft at slower speeds, thus substituting labor and capital for fuel). However, most of the fuel price increase was translated directly into sharply higher operating expenditures.

To estimate what might have happened in the absence of this rapid increase in fuel prices, both jet fuel and gasoline prices were assumed to have risen only as fast after 1978 as prices for other consumer goods. With this adjustment fuel prices would have risen to only about half of their actual level by 1981, so that both air fares and the cost of other travel modes (e.g., intercity travel by automobile) would have been significantly reduced. It was also assumed that none of the improvement in fuel consumption per ASM that followed the run-up in fuel prices would have occurred. This assumption implies that the actual improvement in airlines fuel efficiency after 1978 resulted entirely from efforts to cut fuel costs in response to rising prices, rather than from technological improvements in aircraft or other developments.[18] Since the increase in average fare yields over this period almost exactly matched that of the airlines' total cost per ASM, it was also assumed that yields in each of the years 1980 through 1982 would have been reduced by the full savings in fuel cost per ASM.

Under these assumptions RPMs would have increased in response to lower fares.[19] These effects would have been partially offset, however, by lower gasoline costs for automobiles, which would lower air traffic volumes somewhat by making automobile travel relatively more attractive. Finally, carriers were again assumed to have added 20 percent more ASMs than would have been necessary to accommodate exactly the increased passenger traffic.

The consequences of this simulation of lower fuel costs are displayed in table 3.5. The industry's total fuel expense would have been reduced by approximately $3.8 billion in 1980, $4.2 billion in 1981, $3.2 billion in 1982, and $2.2 billion in 1983. The savings after 1982 are lower due to the stabilization of fuel prices that began in late 1981; indeed, actual fuel prices fell by 5 cents per gallon in 1982. Even with higher traffic volumes, the sharply lower fares permitted by the assumed fuel cost savings would have produced somewhat lower total operating revenue, especially in 1981 and 1982 as the economic recession began to depress passenger volumes. However, these revenue losses would have been offset by even larger savings in

Table 3.5 Effect of fuel price increases on operating expense, revenue, and income of U.S. airlines, 1980–1983

Item	1980		1981		1982		1983	
	Actual	Without fuel price run-up[a]	Actual	Without fuel price run-up[a]	Actual	Without fuel price run-up[a]	Actual	Without fuel price run-up[a]
Fuel cost (¢/gallon)	86.6	51.0	102.1	55.7	96.4	59.0	86.1	60.9
Fuel expense per ASM (¢)	2.3	1.4	2.4	1.4	2.1	1.3	1.9	1.3
Total fuel expense ($ millions)	9,354.1	5,508.4	9,273.6	5,059.2	8,194.2	5,015.1	7,519.4	5,318.6
Total operating revenue ($ millions)	30,549.1	27,611.0	32,360.6	28,813.7	32,247.6	29,631.3	35,174.3	32,636.8
Total operating expense ($ millions)	30,778.1	27,313.5	32,882.2	29,017.2	32,868.2	29,984.7	34,831.4	31,731.4
Net operating income ($ millions)	−229.0	297.5	−521.6	−203.5	−620.6	−353.4	342.9	905.4

a. Assumes that fuel prices increased at the same rate as that of general inflation and airline fares escalated at a correspondingly slower rate. For further detail, see J. A. Gómez-Ibáñez, C. V. Oster, Jr., and D. H. Pickrell, "Airline Deregulation: What's Behind the Recent Losses?" *Journal of Policy Analysis and Management* 3 (Fall 1983).

operating costs.[20] After adjusting for the effects of reduced yields, as well as for the added expense of carrying the higher passenger volumes, the major airlines might have made an operating profit of just under $300 million in 1980. In 1981 and 1982 lower fuel prices might have reduced operating losses by $318 and $267 million, respectively. In 1983 industry operating income might have been over a half billion dollars higher if fuel prices had not increased in prior years. Overall, these estimates suggest that rising fuel prices, through their effect on airline cost structures and fares, were almost as financially damaging as the downturn in traffic volumes from recession.

Deregulation and Airline Industry Earnings

Deregulation has, of course, affected the airline industry's ability to respond to changes in its external economic environment. An intriguing question is the extent to which the airlines' use of the managerial freedoms offered by deregulation (e.g., in pricing, in selecting routes, and in the use of aircraft and other inputs) has actually helped or hurt the industry during the succession of traumatic shocks endured between 1979 and 1983.

Some observers in fact attribute the 1980–1982 industry losses almost entirely to increased price competition, in particular to the proliferation of discount fares that accompanied the relaxation of price and entry controls (see chapter 7). In the early stages of deregulation the airlines indeed did use their pricing freedom to set fares that declined relative to airline costs, as shown in figure 3.2 where the average fare (yield) paid by passengers is compared with a measure of the standard coach fare for the period from 1974 through 1983.[21] Because the coach fare formulas were adjusted throughout this period to reflect changing expenditures entailed in providing air service, the average coach fare shown in the figure can also be viewed as a reasonable index of the trend in air carrier costs. As the figure shows, there was a very slight increase in the differential between the standard coach fare and yield from 1974 to 1977; specifically, yield remained at approximately 94 percent of coach fare. In 1978 and 1979, however, actual yields fell to about 80 percent of full coach fare, as airlines offered an expanded array of discount fares. Beginning in 1980, the range of discount fares broadened and the depth of discounting increased, so that the gap between standard coach fares and average yields continued to increase.[22]

The consequences of this price competition on airline travel and earnings can be estimated using assumptions similar to those employed in the analyses of the effects of recession and fuel prices. Specifically, the effect of

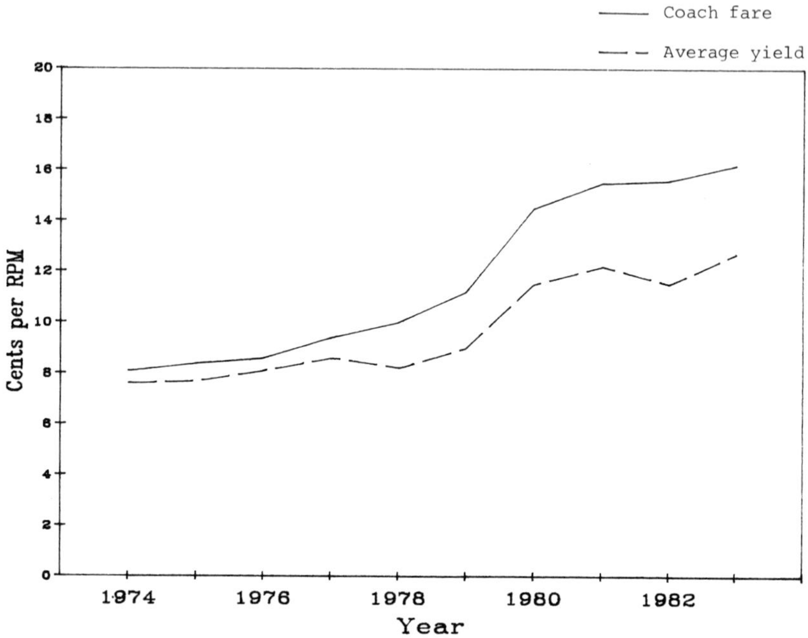

Figure 3.2 Coach fares and average yields, 1974–1983. (Source: *CAB Air Carrier Financial Statistics*, and *Air Carrier Traffic Statistics*, various years.)

fare discounting can be simulated by assuming that under continued regulation average yields would have remained at their historical or prederegulation average level of 94 percent of standard coach fares.

As shown in table 3.6, such an application of CAB fare-setting policies after 1978 would have reduced airline travel to about 88 percent of the levels actually achieved in 1979 through 1982. This projected negative effect of regulatory policy on traffic is due to two factors: a higher overall level of fares; and perhaps more important, a fare structure with only limited or less targeted discount fares.

For the first two years (1979–1980) shown in table 3.6, the airlines under deregulation seemingly were able to limit the use of discount fares primarily to discretionary travelers. At any rate, additional traffic and revenues were generated without disproportionately increasing costs or decreasing overall yield. Thus, as the table indicates, under continuing regulation the airline industry might well have experienced slightly lower profits in 1979 and a considerably larger loss in 1980 than it actually did. By 1981, however, the sharply lower yields per revenue passenger mile under deregu-

Table 3.6 Estimated effects of deregulation on traffic, revenue, expense, and operating income of U.S. domestic airlines, 1979–1983

	1979		1980		1981		1982		1983	
Item	Actual	Regulated[a]	Actual	Regulated[a]	Actual	Regulated[a]	Actual	Regulated[a]	Actual	Regulated[a]
RPMs (billions)	247.1	213.8	235.9	208.6	221.8	201.0	231.0	198.2	250.5	212.9
Operating revenue ($ millions)	33,202.7	29,504.4	30,549.1	27,556.1	32,360.6	31,516.8	32,247.6	30,988.5	35,174.3	33,488.3
Yield (operating revenue ÷ RPMs) (¢)	13.4	13.8	12.9	13.2	14.6	15.7	14.0	15.6	14.0	15.7
Operating expense ($ millions)	33,101.4	29,406.9	30,778.1	27,996.3	32,882.2	31,560.5	32,868.2	31,433.8	34,831.4	33,195.2
Net operating income ($ millions)	101.3	97.5	−229.0	−440.2	−521.6	−43.7	−620.6	−435.3	342.9	293.1

a. Assumes that fares would have continued at the same levels relative to the Standard Industry Fare Level (SIFL) as existed under regulation in the early 1970s inducing reductions in RPMs, ASMs, operating revenues, and operating expenses. For more details, see J. A. Gómez-Ibáñez, C. V. Oster, Jr., and D. H. Pickrell, "Airline Deregulation: What's Behind the Recent Losses?" *Journal of Policy Analysis and Management* 3 (Fall 1983).

lation than those hypothesized under continued regulation began to offset any increase in traffic volume. Apparently discount fare restrictions broke down and an increasing number of travelers utilized discount fares, so that the increased traffic under deregulation raised operating expenses more than revenues. As shown in the table, the higher yield levels that might have prevailed under regulation could have substantially reduced industry losses in 1981 and 1982. By 1983, however, deregulation again appeared to help the airlines' financial performance.[23]

Overall, the pricing freedoms of deregulation seem to have had a mixed effect on industry earnings. To the extent that the airlines can restrict the use of discount fares to price-sensitive travelers and avoid protracted fare wars such as those that occurred in 1981–1982, fare-setting freedom may bolster revenues and operating income. An increased ability to change fares quickly also appears to have allowed the industry to respond to rapidly rising operating costs and to declining demand in ways that sometimes helped earnings. However, the excess capacity that characterized much of the industry at the onset of the economic downturn of 1981–1982 resulted in intense price competition that squeezed revenues at the same time that operating costs were rising at an unprecedented rate. Thus, to the extent that continued regulation would have reduced this price competition, industry losses might have been reduced, at least in those years.

Airline Performance and Financial Markets

Financial markets, by providing an ongoing evaluation of expected future profitability, represent another means of evaluating the financial effects of deregulation. The potential effect of deregulation on equity values was a primary concern of Wall Street prior to 1977. The initial stock market response to the "administrative deregulation" of 1977–1978 and formal deregulation in late 1978 was nevertheless quite positive, as shown in figure 3.3 where the stock market performance of the major airlines is compared to the New York Stock Exchange (NYSE) Composite Index and Transportation Index. An index value of 100 indicates a stock market performance for airlines equivalent to the broader market indexes, an index over 100 a better performance, and under 100 a poorer performance. Although airline industry stocks outperformed the market through early 1979, fuel price increases and subsequent recessions caused airline stock values to plummet through late 1982. The onset of economic recovery in 1983 bolstered airline equity values, not surprisingly since airline earnings have always displayed a strong cyclical pattern (see figure 3.1). However, though

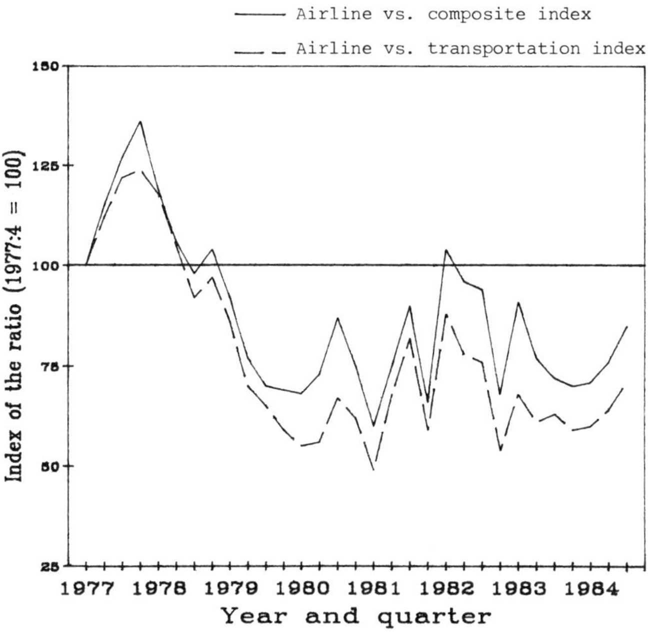

Figure 3.3 Ratio of airline stock index to composite and transportation indexes, 1977–1985. (Source: *Moody's Industrial Manual*, and *Moody's Transportation Manual.*)

airline stocks recovered somewhat in the mid-1980s, airline equity values still lagged the broader market indexes.

The heavy debt loads of many carriers could also be expected to depress equity values and possibly to change airline debt ratings. Although many analysts argued that a principal result of deregulation would be to increase the financial risk of carriers (e.g., because bankruptcy became a possibility with deregulation), the actual experience has been somewhat different. About half of the 14 largest carriers did experience downgradings in 1983 in the midst of the recession, but 3 also experienced upgrades. This degree of rating change was not too different from that of the economy as a whole, where downgradings exceeded upgrades by a ratio of almost three to one. Furthermore, by 1985, four carriers—American, Delta, USAir, and Piedmont—had achieved higher credit ratings than they had ever attained under regulation.

Another measure of cyclical sensitivity and capital market risk is a firm's beta, which indicates how volatile a company's stock is compared to the overall stock market. Betas are estimated by regressing a company's stock

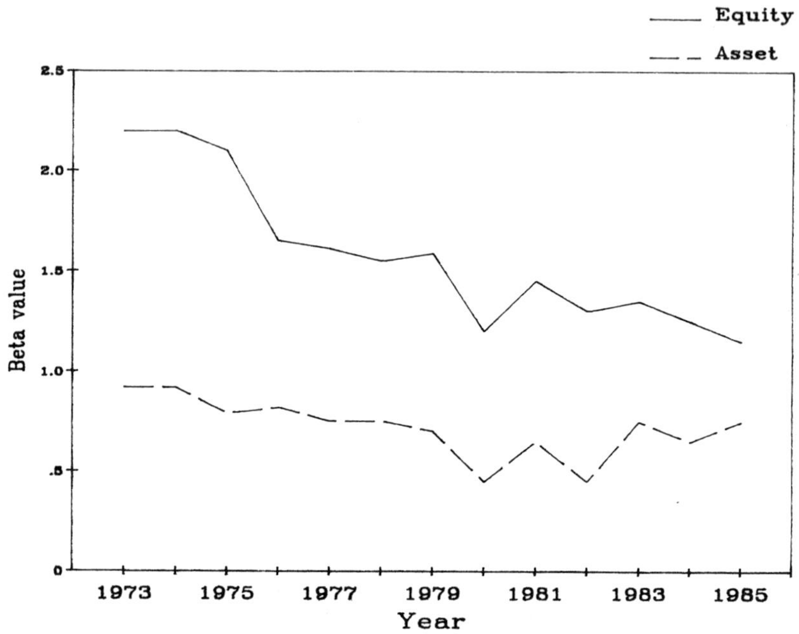

Figure 3.4 Airline equity betas and asset betas, averages, 1973–1985. (Tax rate is assumed to be 30 percent.) (Source: Mark T. Spiegel, "The Effect of Deregulation on the Major Airlines' Risk Structure and Cost of Capital," thesis, Department of Economics, Harvard University, 1986.)

returns on those of a market portfolio: a coefficient value of 1.0 indicates a level of equity risk equivalent to the market as a whole, a value greater than 1.0 greater risk, and a value less than 1.0 less risk. A weighted average of airline equity betas was constructed for 1973 through 1985 and is shown as the top line in figure 3.4. Since market values of equity will reflect the effects of debt held by the firm, conventional equity betas measure both systematic and financial risk. To study changes in the business risk underlying a firm's assets, these two types of risk can be separated by adjusting the observed equity betas by each firm's financial structure to create so-called asset betas.[24] As shown in figure 3.4, these asset betas have also declined somewhat since 1978, although the year-to-year variation has increased. This evidence suggests that though the substantial amount of airline debt outstanding represents a continuing source of financial concern, airline operations are apparently less cyclically sensitive after deregulation than before.

Airline Financial Structure and Investment Capacity

Airline losses in the early 1980s seriously weakened the balance sheets of many airlines, reversing a 1970s trend toward some reduction in the high levels of debt characteristic of the industry. For all airlines as a group, debt as a percentage of total capitalization fell from 64 percent in 1972 to 57 percent in 1977, after which it rose steadily to 68 percent by 1985. Only Northwest, Ozark, Southwest, and USAir had more equity than debt on their balance sheets by 1985, despite the cyclical nature of the airline business.[25] In total, long-term obligations of the major, national, and regional airlines (excluding current obligations, but including capitalized lease commitments) amounted to over $12.6 billion at the end of 1985. Although this represented a decrease of $1.3 billion from 1982, it was still 28 percent above the 1978 level of debt.[26]

The combination of diminished cash flow and growing debt burden has raised questions of whether the airline industry can finance needed capital expenditures. Indeed, the industry's ongoing financial difficulties were reflected in reduced capital spending in the early 1980s. In 1982 spending on plant and equipment fell to slightly less than $3 billion, down 20 percent from 1980.[27] Future investment programs were also revised by many airlines. In the early 1980s Boeing, McDonnell-Douglas, and Airbus experienced cancellations of orders for new aircraft, and other orders were delayed or renegotiated. Orders for commercial jet aircraft totaled only 223 planes worldwide in 1982, far below the 700 new orders placed annually in the 1970s.[28] With the upturn in traffic and profitability in 1984 and 1985, new orders were again placed, causing some analysts to suggest the airlines had committed themselves to substantial overcapacity for the foreseeable future.

Despite the adversities of the early 1980s, it would be premature to conclude that the industry cannot finance its needs. To start, a combination of external economic events as adverse to airline profits as that of the early 1980s—rising energy prices, a double dip recession, and historic highs in interest rates—seems unlikely to recur. And even if it were, the industry obviously learned a great deal from its experiences in those traumatic years. In particular, the industry has proved quite inventive at finding new ways to meet its financial requirements.

Among the more important of these developments has been a greatly increased emphasis on leasing, long an important tool in airline financing. In the context of the industry's weak balance sheets and cash flow, leasing has inherent advantages as a means of equipment financing for most carriers. Leasing has proved particularly attractive for airlines that could not otherwise utilize investment tax credits and accelerated depreciation provisions, especially while the safe harbor leasing provisions of the 1981 tax bill were in effect. When this provision was restricted at the end of 1982, so that only aircraft already on order remained qualified for safe harbor treatment, the airlines shifted from capital to operating leases. In late 1982, for example, American and TWA negotiated five-year lease deals with McDonnell-Douglas for the use of DC-9-Super 80s (MD-80s), an arrangement that effectively shifted the purchase and financing risks to the aircraft manufacturer.[29]

The involvement of aircraft manufacturers in generating investment capital for the airline industry has not been limited to leasing. Instead of selling their used planes to other carriers, airlines in the early 1980s increasingly insisted that trade-ins be part of their new plane purchases. By early 1983 Boeing had 47 unsold secondhand jets, while McDonnell-Douglas had an inventory of 25 to 30 used planes.[30] To save on inventory costs, manufacturers have encouraged the airlines to continue to fly the old planes until a buyer can be found. Thus these trade-in arrangements mainly serve as a form of price discounting and a means of shifting investment expense to the manufacturer.

In the early 1980s airlines also strengthened their balance sheets through various financial restructurings. Early efforts focused on improving liquidity through revision of loan covenants and compensating balance requirements, as well as some deferrals and rate revisions. Some carriers have also sought to bolster equity through negotiations with employees. Specifically, several companies obtained agreements for wage reductions or freezes in exchange for profit-sharing or stock ownership plans (as explained more fully in chapter 6).

Mergers, always the CAB's favorite tool for "bailing out" financially troubled carriers, could also be of importance in a deregulated industry, even though the freedom to enter routes suggests that mergers between airlines may not be as attractive a means of route expansion as under regulation. Other industries have, though, expressed some interest in airline investments or mergers. Norfolk Southern, a major eastern railroad, has invested $38 million in Piedmont Airlines, while Braniff's reorganization was financed largely by Hyatt Hotels. Mergers may offer a number of attractive features to both the outside investor as well as the airline. For the carrier, additional investment capacity is provided while the merger partner may gain access to tax credits and loss-carryforwards that would probably have remained unused by the airlines. These tax benefits are by no means small: at the end of 1983 the airline industry held over $1.5 billion in unused investment tax credits and tax loss carryforwards.[31] Although these tax benefits are substantial, any sizable merger activity probably would also have to be accompanied by the restructuring and write-down of airline debt.

Industry officials believe that a 5 percent return on revenues is necessary if capital investment needs are to be met. The major airlines have only accomplished this three times since 1970—in 1978, 1983, and 1984.[32] During the 1970s the average return was only 2.1 percent, and the first three years of the 1980s did not see any positive returns.[33] Financial considerations alone may thus necessitate considerable restructuring. In this context it is likely that some existing carriers will merge, change substantially, or disappear altogether. Other developments and possibilities unleashed by deregulation, as discussed in the next few chapters, may make this restructuring even more unavoidable.

Concluding Observations

U.S. airlines did not enjoy great financial success during the first five years of formal deregulation. This, however, was at least as attributable to other concurrent events—a sharp rise in energy prices in 1979–1980 and recessions in 1980 and 1982—as to deregulation. Indeed, all else equal, deregulation probably improved the financial performance (as measured by net operating income) of the industry in 1979, 1980, and 1983, though perhaps making it somewhat worse in 1981 and 1982.

By contrast, the economic recessions of the early 1980s had a universally adverse effect on this highly cyclical industry, affecting airline earnings in three major ways. First, the cyclical nature of the industry meant that traffic downturns cut sharply into earnings. Second, the underestimation of the severity and duration of the recession apparently caused airline managements to persist in maintaining capacity levels, resulting in a substantial "overshoot" on capacity that translated into unduly high operating expenses. Finally, this overcapacity, particularly of wide-bodied aircraft, provided the impetus for a prolonged period of price-cutting and fare wars, which lowered revenue yields.

The available evidence also suggests that fuel price increases were very damaging to airline earnings. Rapid escalation in fuel and other input prices after 1979 raised unit costs and necessitated a rapid reversal of the trend toward lower fares, thereby reducing passenger volumes and further squeezing operating margins. Overall, the adverse effect of higher fuel prices was seemingly as great or greater than that of the recessions.

The adversities of the early 1980s inevitably took their toll on airline balance sheets, raising a question of whether the airlines would be able to finance future capital requirements. The airlines' response to these problems has been remarkably creative. Using a variety of approaches—ranging from greater use of leasing to trading equity for lower wages and enhanced productivity—most airlines at least managed to "muddle through" these difficult years. In the longer run, however, either earnings will have to be better than they were in the early 1980s or the industry will likely experience a major restructuring. Of course these two alternatives are not mutually exclusive, and some combination of these solutions may likely occur.

4

The New Entrepreneurs

Prior to deregulation many speculated as to how it might affect the structure of the airline industry. The apparent consensus was that deregulation would lead to a substantial consolidation of the industry so that somewhere between four and six large systems would emerge, each centered around one of the major prederegulation trunks.[1] For example, because of financial strength or protected international franchises, it was commonly speculated that American Airlines, Delta Airlines, Northwest Airlines, United Airlines, and TWA would be among the survivors around which new and larger dominant firms in the industry would be organized.

Not surprisingly, then, mergers and consolidations were expected to be a major phenomenon in the airline industry after deregulation. Several mergers of course have occurred.[2] These consolidations, however, have hardly been of such scope that only three or four systems have come to dominate the industry since deregulation, even though that possibility cannot be excluded in the full passage of time. Specifically, four years after formal deregulation (in 1982) the trunk airlines, far from becoming dominant as a group, had lost 11 points of market share to other types of airlines (5.1 to former intrastate and new entrant jets, 1.0 to commuters, and 4.9 to the local service carriers).[3]

In short, the conventional wisdom about what would happen to the structure of the airline industry under deregulation hardly proved to be the case during the first few years of deregulation. Instead of the expected increase in concentration, the number of certificated competing carriers grew substantially, and the largest prederegulation carriers, the trunk airlines, lost rather than gained market share.[4] Largely overlooked in much of the prederegulation congressional and public debate was the possibility that in creating new opportunities for the larger established carriers, deregulation would create entrepreneurial opportunities for entirely new carriers as well.[5]

One reason these new opportunities were not widely anticipated is that deregulation in actuality proved to be very different from what was discussed before the fact. Specifically, the "deregulation bills" put into the congressional hopper in the mid-1970s, when deregulation first became a serious possibility, were relatively limited in intent.[6] Most did not propose eliminating entry barriers; rather, they sought to enhance competition among the already existing or established firms in the industry. For example, the so-called Kennedy Airline Deregulation Bill (named after its sponsor, the senior senator from Massachusetts) was among the most generous in its proposed entry provisions, but it still would have eliminated the "public convenience and necessity" test for entry only after the fourth anniversary of passage, and even then anticipated only a phased addition of five new carriers on a "fit and able" basis.

All this congressional temerity was dissipated, however, by developments between 1976 and late 1978 when the Airline Deregulation Act finally became law. Specifically, "administrative deregulation" under the successive CAB chairmanships of John Robson and Alfred Kahn had proceeded so far and so quickly that final enactment in 1978 largely amounted to simple codification of what had already happened.[7] The results of this Robson-Kahn administrative deregulation for both consumers and producers seemed so favorable that a quick consensus was created to take the final steps: total abolition of the CAB and an almost immediate adoption of a "fit and able" standard for entry. The final legislation, in short, opened the industry to competition with a thoroughness and speed not anticipated, or even advocated, by most early supporters of deregulation.

The rest of the answer as to why the industry structure did not immediately become more concentrated under deregulation resides largely in the nature of regulation itself. Regulation created incentives for some segments of the airline market to be overpopulated and some underpopulated. Under CAB regulation long hauls were more profitable than short hauls. As a result, when deregulation began, there was a surfeit of wide-bodied aircraft suitable for long-haul service, either already in operation or on order, while there was a deficit of aircraft suitable for short-haul service. Once unleashed from regulation and its accompanying constraints, the overpopulated long-haul segments of the market became subject to intense competition. By contrast, the underpopulated short-haul segments represented unfilled market gaps or niches that could be filled by new entrants.

With deregulation, an airline that could provide a service at less cost was also free to charge a lower fare in hope of garnering a larger market. Conversely, if rates as established by prior regulation were beneath costs in some markets, managements were free after deregulation (with some few exceptions) either to abandon such markets or to raise fares to a fully compensatory level. These freedoms gave birth to entrepreneurship in two major forms.

First, deregulation unleashed a surge of activity by commuter airlines offering scheduled short-haul service in low-density markets using small propeller-driven aircraft. In particular, deregulation greatly expanded the market opportunities for commuter airlines as established trunk and local service carriers used their new freedoms to withdraw from short-haul routes that could not be served profitably with jet aircraft.

A second surge of postderegulation entrepreneurship involved the introduction of simple, no-frills service and low fares in short to medium hauls (200 to 1,000 miles). In these markets most of the new competition came from entirely new jet-equipped carriers or from expansion of what were previously intrastate carriers confined by regulation to operations within one state (e.g., Texas and California). Not surprisingly these new entrant jet carriers were rarely found in the highly competitive long-haul markets.

Each of these entrepreneurial groups—the commuters and new jet carriers—made a distinctive contribution to the airline industry, evoking important and perhaps permanent changes in industry structure.

The New Commuter Operations

To extend air service to the more remote parts of the country and to smaller communities, the CAB had evolved a program of local service subsidies that induced airlines (by the time of deregulation primarily local service airlines and not the trunks) to provide service to small communities; by the mid-1970s most of this service was performed in jet aircraft not particularly well suited to such activity.[8] Such aircraft were actually more efficient in serving longer-haul and more heavily traveled markets. Commuter carriers with more suitably sized equipment were not eligible to receive prederegulation small community subsidies. Before deregulation local service airlines typically used their jets in multistop service from one small community to another during late evening or midafternoon hours with the main economic incentive being the collection of a government subsidy; this also kept these jets available for more remunerative service in higher-density markets elsewhere during the peak business hours.[9] With deregulation and route entry freedoms, these jets could be deployed far more profitably in unsubsidized markets at all times of the day, usually in markets just a bit denser in terms of traffic and a bit further apart than those on subsidy. A concern thus existed even prior to deregulation that insufficient service would be provided to smaller communities. In response to this concern, elaborate provisions were built into the Airline Deregulation Act, limiting the rate at which established carriers could withdraw from small community service and providing various subsidies to induce either the established carriers to continue their small town service or new carriers (including commuters) to enter into such service. Under the deregulation act subsidies were to be awarded on a community by community basis, as determined by bids from carriers providing a stipulated minimum level of service with the lowest bidder among "fit and able" carriers almost always receiving the franchise.[10]

The commuter airlines' niche, even before deregulation, had been to provide service to smaller communities whenever and wherever the larger jet carriers pulled out in search of better opportunities elsewhere. Under CAB regulation the commuter airlines were sharply differentiated in many basic characteristics from the local service carriers. The commuters flew small (19 seats or fewer) propeller-driven planes rather than the 90-seat (or more) jets commonly used by the local service carriers. The commuters had at most two pilots in their cockpits, and sometimes only had one in contrast with three pilots for many jet aircraft. Commuter labor relations were much more informal and flexible; for example, pilots would often help with unloading the baggage or taking tickets, and in general, commuter airline employees were quite willing to do a wide variety of jobs, undertaking whatever needed to be done at a particular point in time or place.

With this combination of smaller, propeller-driven aircraft and more flexible work rules, commuter airline costs were often as much as one-third less than the cost of serving the same markets with jet aircraft.[11] The commuters' costs were often so low that they could even entertain the possibility of profitably serving markets that the local service carriers totally ignored. Indeed, it was in exactly such markets that many of the very earliest commuters had their start.

To some extent, of course, the commuters achieved their lower costs by sacrificing some quality of service and comfort. But the sacrifice was not seen in all dimensions. For example, the commuters, because they operated smaller aircraft, could afford and usually offered, more frequent flights in small markets than the local service carriers operating larger jets. Smaller planes also made it possible for the commuters to provide more direct service between small communities and larger hub airports because they did not have to make intermediate stops to achieve acceptable load factors.[12] Thus, despite the higher top speed of a jet aircraft, commuters, by avoiding intermediate stops, were often able to offer shorter total travel times.

Furthermore, because the commuter airlines' basic service was providing business travelers with connections from small communities to major hubs, they were far more likely to provide more frequent and more conveniently scheduled departures to and from these communities during the popular business travel hours (7 to 9 a.m. and 4 to 6 p.m.).[13] Indeed, between

October 1, 1977, and October 1, 1982, there were 145 communities in which a commuter carrier replaced a departing certificated carrier. For these communities as a group, total weekly departures were 26 percent higher in 1982 than in 1977. Although some 40 percent of those communities had fewer departures, 56 percent had more departures and another 4 percent had the same number of departures.[14] Some of the prior certificated service, however, was provided in propeller aircraft operated by local service airlines. If only the loss of jet service is considered, the increase in departures by replacement commuter carriers is even more striking. Between June 1978 and June 1984, 61 communities lost all jet service.[15] Among these communities total (jet plus nonjet) aircraft departures were on average over 47 percent higher in 1984 than 1978.

By most measures in fact (departure frequency, schedule convenience, and flight time from local small community airports to connections at major hubs) small community service since deregulation has generally improved, although not by as much as has service to larger communities (as indicated by the data in table 4.1). Although some small communities have lost some or all air service since deregulation, as shown in figure 4.1, roughly as many have had service increases.[16] This has happened with a remarkably small input of government subsidy, with total government subsidies actually being lower than they were before deregulation and lower than they would have been on a pro forma basis if regulation had continued.[17] Indeed, by 1984 the annual subsidy payments had fallen to $36 million, down from over $82 million in 1977 and a high of over $121 million in 1981 when both the pre- and postderegulation subsidy programs

Table 4.1 Postderegulation changes in weekly airline service by airport size, June 1, 1978–June 1, 1984

Airport size[a]	Percent change in aircraft departures	Percent change in seat departures
Large hub	35.5	38.3
Medium hub	38.5	36.1
Small hub	19.1	7.9
Nonhub	9.3	−9.7
Total	28.1	29.9

Source: *Official Airline Guide*, June 1978 and June 1984, as reported in Civil Aeronautics Board, "Report on Airline Service, Fares, Traffic, Load Factors, and Market Shares, Service Status on June 1, 1984," table 16.

a. A large hub is defined by the Federal Aviation Administration (FAA) as an airport that enplanes 1.00 percent or more of total U.S. enplaned passengers. Similarly a medium hub enplanes between 0.25 and 0.99 percent; a small hub enplanes between 0.05 and 0.24 percent, and a nonhub enplanes less than 0.05 percent.

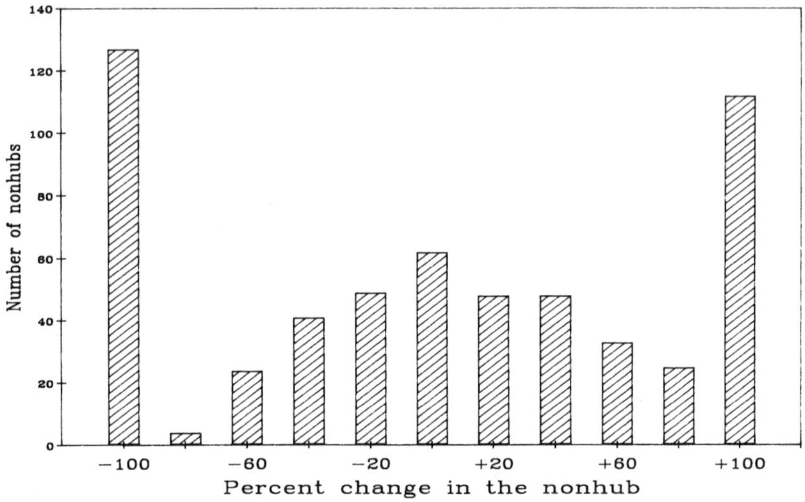

Figure 4.1 Distribution of changes in weekly departures at nonhubs, September 1978–September 1984.

were in operation.[18] In short, commuter airlines have not only typically provided service at lower unit costs than predecessor local service airlines but have also provided a service that has had more frequent and conveniently timed departures. A service trade-off has thus existed between the greater comfort and roominess of the jets and the schedule convenience and directness of the commuter prop flights.

As yet another service improvement, but one with a high potential cost in reducing effective competition, commuter feeder services have also become better integrated with longer-haul jet services since deregulation, mainly through marketing alliances between commuters and large jet carriers. Although the Allegheny Commuter System, which began in 1967, might be considered a prototype for these alliances, the alliances didn't begin to spread throughout the industry until late 1984 and 1985. The speed with which these alliances subsequently grew was remarkable. For example, at the beginning of 1985, marketing alliance agreements were in effect at 20 different hub airports involving 7 major airlines and 17 commuter carriers. Less than a year later by November 1985, the 13 largest jet carriers had alliances with 39 different commuter carriers at 33 of the nation's largest airports.

These alliances have the common feature of the smaller carrier sharing the larger airline's two-letter designator codes in the Official Airline Guide (OAG), in computer reservations systems, and on tickets. These codes have traditionally been used to identify the carrier specifically providing the service, not flights operated by others however affiliated.

Many participants in the commuter airline industry have argued that these code-sharing alliances owe their existence in large part to the way in which online connections are favored over interline connections in computer reservations systems. Although the precise manner in which flights are selected for display on a travel agent's computer reservations system terminal varies among the different systems, all the major systems place a penalty on interline connections relative to online connections. (Discussions of other impacts of computer reservations systems are found in chapters 5 and 8.) Through code sharing a commuter carrier's flight connections to its marketing partner are treated as online connections, whereas a competing nonaligned commuter's flights are treated as interline connections. Because of the preference given online connections in the computer reservations system display, commuters with code-sharing alliances can achieve a considerable competitive advantage over commuters who do not participate in such arrangements.

Code-sharing alliances are also usually accompanied by preferential access to joint fares. For example, a passenger in Flint, Michigan, wishing to travel to Boston, Massachusetts, during the first week in November 1985 had the choice of flying from Flint to Detroit via either Simmons Airlines or Fischer Brothers Aviation and connecting to a Republic Airlines flight from Detroit to Boston. Simmons had a code-sharing marketing alliance with Republic in Detroit, whereas Fischer Brothers did not, so Republic offered joint fares to Simmons but not to Fischer Brothers. The result was that not only did the Simmons connections appear first in the computer reservation systems, but the trip to Boston beginning in Flint with Simmons cost $200, whereas the one beginning with Fischer Brothers cost $285 even though both connected with equal convenience to the same Republic flight.

As another common and very real advantage to both commuter carriers and passengers, virtually all alliances feature close coordination of schedules between commuters and major carriers, allowing convenient connections for commuter passengers with the flights of the major carrier. Most alliances also involve locating the commuter gates on the same terminal concourse as the major carrier, thus providing short walks between connections and easier transfer of baggage between flights. Close schedule coordination and adjacent gates were common, but not universal, features of commuter-jet carrier cooperation prior to the spread of marketing alliances. Some alliances also involve the major carrier taking over the reservations and cost- and revenue-accounting functions from the commuter carriers with resultant cost savings. At least one set of alliances, those with American Airlines, also provide the commuter with cost savings from bulk fuel purchases and quantity discounts on the purchase of commuter aircraft.

In developing their relationships with the commuter carriers, the major airlines, with some important exceptions, have typically preferred code-sharing alliances to buying commuters or starting their own commuter operations. One apparent reason to prefer a code-sharing alliance to ownership is that employees of a separate company are less likely to be able to obtain the same wage, benefit, and work rule package as that available in the major company. As already noted, part of the reason commuters can serve short-haul, low-density markets so cost-effectively is their lower wage structure and more flexible work rules. Although some of the major airlines have been able to establish dual wage and work rule structures (as will be discussed in chapter 6), most commuter wages are still below the lowest or "B-scale" wages of the major airlines.

A second reason to prefer code sharing is that the contractual arrangements appear to allow the major to control the commuter's behavior at far less cost than outright purchase. Moreover, should any of the elements of the arrangement not work out as expected, the risk to the major carrier is far less than if the commuter were owned.

Nevertheless, as a consequence of code sharing and related developments, the commuter airline industry's structure has been fundamentally changed. The consensus among commuter airline operators is that the competitive advantages of these alliances are such that a commuter must belong to one in order to compete for feed traffic at a major hub. Indeed, by the end of 1985 all but a few of the major commuters had joined alliances. But once in an alliance, a commuter typically has far less independence in making operating and route decisions than before. Specifically, an aligned commuter is discouraged from scheduling flights that would feed the flights of the major airline's competitor. The probable result is that in a small community generating enough traffic to support only one commuter airline, flights will be timed to connect conveniently to only one carrier in the nearby hub. Similarly an aligned commuter is likely to be discouraged from offering a service that might be considered competitive with the major airline, such as service in jet aircraft. In the future therefore, should marketing alliances continue to dominate the commuter industry, commuters may provide less of a potential competitive check on major carriers than they otherwise might have.

Anther interesting aspect of code-sharing relationships has been a tendency among the majors to select only one commuter carrier to feed each hub. Using only one carrier per hub avoids a problem observable in the early and pioneering experience of the Allegheny Commuter System; there, disputes arose among commuters serving the same hub about who would get Allegheny's approval to enter a new feeder market. However, if a single commuter provides all the short-haul feed to a major carrier at a hub, and in the process forces the remaining independent commuters from that hub, the major may become dependent on that feed and face a difficult position should trouble befall the commuter or the commuter want to negotiate better terms. Maintaining at least two carriers per hub would also make it more difficult for another trunk simply to buy the feed at a hub.

Formal alliances between the major trunks and commuters may also help alleviate another lingering "service deficiency" of commuter operations: an unfortunate tendency of commuter carriers not to achieve quite as good an overall safety record as their jet predecessors. On average over the 1970 through 1983 period a passenger boarding a commuter was about three times as likely to be killed as a passenger boarding a jet.[19] This inferiority, though, appears to be primarily a function of two considerations: the different characteristics of commuter operations (more landings and takeoffs per million passengers or passenger miles, etc.) and the limited experience of the commuter airlines which, to a considerable extent is attributable to the simple fact that these airlines did not emerge as a serious element in the industry until a relatively late date (the early 1970s).[20] Actually the older, more experienced, better-financed, and larger commuter airlines have a safety record that compares well with both the established trunk and local service airlines. The 20 largest commuter airlines averaged 1.12 passenger fatalities per million enplanements between 1970 and 1980, while the rest of the commuter industry experienced a rate of 5.91; at the same time the rate for certificated jet carriers was only 0.91.[21] Furthermore the Allegheny commuters, perhaps reflecting the added discipline and supervision of their alliance status, actually achieved a slightly better safety record than the certificated jet carriers during those years.

Much of the inferiority in the safety performances of the commuter airlines in the 1970s thus seems attributable to the activities of the newer and less established of these carriers. Toward eliminating that discrepancy, the Federal Aviation Administration (FAA) in 1978 imposed stricter safety standards on commuter operations.[22] In the first five years following the tighter safety standards, the fatality rate for the commuter industry was a notable 30 percent lower than in the prior four years.

Given this safety advantage of the established and larger commuter operations, the commuter industry has been characterized by an unfortunately high rate of turnover both before and after deregulation. For example, only 79 of the 187 commuter carriers operating in September 1978 were still conducting scheduled passenger operations in February 1984.[23] Some of the no-longer-operating carriers merged with surviving carriers while others cut back to offer only on-demand "air taxi" services. This turnover of course was concentrated among the smallest and least experienced carriers. As many of these carriers went out of business, some of their markets were taken over by existing commuters and other new commuter airlines were formed so that the total number of commuter airlines operating in the United States was not changed dramatically in the first few years after deregulation. The spread of marketing alliances may, however, change that by forcing a consolidation and stabilization of the industry. Postderegulation recessions have also no doubt contributed to a rate of turnover somewhat higher than might be expected in the long run, since severe recessions are particularly damaging to an industry such as commuter airlines which are comprised largely of small and often undercapitalized businesses.

Prior to deregulation commuter airlines were also effectively proscribed from operating aircraft that could carry more than 19 passengers, a fact that may have contributed to both their inferior safety record and lack of some service amenities. Aircraft seating up to 30 were permitted after 1972, but few such aircraft were available. After deregulation the seating limit was raised so that commuter airlines could use planes large enough to carry 60 passengers. Moreover after deregulation commuters wishing to fly still larger aircraft could easily become certificated carriers and be free of all aircraft size regulation, an option not available under regulation. An important consequence of the prederegulation size constraint was that no effective commercial market existed for planes capable of carrying passengers in the 20- to 60-seat range. Indeed, prior to deregulation the commuter airlines tended to use airplanes basically developed for other purposes—such as gaining access to outlying bush country or providing private corporate aircraft services. With the commuter industry established and achieving a substantial scale after deregulation, aircraft explicitly designed for this market have emerged and should provide a better match between the needs of the commuter airlines and their passengers than predecessor aircraft. In particular, with these new planes the commuters should be able to achieve lower costs in "medium-density" commuter operations. Also the additional investment required to move from an existing low-scale operation to a larger scale should not be so large in the future; this suggests that the commuters eventually could become more of a "market contestability" threat to larger operators, although this may be more than offset by the emergence of marketing alliances.

In essence, these newly developed and larger commuter aircraft will reinforce a rather remarkable aspect observable even prior to deregulation in small-scale, low-density, small town airline operations. Specifically, and counter to much conventional wisdom, commercial airline operations appear subject to only limited aircraft scale economies, even at very low operating densities. Apparently, unit costs can be kept relatively low in low-density airline operations by carefully matching plane size and departure frequency to the characteristics of the market; done properly, the unit costs of serving a very low-density market may not be too much higher than those of serving a very large-scale, high-density market.[24] And exceptions to this rule have mainly been in the range where 20- to 60-seat planes (previously unavailable) would appear particularly suitable.

Lifting the technical limits on plane size of commuter operations may also help alleviate the commuter airlines' most obvious deficiency, a relative lack of comfort in their planes. Of course this deficiency should be far more tolerable in the short-haul, usually less than one hour, hops of commuter airlines than in long transcontinental or international flights of jet carriers. Nevertheless, there can be little doubt that many travelers originating in or flying to very small cities miss the creature comforts that were previously available in subsidized jet services and are not available in the small propeller commuter planes (usually unsubsidized) that have replaced them. Assuming that it is easier and less expensive to provide these creature comforts in larger planes, the mere lifting of the upper limit on commuter plane size should help alleviate the problem. To the extent, moreover, that the unleashing of the commuters under deregulation has expanded their operations, and therefore their total demand for aircraft, it may also prove possible to provide better comforts in commuter planes at lower than expected costs as a consequence of possible scale economies in aircraft production.

The New Entrant Jet Carriers

The emergence of the new entrant jets was almost surely the least anticipated major event of deregulation prior to the fact. Under regulation, as noted earlier, the population of scheduled airlines was remarkably stable: essentially all the trunk airlines existing at the time of deregulation were created by grandfather rights granted at the time regulation was first formalized in 1938.

The only substantial new entry into the ranks of scheduled carriers (but not trunks) was the creation of local service carriers in the early post-World War II years.[25] Furthermore, not only did historical experience and precedent suggest a stable number of carriers but most of the early legislative proposals for deregulation did not really anticipate fully opening up entry into the industry.

Again, the specific niches served by the new jet entrepreneurs were largely markets left vacant because of previous regulatory policies. Regulation dampened incentives to keep costs under strict control. Even if lower costs were achieved, no one was permitted to reflect these costs in lower rates nor, for that matter, in developing new markets, since entry into new markets was rigidly controlled by the CAB. Indeed, under regulation one of the common ways to capture or gain entry to a new market was to be extravagant; for example, an airline, to prove an "affinity of interest" with a community that it sought CAB approval to add to its route structure, might develop lavish new hotel facilities in that community or promise service in large planes (that were not justified by market scale). And of course under regulation it simply did not pay to serve some routes because the rates permitted by the regulators did not allow a profitable return given the technology available (which in turn was strongly influenced by past regulatory policies). These unprofitable markets under regulation, as already noted, tended to be medium to short haul and relatively low-density routes.

In keeping with the identity of these underattended market niches, most of the new entrant jet carriers attempted to do something that predecessor established carriers did not. In most instances they either entered a market that was not previously served or well served or entered a previously well-served market while offering substantially lower fares.

Offering low fares is of course more easily sustainable if costs are kept low. The new entrants typically achieved lower costs than the old established carriers in a variety of ways, including being less unionized and paying lower wages with less restrictive work rules, flying their aircraft more hours per day, allowing more managerial discretion in making labor assignments, using less expensive satellite airports or terminals, eliminating "unnecessary" service frills, encouraging travelers to carry their own luggage (sometimes even quoting special charges for luggage that was checked), not interlining reservations or luggage, eliminating meal services, and using less comfortable and more closely spaced seats.

Table 4.2 Comparison of various airlines' costs for serving 200-mile markets

	Actual			Adjusted[a]	
Cost category	Southwest	Piedmont	United	Piedmont	United
Flight crew	$ 130	$ 251	$ 460	$ 251	$ 307
Aircraft, fuel, landing fees, and aircraft servicing	1,125	1,469	1,683	1,374	1,359
Cabin crew	70	86	149	72	124
Passenger specific costs	349	927	989	1,122	1,171
Overhead (excluding aircraft)	136	134	332	144	338
Fully allocated costs	1,900	2,867	3,613	2,963	3,298
Fully allocated costs per passenger	24	47	58	37	42
Seats per aircraft	118	110	103	118	118
Load factor	0.67	0.56	0.60	0.67	0.67

Source: CAB, "Domestic Fare Structure Costing Program, Version 6, update." Data are for 12 months ending June 30, 1981, as reported in David R. Graham and Daniel P. Kaplan, "Competition and the Airlines: An Evaluation of Deregulation," Staff Report, Office of Economic Analysis, U.S. Civil Aeronautics Board, December 1982, table 4.1
a. Adjusted costs assume crew complements, landing fees, load factors, seating densities, and aircraft utilization are the same for United and Piedmont as are observed for Southwest.

Typical savings possibilities are as shown in table 4.2, wherein Southwest Airlines (a former intrastate carrier that has expanded into interstate markets and whose costs are similar to those achieved by new entrants) is compared with Piedmont (a fairly typical local service carrier) and United (the largest of the established trunks). Southwest's cost advantage is substantial and comes not only from lower wages and less restrictive work rules but also from other operational differences. Not surprisingly the established carriers have responded to their cost handicaps by attempting to curb their costs, as discussed in detail in chapter 6.

The established airlines have been reluctant, however, to pursue certain cost economies popular with the new entrants. In particular, the established airlines have shown little inclination to follow the new entrants in abandoning interlining privileges, apparently viewing (perhaps mistakenly) interlining as a major competitive service advantage. Reportedly, though, some of the very biggest established carriers (in particular, American) have pondered the possibility that their systems are large and comprehensive enough to *consider* "going it alone," thereby enhancing the need for smaller airlines, particularly commuters, to become "captive" or subservient to a trunk through code-sharing alliances or similar arrangements.

The new entrants have also not always been cost-cutters or service stingy. In a few instances, the new entrants have chosen to compete by offering more and better service at the same or slightly lower fare than was previously available. New York Air, for example, competing with the Eastern Shuttle on the Northeast Corridor made newspapers, food services, and even wine tastings available on some of its flights—all amenities not previously available on the spare, almost astringent, shuttle service.

Even though the new airlines have proliferated, and some individual new jet entrants have grown spectacularly, they have not provided a comprehensive alternative to the established airlines. Indeed, of all the new entrants, only People Express was in a position as of 1985 to provide near-nationwide service. Certain routes and sections of the country have seen relatively little of the new entrants, whereas other areas have experienced a great deal of such activity.[26] As a consequence the new entrant jets accounted, even on a most generous counting, for only 5 to 10 percent or so of the total U.S. domestic airline market as of 1985. At some hub airports, however, the new entrants had become significant factors. By March 1984 there were seven large hub airports where a single new entrant had more than a 10 percent share of capacity, with the largest being People Express's 41.3 percent share at Newark.[27] Similarly there were six medium hub airports where a single new entrant had more than a 25 percent share, with the largest being Southwest's 62.1 percent share at El Paso.

Of course, the mere existence of new entrants could exert an influence that extends beyond those markets in which they directly participate. A long standing and standard concept of industrial economics is that the very presence of potential competitors can exercise a discipline even on markets where the potential competitors are not directly involved. Whatever the form in which this concept is expressed—entry preventive pricing, dynamic limit pricing, workable competition, or market contestability—the essential conclusion remains much the same: potential competition, all else equal, will exert a downward pressure on prices.[28] And the airlines should be no more exempt from this rule than other industries; to the contrary, there are reasons for believing that airlines may be above average in their vulnerability to such pressures.[29] From the standpoint of public policy, in fact, it is in this very potential for creating new forms of competition where it did not previously exist, for exerting pressures to keep costs under control, for creating incentives to explore new service and price combinations that better satisfy travelers' needs, and so on, that the significance of the new entrants may reside.

Conclusion

Deregulation has unleashed entrepreneurial skills in the airline industry well beyond what most observers expected prior to the fact. This new entrepreneurship has been particularly evident in two specific sectors: commuter operations and jet operations on medium- to short-haul, moderate-density routes. These new carriers have played central roles in three of the principal developments in the airline industry following deregulation: rationalizing small community service, broadening the range of fare and service offerings, and improving productivity and lowering cost structures.

Specifically, commuters have helped solve one of the major public policy problems anticipated with deregulation, ensuring a continuation of "essential" air service to small communities while maintaining an acceptable standard of service and safety. Furthermore they apparently have done so at less total cost to the economy and to governments than would otherwise have been the case.

The new entrant jet carriers, with their simplified fare structures, have also helped spread unrestricted low fares. They have done this by their own pricing policies and by competing away the restrictions placed on discount fares in the markets where new entrants have contested the established carriers.

The new entrant jet carriers have also been a force in lowering airline costs. The increased competition fostered by deregulation would have increased pressure on the airlines to lower their costs to some extent even in the absence of the new carriers. The new entrants have demonstrated just how low costs can be driven by streamlining service offerings and being free of the work rule restrictions of unionized labor. In essence, the new airline entrepreneurs have forced both labor and management of the old established carriers to rethink their old established ways and procedures, thus bestowing a potentially permanent benefit whatever might happen to the industry's structure in the future.

5

Responses of the Old Guard

With deregulation the old guard—those established trunk carriers operating under grandfather rights since 1938 and the local service airlines created shortly after World War II—suddenly faced the prospect of both competing with one another and competing with low-cost new entrant carriers. They had to and did develop new competitive strategies, as routes, equipment, and fares all became matters of free choice for airline managements.

Route Strategies

The Deregulation Act of 1978 enabled all applicants found "fit, willing, and able to properly perform air transportation" to be granted certificates for a route even though they might divert traffic from an existing carrier. In fact, after deregulation the CAB processed route applications so quickly that an existing carrier could get authority to serve virtually any domestic route without much delay.[1] The Deregulation Act also made it possible for a carrier to stop serving a route, again with minimal delay in most cases, so long as essential air service was not threatened. Even where a carrier's withdrawal would leave a community with too little air service, the CAB was usually able to find a replacement carrier quickly.[2]

Thus airlines were able for the first time to begin fashioning the precise type of route network they wished to serve. A carrier's route development was still constrained in the short run of course by its own historical service patterns and those of its competitors and by its fleet of aircraft on hand. Development was also restricted to some extent by the inexperience of most airline managements in strategic route planning, especially in a deregulated environment. Indeed, route strategies that had proved successful in a regulated environment did not always find continued success under deregulation.

At the beginning of deregulation, the route strategies available to and pursued by the airlines seemed classifiable into one or more of the following seven categories:

1. hub strengthening
2. establishing longer and stronger routes
3. network extension through internal growth

4. network extension through merger
5. regional rationalization
6. seasonality reduction
7. opting out (i.e., changing very little or abiding by the status quo).[3]

These strategies, as discussed next, were not mutually exclusive and were frequently used in combination.

Hub Strengthening

All of the established carriers undertook some degree of hub strengthening.[4] Hub and spoke route networks have long been a dominant feature of domestic airline route strategies, but prior to 1978 CAB regulation severely hampered the rational development of such networks. The basic notion of a hub and spoke system is that flights from many different cities converge on a single airport—the hub—at approximately the same time, and after giving the passenger sufficient time to make connections, all then leave the hub airport bound for different cities. Such a convergence of flights on a hub is often called a "connecting complex" or "connecting bank," and a passenger on any of the incoming flights of a complex has a convenient connecting opportunity to any of the cities served on the outgoing flights of the same complex. The main advantage of such a system is that by collecting passengers bound for all the spoke cities, less dense markets can be served more frequently, and usually more cheaply, than if all city-pair markets were served only by direct flights. A disadvantage of course is that hub and spoke service is usually connecting or in a few cases one-stop service instead of the nonstop service passengers prefer. Furthermore, if too many flights are involved in one connecting complex, an airport's capacity can be overstrained with attendant losses in service quality and operating efficiencies.

The more spokes in a hub and spoke system, the more connecting opportunities; therefore large systems have advantages over small systems (at least up to the point at which the hub airport's landing and takeoff capacity becomes saturated). Any city in which a single carrier has 50 or more daily departures can be defined as a possible hub, since 50 departures usually is considered a minimum level needed to run substantial morning and evening connecting complexes.[5] Using that definition, carriers can be placed into three categories, depending on their network characteristics prior to formal deregulation:

1. Carriers with no hubs (serving no airports with 50 or more daily departures).

2. Carriers with a single hub (only one airport with 50 or more daily departures).

3. Carriers with multiple hubs (more than one airport with 50 or more daily departures).

"No-Hub" Carriers Prior to Deregulation

As of 1976, prior to deregulation, there were only three carriers with no domestic hubs: Piedmont, Texas International, and Pan Am.[6] After deregulation all developed hubs.

As regulatory restraints relaxed, Piedmont undertook development of a hub at Charlotte, where by 1981 it had increased daily departures from 18 to 53 while reducing departures at Roanoke, Washington-National, and Atlanta—cities that had played a more prominent role in Piedmont's system in 1976 than had Charlotte. By 1984 Piedmont's strategy had emerged clearly with the development of major hubs at both Charlotte and Baltimore, each with 147 daily departures. By 1984 Piedmont had also organized a move into midwestern markets around the development of a small secondary hub at Dayton.

Similarly, after deregulation, Texas Air built a hub at Houston by increasing daily departures from 43 in 1976 to 58 in 1981 while decreasing operations at Dallas/Fort Worth. By 1984 Texas Air had merged its operations with Continental Airlines, and the combined carrier had a dual hub system with hubs at Houston (161 daily departures) and Denver (127 daily departures) accounting for 45 percent of the combined carrier's domestic departures. Indeed, between 1976 and 1981 Continental, even without Texas Air, had virtually doubled daily departures at Denver from 57 to 113.

Pan Am had not developed a strong hub at any of its cities by 1981 as it was absorbed with consolidating operations following its mereger with National. Pan Am, as discussed in chapter 3, was also plagued with severe financial difficulties that limited its options. By 1984, however, Pan Am had developed hubs at New York-Kennedy and Miami. These hubs were designed to provide Pan Am with domestic feed for its international routes, a feed that Pan Am had sorely lacked prior to deregulation.

Single-Hub Carriers

Braniff, Frontier, and Western were all single-hub carriers in 1976. Following deregulation, Braniff undertook a major expansion around its Dallas/Fort Worth hub, a pattern arrested by Braniff's bankruptcy in May 1982. A substantially smaller Braniff resumed operations in March 1984, with Dallas/Fort Worth again the major hub.

Frontier remained committed to Denver as a single hub, increasing daily departures from 105 to 133 between 1976 and 1981, with a further increase to 165 by 1984. Frontier was acquired by People Express in 1985, with the combined airline operating two major hubs at Denver and Newark. Subsequently, in 1986, Frontier went into bankruptcy, with some of its Denver operations acquired by United Airlines, thus greatly augmenting United's already very large Denver hub. The remainder of Frontier was eventually acquired by Tèxas Air through its acquisition of People Express; since Texas Air also owned Continental, Continental's presence in its Denver hub was further augmented.

Western did very little to the structure of its route network between 1976 and 1981, except to cut total system departures by more than 20 percent. Los Angeles remained its single hub during this period with the level of daily departures remaining essentially unchanged. By 1984 Western had embarked on a new route strategy centered around a hub at Salt Lake City where daily departures were increased to 99 from a 1981 level of only 35. Los Angeles remained a secondary hub with about the same level of departures (74) as it had in both 1976 (77) and 1981 (76). In 1986 Western was acquired by Delta Airlines, thus adding potential western U.S. hubs to Delta's traditional eastern presence.

Multiple-Hub Carriers

Following deregulation, two carriers, Northwest and Ozark, that had two hubs in 1976 changed to being single-hub carriers. Northwest entered deregulation with hubs of similar size at Minneapolis/St. Paul (76 daily departures) and Chicago (60 daily departures); by 1984 Minneapolis/St. Paul had been increased to 103 departures, while Northwest's domestic operations at Chicago had been cut to 32 daily departures. In 1986 Northwest acquired Republic, a carrier that also had its principal hub at Minneapolis/St. Paul. In somewhat parallel fashion Ozark in 1976 operated hubs at St. Louis (71 departures) and Chicago (56 departures), but by 1984 St. Louis had emerged as Ozark's sole hub with 151 departures, with departures at Chicago cut to 20. In 1986 Ozark and TWA, another carrier with its primary hub at St. Louis, proposed were merged.

Delta and Eastern, both multihub carriers prior to deregulation, adopted very similar strategies that focused on tremendous increases in departures at Atlanta. Between 1976 and 1984 Delta increased its Atlanta departures from 237 to 417, while Eastern increasd its Atlanta departures from 244 to 347. Delta added a second hub at Dallas/Fort Worth, with an increase in daily departures from 52 to 202 between 1976 and 1984, while

Eastern increased its departures at Houston from 22 to 98 over the same period. Both also reallocated flights among their other secondary hubs, increasing at some while decreasing at others. From late 1984 on, moreover, Eastern retreated from its Houston hub and emphasized instead development of a major Kansas City hub. Both Delta and Eastern were involved in mergers that made them part of nationwide systems. Delta acquired Western, with its hub at Salt Lake City, and Eastern was acquired by Texas Air, with its hub at Denver.

USAir also adopted a route strategy centered around a large buildup in daily departures at its primary hub, Pittsburgh, which went from 129 departures in 1976 to 263 in 1984. USAir also reallocated flights among its secondary hubs with the main adjustments being increases at Philadelphia and Washington-National and decreases at Buffalo.

American and TWA adopted strategies of shifting or relocating their primary hubs. American entered deregulation with its primary hub at Chicago but between 1976 and 1981 undertook a major expansion at Dallas/Fort Worth from 114 to 213 daily departures while cutting back at Chicago from 154 to 133 departures. By 1984 American had continued to build Dallas to 290 daily departures while rebuilding Chicago to 203 departures. In 1976 TWA had 108 daily departures in Chicago and 85 in St. Louis. By 1984 TWA had built St. Louis into its primary hub with 174 daily departures while cutting operations at Chicago to only 23 daily departures. During the same period TWA also built domestic operations at New York-Kennedy to provide feed traffic for its international operations.[7] As noted, TWA's merger with Ozark also helped build its St. Louis hub.

United strengthened its primary hub at Chicago while building its secondary hub at Denver. Between 1976 and 1981 United held Chicago roughly constant while building Denver and cutting back at San Francisco, Los Angeles, and Cleveland. Between 1981 and 1984 United undertook a major expansion at Chicago from 206 to 312 daily departures while continuing to build at Denver and restoring San Francisco operations to a level somewhat greater than 1976.

Finally, Republic, like Pan American, spent much of the period attempting to solve various problems bequeathed by mergers and attendant financial difficulties. But by 1984 a primary hub had emerged at Minneapolis/St. Paul with 122 daily departures (up from 48 in 1976) and with secondary hubs at Detroit (91 daily departures up from 53 in 1976) and Memphis (87 daily departures up from 46 in 1976). The western portion of Republic's route network was increasingly concentrated on Phoenix with

59 daily departures. Republic's largest hub, Minneapolis/St. Paul, accounted for only about 10 percent of its total daily departures in 1984, the smallest share at a primary hub for any of the trunk or former local service airlines. Republic's merger with Northwest, of course, created a combined airline far more focused on Minneapolis/St. Paul than Republic had been.

Competitive Aspects of Hub Development

Hub strengthening has changed the patterns of passenger flows at the hub airports. At Atlanta, the premier example of a connecting hub both before and after deregulation, over half the passengers (52 percent) boarding aircraft were making online connections in 1976. By 1980 the figure had climbed to 60 percent. Nor was Atlanta's experience unique. In 1976 an average of 21 percent of boarding passengers at five interior hubs—Dallas/Fort Worth, Denver, Minneapolis/St. Paul, Pittsburgh, and St. Louis—were making online connections. By 1980 the average for these airports had climbed to 29 percent.

Even more important, as a consequence of hub stengthening several of the nation's major hub airports became dominated by one or two carriers. Table 5.1 shows the share of capacity measured by weekly seat departures as of 1984 by each carrier at its primary hub as well as the change in that share since 1978. As the table indicates, three carriers came to dominate their primary hubs by 1984: USAir with 75 percent of Pittsburgh, Western with 69.2 percent of Salt Lake City, and Piedmont with 67.1 percent of Charlotte. Moreover near duopolies appeared at Atlanta where Delta and Eastern combined had 89.1 percent, at Minneapolis/St. Paul where Northwest and Republic (merged in 1986) accounted for 78.4 percent, and at St. Louis where TWA and Ozark (also merged in 1986) totaled 80.2 percent. Similarly there were four other larger hubs where two carriers combined for more than half the capacity.

Carrier domination of a hub airport could become a barrier to entry. Specifically a new entrant could be at a severe disadvantage in entering a dominated hub because the entering carrier typically would be offering interline connections in competition with the dominant carrier's online connections. In such a situation not only must the entering carrier battle consumers' usual preference for online connections over interline connections, but the preferential treatment commonly given online connections in computer reservations systems could make it difficult for travelers even to learn from their travel agent of possible interline connections with the entering carrier. Moreover, if joint fares were not offered for interline connections, as described in the previous chapter for connections between

Table 5.1 1984 capacity shares of major airlines at their primary hubs and change of share between 1978 and 1984

Airline	Primary hub	Capacity share as of March 1984 (%)[a]	Change of share (in percentage points) from March 1978 to March 1984
American	Dallas/Fort Worth	40.6	+19.2
Braniff	Dallas/Fort Worth	10.1	−23.0
Continental	Denver	15.0	− 7.9
Delta	Atlanta	51.0	+ 4.0
Eastern	Atlanta	38.1	− 1.5
Frontier	Denver	22.8	+ 5.4
Northwest	Minneapolis/St. Paul	48.8	+ 0.6
Ozark	St. Louis	24.6	+ 4.4
Pan Am	New York	15.5	+ 4.8
Piedmont[b]	Charlotte	67.1	+53.3
Republic	Minneapolis/St. Paul	29.6	+12.5
TWA	St. Louis	55.6	+16.4
United	Chicago	34.1	+ 7.2
USAir	Pittsburgh	75.0	+29.8
Western[b]	Salt Lake City	69.2	+29.4

Source: *Official Airline Guide*, March 1984 and June 1984, as reported in Civil Aeronautics Board, *Report on Airline Service, Fares, Traffic, Load Factors, and Market Shares*, issue 30, June 1984, table 1, pp. 49–60, and issue 31, September 1984, table 1, pp. 7–17.
a. Capacity share measured in weekly seat departures.
b. Piedmont and Western data are for June 1978 and June 1984.

nonaligned commuters and jet carriers, the entering carrier would have to absorb all of the joint fare reduction to offer a competitive connecting fare.

Code-sharing alliances between commuters and major carriers can also strengthen the anticompetitive aspects of hub dominance. If a carrier can "lock up" the commuter feed to a hub, entry by another jet carrier would be even more difficult than if the entering carrier had equal access to feed traffic from surrounding small communities (as might be expected if commuter carriers remained independent). Although the number of passengers a commuter carrier brings to a hub might be small in relation to total enplanements at the hub, it may not be that small in relation to traffic originating at the hub. Thus access to a share of the commuter feed could make a difference to an entering carrier. Moreover in the airline industry the marginal costs of adding passengers to an established flight are often low so that a consistent diference of a few extra passengers can have a disproportionate impact on the profitability of a flight.

Finally, if all these strategies—penalizing interline connections in the computer reservations systems, "cornering" the commuter feed, and the selective use of joint fares—proved inadequate to discourage entry at a hub, a further step would be for the dominant carrier to refuse to interline baggage or even tickets or, in other words, to "go it alone." As mentioned earlier, such a strategy might be particularly appealing to the very largest trunk airlines, and thus developing the potential to "go it alone" may have been a partial reason for the merger activity of 1985–86. Without interlining, a connection between two different carriers would still be possible, but probably more expensive without joint fares and logistically more difficult with passengers responsible for transferring their own baggage and arranging separate tickets.

Successful entry into a hub dominated by another carrier would be likely in only two types of situations. The first would be where a carrier with a dominant hub elsewhere entered the market as a spoke to its own hub. The second would be where the dominated hub was one end to a city-pair market of sufficient density that an entrant could survive on its share of origin and destination traffic alone. In this situation carriers without a dominant hub (e.g., new entrant jet carriers) might participate, albeit at a disadvantage. Of course such a disadvantage might be overcome, at least in part, with lower fares or service innovations.

A hub and spoke system is based, obviously, on connections. As connecting banks become larger, more gates are needed, and more time is required for all the aircraft to arrive and depart. The results are longer walks between gates and longer waits for connecting flights. Large hub and spoke systems are therefore vulnerable to overflight strategies where a competing carrier offers nonstop service between two spoke cities, thereby bypassing hubs and their connections altogether. Still another potentially effective form of competition would be to offer flights over an alternate hub, where a destination or origin city serves as the end of a spoke for more than one hub.

On balance, though, hub strengthening could pose a threat to the market competition needed for deregulation to achieve its goals. Carried to an extreme, and tied to control of computer reservation systems, the threat might warrant antitrust or some similar public policy response. Still, the extent of the anticompetitive threat might also be easily exaggerated as there are clearly self-contained limits on the extent to which hub-building route strategies can be pursued.

Longer and Stronger Route Strategies

A major characteristic of the CAB-regulated operating environment was that the standard fares for long flights were structured to provide a larger margin over costs than that provided by the standard fares for short flights. As a result, many in the airline industry believed that longer routes were inherently more profitable than shorter routes and that with deregulation airlines should aggressively pursue route- and flight-lengthening strategies.

In fact, the old guard airlines did pursue such route-lengthening strategies immediately following deregulation. Thus the trunk airlines increased their average domestic stage length (the average length of an aircraft flight between takeoff and landing) by 21 percent (from 596 to 721 miles) between 1977 and 1982, as contrasted with only 9 percent between 1970 and 1977 (from 545 to 596 miles). Similarly the local service airlines, starting with an average stage length of only 154 miles in 1970, increased that average by 34 percent (to 206 miles) by 1977. But when deregulation released the local service airlines from many of their requirements to serve small communities, they increased that average stage length by a dramatic 74 percent (to 358 miles) between 1977 and 1982.

Strikingly, the three trunk carriers (American, United, and Pan Am) that had traditionally specialized in long-haul flights experienced an appreciable increase in their average stage length after deregulation. In part these increases may have been a by-product of past CAB route policies. None of these carriers had been particularly successful in obtaining new domestic routes in the 1970s. American and United, as two of the largest and financially strongest carriers, were caught by the CAB policy of awarding long-haul routes to smaller or financially weaker carriers in an attempt to promote industry stability or firm size equality. Pan Am, as a CAB-designated international carrier, had been almost totally constrained in its attempts to obtain domestic route authorities. Part of the move into longer routes by these airlines may thus have represented a "pent-up demand" to serve specific markets.

The move into longer routes by the trunk airlines may also have been due to the substantial fleet of wide-bodied aircraft suitable for long hauls that these carriers had at the beginning of deregulation. Table 5.2 shows wide-body capacity as a fraction of domestic fleet capacity for the trunk carriers. In 1977 American, Pan Am, and United were three of the five carriers most heavily dependent on wide-bodied aircraft. Thus their move into longer routes may also have represented an attempt to utilize these wide-bodied aircraft more effectively. As can also be seen in table 5.2, most trunk carriers did not add substantially to wide-body capacity following deregu-

Table 5.2 Wide-bodied aircraft capacity as a percent of the domestic fleet by airline 1970–1981

Carrier	1970	1977	1981
American	5	26	32
Braniff	0	4	8
Continental	6	34	21
Delta	0	21	28
Eastern	0	14	33
Northwest	7	63	49
Pan Am	0	72	47
TWA	0	24	28
United	2	27	39
Western	0	18	23

Source: Derived from CAB Form 41.

lation, despite the fact that some modest addition of the fuel-efficient wide-bodies might have been useful during the runup in fuel prices starting in mid-1979. Indeed, as traffic fell in the recession of 1982, many of the trunks apparently felt that they had too many wide bodies, so many wide-bodied aircraft were mothballed or "thrown into" so-called fare wars on transcontinental and other long-haul routes.

Network Extension through Internal Growth

Table 5.3 shows the total number of domestic airports served by each trunk and local service airline in July 1976, 1981, and 1984. The trunk airlines were modest in their expansions between 1976 and 1981, with only TWA and American adding, on net, more than 10 airports to their networks. By contrast, between 1981 and 1984 all of the trunks increased their networks by at least 10 airports except Braniff, newly reorganized after bankruptcy, and Northwest, which added 8. Overall, from 1981 to 1984 the trunks increased the average number of airports served by 34 percent.

The local service carriers focused initially on dropping small communities (nonhubs) they no longer wished to serve. All the local service airlines also added large hubs to their route networks. Moreover most dropped small hubs and added medium hubs. The striking trend among the local service airlines was thus the increase in the average density of the markets they served. The trunks also used airport additions and deletions to drop smaller communities and add larger ones so as to move into denser markets. Since the trunks under regulation were not burdened with as many small

Table 5.3 Number of airports served by major airlines, 1976–1984

Carrier	July 1976	July 1981	July 1984	Percent change, 1976–1981	Percent change, 1981–1984
Trunks					
American	48	64	91	33	42
Braniff	40	45	22	13	−51
Continental[a]	58	55	67	−5	22
Delta	73	73	113	0	55
Eastern	71	73	93	3	27
Northwest	35	42	50	20	19
Pan Am	40	27	41	−33	52
TWA	38	55	68	45	24
United	89	81	129	−9	59
Western	33	31	58	−6	87
Local service					
USAir	52	57	69	10	21
Frontier	90	78	90	−13	15
Ozark	46	47	53	2	13
Piedmont	49	43	75	−12	74
Republic	160	148	102	−8	−31

Source: Derived from the *Official Airline Guide*, issues of July 1, 1976, July 1, 1981, and July 1, 1984.
a. Includes Texas Air for 1976 and 1981.

communities on their certificates as the locals, their moves out of small communities were not nearly so dramatic. Indeed, only United and Western dropped on net more than two nonhubs by July 1981, and even they dropped only nine and seven, respectively.

The local service airlines pursued network extension strategies along with a fleet strategy of phasing out their remaining turboprop aircraft. All local service airlines operated turboprop aircraft in 1978. By 1981, most had made the transition to all-jet operations while the others had substantially reduced both the number and proportion of turboprops in their fleets.

The markets abandoned by the local service carriers had two characteristics that worked against continued service by an all-jet fleet: they enplaned relatively few passengers, and they involved fairly short flights. The jets these carriers were adding to their fleets seated about twice as many passengers as the turboprops that were being replaced. Thus to continue serving small nonhub markets with jets almost certainly would have resulted in unacceptably low load factors. Jets, to a far greater degree than turboprops, also pay a very heavy fuel consumption penalty for short flights.

After the Iranian revolution in 1979, fuel price increases made low-density, short-haul jet service doubly infeasible.

A change in the total number of airports served is of course only one measure of the extent to which an airline can use the freedoms of deregulation to improve market position. A more accurate measure in many ways, especially of the costs incurred, would be the sum of old airports dropped and new ones added, that is, total station changes. Any station change would represent an expense since one-time costs are associated with both opening a new station and closing an old one. The airlines varied considerably in the extent to which they incurred these costs during the early years of deregulation, as shown in table 5.4 which reports the number of station changes (openings plus closings) between October 1978 and December 1981. To place these changes in the context of the size of the airlines' total system, the table also reports the ratio of station changes to the number of stations (airports) served in July 1976.

Three of the airlines, Braniff, TWA, and Texas Air, had more station changes than the total number of stations they served in 1976. These

Table 5.4 Airline station changes, October 1978–December 1981

Carrier	Station changes	As a fraction of 1976 stations
Trunks		
American	35	.73
Braniff	43	1.08
Continental	21	.68
Delta	22	.31
Eastern	29	.41
Northwest	7	.20
Pan Am	28	.70
TWA	40	1.05
United	29	.33
Western	20	.61
Local service		
USAir	37	.70
Frontier	53	.59
Ozark	28	.61
Piedmont	31	.63
Republic	61	.54
Republic-West	21	.44
Texas Air	39	1.03

Source: Derived from *Official Airline Guide*, various issues and CAB Staff Study, *Report on Airline Fares, Service, and Load Factors*, various issues.
Note: Station changes are defined as the sum of station openings plus station closings.

carriers all had unsettled route strategies in the early months following deregulation and opened new stations that were subsequently closed. Such "mistakes" were costly since they incurred both opening and closing costs for stations that almost certainly generated operating losses while they were served and offered little ongoing potential for profitability (or otherwise they presumably would not have been dropped).

The other airlines appeared to have had more purposeful, or at least more subdued, station and route development strategies, but the striking feature of table 5.4 is how high the ratios are for all but a few carriers. Indeed, only five of the 17 airlines had ratios of less than 0.50.

Hub strengthening coupled with moves into denser markets should have enabled carriers to improve their station utilization, thereby spreading any fixed station costs over more flights. As shown in table 5.5, between July 1976 and July 1984, all the airlines (except Braniff) increased their daily departures per station at their dominant hubs (and substantially so in most cases).

Table 5.5 Average daily aircraft departures per station by airline July 1976 and July 1984

	Dominant hub[a]		Secondary cities[b]	
Carrier	July 1976	July 1984	July 1976	July 1984
Trunks				
American (2)	134.0	246.5	14.0	7.0
Braniff (1)	146.0	78.0	7.4	3.4
Continental (2)	69.5	144.0	9.5	4.9
Delta (2)	144.5	309.5	13.6	10.4
Eastern (2)	167.5	211.5	12.3	10.7
Northwest (1)	72.0	103.0	8.1	5.1
Pan Am (2)	35.5	65.0	7.7	4.1
TWA (2)	60.0	111.5	14.6	4.8
United (2)	151.5	242.0	11.1	6.5
Western (2)	56.5	86.5	8.1	4.1
Local Service				
USAir (2)	102.0	162.5	12.1	9.6
Frontier (1)	105.0	165.0	5.4	4.3
Ozark (1)	71.0	151.0	8.2	4.2
Piedmont (2)	9.5	147.0	8.3	8.9
Republic (2)	50.5	106.5	7.9	8.3

Source: Derived from *Official Airline Guide*, issues of July 2, 1976, and July 1, 1984.
a. Dominant hubs were the one or two largest hubs for each carrier in July 1984. The number for each specific carrier is shown in parentheses.
b. Secondary cities were all cities for a carrier other than that carrier's five most frequently served points in July 1984.

By contrast, none of the trunks increased their daily departures per station at secondary cities, and some, notably TWA, registered substantial drops. The local service airlines did little better, despite starting from a base of fewer departures per station and pursuing a deliberate policy of abandoning their smallest markets. Only Republic and Piedmont increased departures per station at their secondary cities, and then only slightly, while the others all experienced decreases. These changes should be viewed in the context of total RPMs for the major airlines being about 38 percent higher in July 1984 than in July 1976 and system load factors also being higher in July 1984.

In explanation of the patterns observed in table 5.5, most carriers seemingly expanded the number of cities they served more rapidly than their fleet of aircraft. Apparently some carriers felt it important to establish themselves in the cities they wished to serve as quickly as possible, even if it meant not serving those cities as frequently as they might ultimately hope. The slow expansion of fleets was also aggravated by the fuel price increases that began in the third quarter of 1979 which rendered about one quarter of total jet capacity economically obsolete.[8] Nevertheless, even if average daily departures per airport by individual airlines dropped somewhat, competition seemingly increased as a result of the route freedoms of deregulation: between 1976 and 1984 the average number of carriers serving each point increased 48 percent from 2.47 to 3.67.[9]

Network Extension through Merger

Several carriers chose to extend their route networks quickly through merger rather than rely solely on extension through internal growth. The first major postderegulation merger was that of Pan Am and National. Pan Am, which had been confined by CAB regulation largely to international routes, quickly tried to meet its need for a domestic feeder system by the merger with National.

National not only had an existing route network among east coast population centers but also a fleet of fuel-efficient DC-10s and B-727-200s. The B-727-200s were excellent hub and spoke feeder aircraft, and the DC-10s could be used to replace Pan Am's aging fleet of long-haul aircraft. The merger, however, did not immediately bring the desired benefits. Integrating the work forces of the two airlines proved more troublesome than anticipated, with particular difficulty encountered in merging the seniority lists of the unionized employees.

A second major merger immediately after deregulation was the combination of North Central, Southern, and later Hughes Airwest into Republic Airlines. The combined route networks of these three local service airlines covered most of the country, making the newly formed airline of national stature. Integrating these separate route networks into a cohesive system, however, proved quite difficult. As noted earlier, Republic did not immediately consolidate its operations around one or two strong hubs but rather operated at least five rather weak hubs so that Republic, though it had a presence in many markets, was not particularly dominant anywhere. Eventually, this ambiguity was resolved when Republic merged with Northwest in 1986, giving the merged airline a commanding 80 percent position in the Minneapolis hub and considerable strength in Los Angeles, Seattle, Detroit and elsewhere as well.

After a hiatus in major merger activity in the early 1980s—apparently because of the general economic malaise of the industry and growing recognition that mergers were not needed to acquire new routes under deregulation—mergers again became fashionable in the mid-1980s. In 1985 People Express acquired one of the largest commuter airlines (Britt) and Frontier, only to find itself overextended in 1986; this forced, in turn, a "divesture" of Frontier through bankruptcy, and then People Express' absorption by Texas Air. In 1985, too, United acquired Pan American's Pacific operations in a classic use of merger to extend routes (since international operations were not deregulated and still subject to government controls). In 1986 Delta merged with Western in an end-to-end merger that seemed primarily motivated by considerations of network expansion.

By contrast, several other mergers proposed or consummated in the mid-1980s seemed more motivated by notions of scale economies or market control than by network extension. Neither TWA's merger with Ozark nor Northwest's with Republic involved much in the way of network extension. Texas Air's additions of Eastern, People Express, and the remnants of Frontier to its existing positions in Continental and New York Air seemed to involve both network expansion and consolidation of market positions, particularly in the Northeast corridor and at Denver. Piedmont's acquisition of Empire also apparently involved both market and route extension considerations, but probably more of the latter than the former. All in all (and as discussed more fully in chapter 12), as the deregulation experience matured, mergers reemerged as a major strategic possibility, but with market control and pursuit of scale economies becoming at least as important motivations as network extension.

Regional Rationalization

Another route strategy alternative for airlines after deregulation was rationalization of their route networks by focusing on a particular region of the country. The local service airlines in particular were expected to become dominant in a geographic area first and then perhaps extend their routes to more distant destinations.

In essence, the hub-strengthening strategies that almost all carriers pursued did tend to develop a strong market presence in a specific geographic area. The larger carriers, though by dint of pure scale, staked out a larger area than the smaller ones. A special form of regional rationalization open to the local service airlines, however, was to drop service to small communities and redeploy their aircraft to denser markets within the region.

Three of the local service airlines, Frontier, Ozark, and Piedmont, seemingly pursued an initial policy of building regional strength. For example, of the 18 stations Frontier added between July 1976 and July 1981, 15 were within its traditional service area. Similarly both Ozark and Piedmont concentrated their expansions either within or on the periphery of their established service areas.

Collectively the carriers' route development strategies have also involved some shifts in regional emphasis for the entire airline system. These shifts can be seen most clearly by comparing the hubs at which individual carriers increased daily departures with those at which they decreased departures. Table 5.6 lists those hubs at which carriers increased their daily departures by 50 or more between July 1976 and July 1984. Eleven of the 17 hubs in the table, including the three with the largest increases, represent centrally placed connecting locations for the rapidly growing southern and western portions of the country. This pattern suggests that prederegulation CAB route regulation may not have permitted the airlines to respond fully to demographic and locational changes in the U.S. population.

Such a tendency is further evident in table 5.7, which lists those hubs at which a carrier decreased daily departures by 25 or more. Twelve of the 16 hubs subject to decreases were either northern industrial cities (e.g., Cleveland, Pittsburgh, and Chicago) or coastal cities (e.g., Los Angeles, Miami, and New York) with little opportunity to build as connecting domestic hubs because of obvious geographical limitations. In the cases of Chicago, Dallas/Fort Worth, and Pittsburgh, another motivation may have been to withdraw from a hub dominated by other carriers.

Table 5.6 Hubs with an increase of 50 or more daily departures, July 1976 to July 1984

Carrier	Airport	Change in daily departures
Delta	Atlanta	180
American	Dallas/Fort Worth	176
Delta	Dallas/Fort Worth	151
Piedmont	Baltimore	146
USAir	Pittsburgh	134
Piedmont	Charlotte	129
United	Chicago	104
Eastern	Atlanta	103
TWA	St. Louis	89
Continental	Houston	87
Ozark	St. Louis	80
United	Denver	77
Eastern	Houston	76
Republic	Minneapolis/St. Paul	74
Western	Salt Lake City	63
Continental	Denver	61

Source: Derived from *Official Airline Guide*, issues of July 1, 1976, and July 1, 1984.

Table 5.7 Hubs with a decrease of 25 or more daily departures, July 1976 to July 1984

Carrier	Airport	Change in daily departures
TWA	Chicago	−85
Braniff	Dallas/Fort Worth	−68
Continental	Dallas/Fort Worth	−54
United	Cleveland	−44
United	Pittsburgh	−42
Braniff	Kansas City	−39
Ozark	Chicago	−36
Delta	Chicago	−33
American	New York (LGA)	−31
American	Los Angeles	−29
Continental	El Paso	−29
Northwest	Chicago	−28
Republic	Milwaukee	−27
TWA	Los Angeles	−26
Delta	Miami	−25
United	Los Angeles	−25

Source: Derived from *Official Airline Guide*, issues of July 1, 1976, and July 1, 1984.
Note: A negative number indicates a decrease in daily departures.

Seasonality Reduction

Airline travel has distinct seasonal variation, particularly travel for leisure purposes. For example, southern vacation markets, particularly those in the southeast, are most frequently visited in the winter, while east and west coast vacation markets are more often visited in the summer. The result is that east–west markets, and the carriers that serve them, tend to have more passenger demand in the summer and north–south markets relatively more demand in the winter.

This seasonal variation can make it difficult for airlines to utilize their capacity year-round. For a carrier with a predominant east–west route network to have sufficient capacity to meet the summer demand, it will most likely have aircraft that will be underutilized in the winter. In principle, deregulation should have allowed carriers to enter markets that have peak demand in their off-peak season, thus improving aircraft utilization.

Several carriers, in fact, seemingly pursued such strategies after deregulation. Eastern and Delta, predominantly north–south carriers with their greatest strength in the eastern half of the United State, entered several western markets. TWA, an east–west carrier, entered new Florida markets and increased its service in others it already served. USAir, a northeastern regional carrier under regulation, added southern and southwestern markets with winter travel peaks. Many of these route openings were also accompanied by special promotional fares. Despite such moves, however, no dramatic reduction in seasonal variation of passenger traffic is evident for most carriers. The seasonality embedded in the historically established route networks apparently could not be easily overcome by simply entering a few counterseasonal markets.

Opting Out

The final route strategy was to do very little, in essence, to opt out of making major adjustments to compete in a deregulated environment. The only carrier that seemed to take this approach in the first years following deregulation was Western Airlines. Western became involved in merger discussions with Continental shortly after the beginning of deregulation. During those discussions Western made very few changes to its route network, as if simply waiting to merge before responding to deregulation's freedoms. The merger subsequently did not take place and Western belatedly began to respond to deregulation by establishing a major hub at Salt Lake City, as described earlier. Ultimately Western also found its merger partner when in 1986 it agreed to an offer from Delta.

Fare Strategies

Strategic route development considerations spilled over directly into the established carriers' fare policies. For example, several carriers used discounts to stimulate additional feeder traffic so as to develop existing hub and spoke networks. Discounting has also been an important element in developing new hubs or expanding old ones, as shown by Eastern in Kansas City and United in Denver. The use of discounts for hub strengthening appears, however, to be limited to the more competitive airports; for example, USAir's dominance in Pittsburgh has resulted in very little discounting in that city. Fare discounts have also been commonly used to develop new routes to counterbalance seasonality or to get travelers to extend their trips on a carrier as that carrier extended its network into new areas. Thus Piedmont heavily discounted new long-haul flights from Charlotte in order to retain passengers who had previously flown Piedmont on short-haul legs and then changed to other carriers for the long-haul segments.

Generally, fare discount strategies have emerged in four basic situations: (1) established carriers battling for market share, (2) market entry by an established carrier, (3) market entry by a "new entrant" carrier, frequently with a lower cost structure than the incumbent carriers, and (4) deep discounting as a result of cash flow problems and financial distress. Each of these cases has had distinct aspects and consequences.

Case 1: Established Carriers Pursuing Market Share

Fare wars typified by two or three incumbent major carriers battling for market share frequently reflected attempts to stimulate traffic in the face of falling load factors or to reduce the seasonal traffic imbalances that characterize many markets. The magnitude and duration of these pricing revisions is difficult to ascertain from publicly available data: though some carriers have reduced prices, other airlines have tended not to lower quoted fares but instead have increased the percentage of seats sold at discount.

Price-cutting among incumbent carriers has also been used to increase market share as part of a hub-strengthening strategy. In some instances this has even spilled over into an extension of discount fares into smaller markets where such fares were previously unavailable.

Nevertheless, market-share price competition among established incumbents has tended to be controlled, in both depth and duration. Fare reductions, for example, have frequently been put into effect with announced termination dates. There is only limited evidence of escalation of discounting beyond the initial stage. Following the introductory period, fares have often returned to previous levels with little permanent change in fare structure, with the possible exception of more discount fares being available in some smaller markets.

Case 2: New Entry by an Established Carrier

Entry by established carriers into new markets has often been marked by promotional low fares to "buy-in" to the market. Of course many products, from laundry detergent to magazine subscriptions to record clubs, commonly are offered initially at substantial discounts to attract consumers. The extension of entry and fare freedoms has thus resulted in air carriers behaving more like firms elsewhere in the economy. When confronted, the incumbent carriers have tended to match the entrants' low introductory fares quickly. This reaction is usually intended as a signal that the incumbents will protect their market share aggressively and that further expansion would be unprofitable for the new entrant.[10]

Although traffic volumes have tended to increase substantially in response to such discounting, frequently it is not enough to offset the additional capacity introduced by the new entrant. These price wars appear to be self-limiting, however, with carriers recognizing that beyond some point additional discounting would serve only to dilute yields to unprofitable levels. Although fares have tended to rise sharply after these wars subside, long-run average prices and yields have usually remained below former levels. In addition a variety of lower promotional and discount fares have become permanently established.

The 1980 transcontinental fare war aptly illustrates the type of price war triggered by market entry by an established carrier. As shown in figure 5.1, New York–California unrestricted coach airfares fell precipitously in July 1980. Although entry by such prederegulation charter carriers as World Airways and Capitol Airways was part of the explanation, the extremely low unrestricted fares prevailing during the summer of 1980 mainly resulted from the entry of Eastern into the market and the competitive responses of the incumbent carriers (particularly American). The price discounting that ensued was a result of substantial new capacity and a struggle for market share among established carriers with approximately the same cost structures.

The response of traffic to the new low fares was dramatic. New York–San Francisco and New York–Los Angeles traffic increased by 34.8 and 12.6 percent, respectively, in the third quarter of 1980 over the third quarter of 1979, whereas passenger volumes in all domestic markets declined by

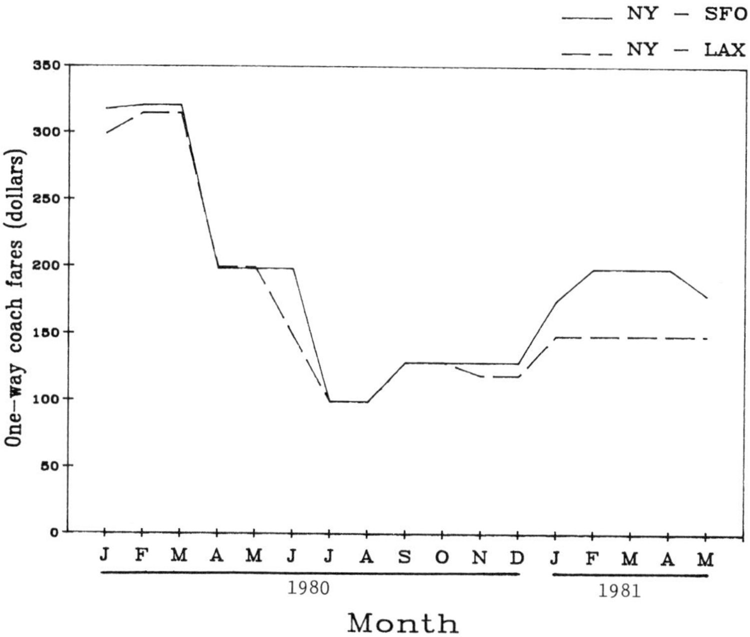

Figure 5.1 New York to California fare wars of 1980–1981.

12.9 percent over the same period. Consumers were apparently diverted from other vacation markets to California, and many travelers rearranged schedules to take advantage of the low fares. For example, passengers traveling between Philadelphia and Los Angeles saved over $200 by backhauling to New York and using the low New York–Los Angeles fare rather than flying directly. In fact, for markets up to 750 miles west of New York or east of Los Angeles, it was generally cheaper to backhaul to either coast and use the low transcontinental fare.

The entry of Eastern (and to a lesser extent, World Airways) also affected market shares. The new entrants garnered about 20 percent of the market in June and slipped back to about 15 percent by October. Thus, though the new entrants were able to establish themselves, the incumbent carriers remained dominant.

Although transcontinental prices in late 1980 increased sharply, a variety of new, high-discount promotional fares continued to be offered. Indeed, since the summer of 1980, average transcontinental yields have remained lower than on most comparable routes elsewhere in the domestic system.

Case 3: Entry by "New Entrant" Carriers

As noted in the last chapter, one of the most publicized effects of deregulation has been the formation of entirely new airlines. These new entrants typically have lower costs than established carriers and have attempted to exploit this advantage by setting low fares, as shown in table 5.8. These low fares have been aimed at establishing market presence and generating traffic volume among price-sensitive travelers (many of whom were not previous air travelers). Since these new entrant carriers generally have not provided substantial increases in capacity (at least initially), the established carriers have responded to the new entrant's low fares mainly by instituting matching discounts that are capacity controlled. In some cases an adjustment has also occurred in unrestricted fare levels. For example, New York Air's entry into the Boston–New York–Washington corridor with a $45 peak New York–Boston fare caused Eastern to reduce its shuttle fare from $56 to $49 during peak periods, and to match New York Air's fare on off-peak flights.

Initially, few attempts were made by the established carriers to drive the new entrants totally out of the market. In part this may have been due to cost differentials, but it also appears that the new entrants' low prices often so expanded the market that only a few passengers were taken from the incumbent carriers. As time passed, some of the entrants grew and became more aggressive. The established carriers also became more experienced in responding to the new entrants, finding ways through capacity controls to limit discounts to passengers ostensibly most sensitive to price. As a consequence the new entrants were confronted increasingly with stiff competitive responses from the old guard, to the point that in some cases the new entrants were actually forced to withdraw.

Table 5.8 Comparison of fares of new entrants and established carriers in selected markets, August 1982

Market	Major carrier coach fare	New entrant fare
Boston–New York	$ 56	$ 35
Washington–Boston	79	49
Chicago–Washington	189	109
Boston–Jacksonville	149	119
Cleveland–New York	154	99
Columbus–New York	166	65
St. Louis–Chicago	104	69
New York–Raleigh/Durham	149	79

Source: *Official Airline Guide*, August 1, 1982.

Case 4: Financial Problems

Severe fare wars have sometimes resulted when a financially troubled carrier has slashed fares to generate cash. Such fare cuts have often been of substantial depth. It has been suggested that such prices in some markets have fallen below average cost at full load, resulting in breakeven load factors in excess of 100 percent. Though obviously not sustainable over a long period, such fares can bring in cash to meet pressing financial liabilities. In markets where the financially troubled carrier has a strong presence, competitors have responded by matching fares to preserve traffic volume, apparently hoping that the deep fare reductions would be short-lived.

The premier example of a "cash flow" fare war was the intense price competition in Dallas markets that resulted from Braniff's financial problems. Undertaking rapid expansion in 1979, Braniff purchased 41 new aircraft in three years at a cost of $925 million. The carrier's debt service costs exploded as interest rates rose steadily, since much of Braniff's bank debt was linked to the prime rate. At the time Braniff filed for bankruptcy in May 1982, annual debt service costs exceeded $125 million. Braniff lost $160.1 million in 1981 and another $41.4 million in the first quarter of 1982.

As Braniff's strategy changed in 1981 and 1982 from profitable growth to staying aloft, the airline was forced to adopt severe price cuts to generate cash. In January 1982 Braniff removed all discount restrictions, instituted single-class service, and slashed fares an average of 45 percent. The extent of these cuts in three markets is shown in figure 5.2. Fares from Dallas to Los Angeles, New Orleans, and Denver fell 46, 64, and 47 percent, respectively. American Airlines, with 42 percent of its flights in markets also served by Braniff, quickly responded by matching Braniff's fares. Industry analysts have estimated that these fare cuts reduced American's 1982 revenues by $65 million.[11] Matching Braniff's other discounts (two-for-one tickets, etc.) reduced American's yield even further. Other airlines matched Braniff's fares, including some carriers (Continental and Western) that were also in financial difficulty. Having other carriers match its fare reductions effectively prevented Braniff from garnering enough additional traffic to make it through to its traditionally profitable third quarter. After Braniff filed for bankruptcy in May 1982, the other carriers quickly moved to increase fares. American, for example, restored fares to their June 1981 level and imposed restrictions on discount fares.

A somewhat more complex fare war was initiated in the Florida markets during early 1982, prompted in part by the financial problems of Pan Am and Air Florida. Pan Am, with the appointment of Edward Acker as chairman in late 1981, adopted a cut-rate fare strategy in the New York–

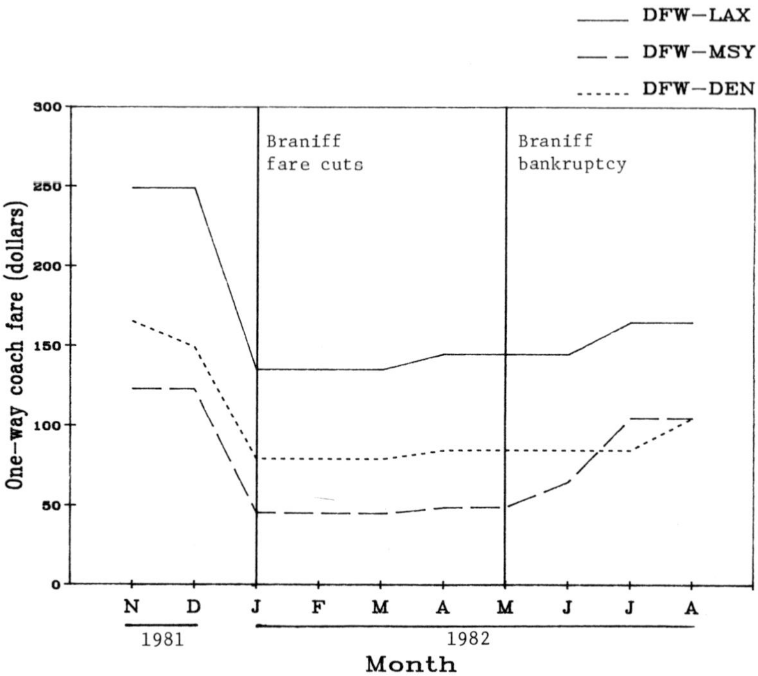

Figure 5.2 Fare wars in Dallas markets, 1981–1982.

Florida market. Previously Air Florida (under Acker's leadership prior to his move to Pan Am) had maintained a much lower fare structure than Delta and Eastern, with the two major carriers countering with selective, capacity-controlled discounts (apparently made effective because of perceived service differentials and Air Florida's small market share). Pan Am's cut-rate policies of early 1982 thus introduced large-scale price discounting in a market already characteriszed by low fares and excess capacity. As market shares of the dominant carriers eroded, they responded by reducing unrestricted coach fares from $149 to $103. Fare-cutting continued from January through March 1982 with considerable uncertainty about how long the fare war would persist. Air Florida introduced connecting flights to other Florida cities for $10; Florida fares from other east coast cities also fell to prevent diversion of travel through New York. In March, however, Delta and Eastern announced they would not be underpriced on any flight. Given the strong market position of these two carriers, the action clearly signaled that further price-cutting might not increase revenues, with the market thus regaining some semblance of stability by late 1982.

These fare wars of 1982 reemerged during 1984, but in a very different guise. The 1984 discounting began with the emergence of both Braniff and Continental from bankruptcy. With their operating costs dramatically reduced, these two carriers began a series of price promotions to rebuild market share. They were joined by the new entrant, People Express, which had doubled its fleet size in the previous 18 months and was aggressively entering new markets.

The major airlines responded, but more selectively than before. Rather than slicing fares across the board, they placed more restrictions on their cheap fares, limited the number of discount seats, and cut prices only where the low-cost airlines challenged them on routes central to their operating strategy.

In late summer of 1984, for example, Eastern faced tough price competition from Continental in Houston while People Express and a half-dozen smaller carriers began a wave of price-cutting on routes between New York and Florida. Realizing that matching prices in both markets would result in sizable losses, Eastern reduced its Houston capacity by more than half and shifted it to Florida. The increased Florida capacity and a short-lived fare reduction from $159 to $99 for a New York–Florida ticket signaled Eastern's intention to preserve its position, and discounting subsided in the Florida market. The series of events did have long-term effects, though, as unrestricted fares between New York and Florida subsequently stabilized at roughly $130.

United's response to People Express' entry into Chicago illustrated another use of capacity management as a competitive tool. In August 1984 People Express began Newark–Chicago service for $79 peak and $59 off-peak, with no additional restrictions. These fares were less than one-third of the previous unrestricted fare of $258 charged by United. United responded by advertising that it would match the low fares while preserving amenities such as free baggage handling and in-flight meals. However, tickets at these prices were subject to both advance-purchase and minimum-stay restrictions. Unrestricted coach fares were also offered, for $119 peak and $99 off-peak. The number of discount seats being offered was carefully managed by United. Like that of most major carriers, United's computer system plans seating allotments up to a year in advance. The number of discount seats offered is determined by historical selling patterns. If a particular flight is not filling up with full-fare passengers as rapidly as expected, more seats can be opened up for discounts, and vice versa. Thus the balance of discount and full-fare tickets can be continually revised and carefully targeted to respond to new competition. Basically, the ability to manage the number of seats available at each price has enabled the old airlines to initiate and respond quickly to price and entry competition, and thus fundamentally to alter the marketplace for air travel.

Summary

The dominant route strategy of the established carriers after deregulation was to build their hub and spoke operations, thereby emphasizing their primary strengths (large-scale computer reservation systems, large-scale terminals, mechanized baggage handling, etc.) vis-à-vis the new entrant carriers. They also added new airports and discontinued service at others so as to extend the geographic coverage of their networks and to increase their average stage lengths. These steps not only reduced costs but also allowed the carriers to offer such service attractions as enhanced single-carrier service and additional frequencies. The net effect has been to create an industry where particular airlines have come to dominate certain hubs, suggesting an element of potentially diminished competition, though most major city-pairs are served by more carriers than before, pointing to an element of increased competition.

It is of course possible that the carriers' emphasis on hub and spoke operations may recede as they reequip during the 1980s and 1990s with smaller- and medium-sized fuel-efficient aircraft (MD-80s, B-737-300s, B-757s, and B-767s) better suited to "flyover" strategies that avoid major hubs. Direct flyover operations also eliminate connections and thereby improve service for many travelers. Any increase in congestion delays at major hubs would, of course, only heighten any tendency to supplant hub and spoke strategies with flyovers. Nevertheless, immediately following deregulation both marketing and cost considerations dictated a strong emphasis on hub and spoke network development for the established carriers. In addition, to the extent that large hubs create some barriers to entry by smaller airlines, they are likely to remain a part of the established carriers' strategies for some time to come.

The established carriers used their new found freedoms in fare setting to complement their route strategies. Specifically, fare discounting emerged when this was useful in developing new hubs or adding spokes (and thus strengthening established hubs). Low "introductory" fares were also a common means employed by the established carriers to establish presence in entirely new markets. Discounts, usually done in a highly selective and quantity-controlled fashion, also were used by the established carriers to meet challenges to their market shares posed by the entry of entirely new carriers into particular markets or city-pairs. However, when established carriers initiated price cutting as a promotional and marketing tool for new entry, or as a means of utilizing excess capacity, these reductions in most cases have been short-lived and self-limiting, with long-run fare levels and market shares being only somewhat modified. By contrast, where new airlines have initiated fare cuts to generate traffic and market position, the result has more often been persistently lower fare levels and a greater variety of discounts.

Finally, discounts, sometimes approaching truly unsustainable "fare war" levels, were unleashed in certain markets where one of the participating carriers (sometimes new, sometimes old) needed immediate cash flow to fend off bankruptcy; in these cases the other carriers' strategies became simply that of more or less meeting the fare cuts and hoping that they could survive until "normality" returned. Fare wars due to such financial problems have tended to end either when a bankruptcy occurred or when larger carriers responded so aggressively that they convinced others that they would do whatever was needed to protect their market shares.

In general, a deregulated environment and the emergence of low-cost new entrant jet carriers has forced the established carriers to look for new ways to compete on the basis of both fares and service. In addition to changing their route and fare strategies, a second major theme of the established carriers in responding to this challenge has been a concerted effort to improve their overall productivity, thereby lowering their costs. As documented in the next chapter, this they have done, although probably not to the point of immediately matching the performance of their very lowest cost competitors.

6

Productivity, Employment, and Labor Relations

Prior to the fact, the principal concern in airline labor circles was a perception that deregulation might somehow threaten job security by reducing total employment in the industry or, even more likely, reducing employment at certain airlines unable to cope with a dereguated competitive environment. The airline unions felt that senior employees left without work because of these developments should have a priority claim on any new jobs that became available elsewhere in the industry.

Predicting deregulation's eventual effects on employment is neither a simple task nor an issue on which widespread consensus is easily achieved. Employment at a particular airline can be influenced by many considerations ranging from differences in regional economies to managerial styles. Similarly total airline employment is determined by the interaction of several elements, including total airline industry output, the productivity of the various factors of production, and the mix of these factors used to produce airline services. Deregulation might have a very mixed impact on these various influences.

On the positive side, deregulation could be expected to increase airline employment by increasing the number of people flying. Based on the experiences with administrative deregulation from 1976 to 1978, lower fares had apparently stimulated more travel than otherwise would have occurred and induced travelers to switch from autos to air for more of their trips.

On the negative side, feeding labor's concerns about job security, the prospect of productivity improvements was a major argument in favor of deregulation in the congressional debate prior to the passage of the Deregulation Act. Comparisons of the CAB-regulated airlines and the largely unregulated intrastate carriers in Texas and California revealed that the intrastate carriers had achieved both higher productivity and substantially lower costs.[1] The intrastate carriers were also believed to have kept costs down by reducing restrictive work rules and lowering wage rates. Organized labor found both of these trends discomforting, particularly since the intrastate carriers were frequently nonunion.

These and other issues concerning the impact of deregulation on airline labor are examined in this chapter. To start, productivity changes among the major airlines following deregulation are analyzed. The discussion then turns to how the conditions of employment, in terms of wage rates, work rules, and job security, have changed in response to the increased competitive pressures of deregulation. Finally, the net effects of these competing forces on the amount of airline employment are assessed for the 12 established major jet carriers who prior to deregulation were largely unionized and where the possibility of employment losses was of particular concern to organized labor.

Airline Productivity

The U.S. airline industry has been characterized by high rates of productivity growth throughout most of its history. In the 10 years prior to World War II, output per employee in the industry grew at an average annual rate of just over 10 percent.[2] Following World War II, productivity growth remained high with total factor productivity growing at 8 percent per year between 1948 and 1966, the highest of any major industry.[3] Airline productivity clearly was helped by rapid technological development, most notably the introduction of jet aircraft in the early 1960s. Productivity continued to benefit from technological improvements throughout the late 1960s and early 1970s with the introduction of more efficient fan jet engines and wide-bodied aircraft.

Following deregulation, several operational and marketing changes further improved productivity; these included increased aircraft utilization, higher load factors, and, as will be discussed later, negotiation of less restrictive work rules for many airline employees.[4] These and other improvements stemmed from increased airline incentives to be productive and a dramatic increase in the long-run penalties for being inefficient. To be sure, operating economies had always been sought in the airline industry, but under regulation the penalty for not having the lowest costs had not been severe. The CAB allowed all carriers to have at least some monopoly routes and relatively few routes had more than two jet carriers. Of probably more importance, the CAB's restrictions on price competition prevented a low-cost carrier from charging lower fares, and thereby gaining market share.

With deregulation and fare freedom, however, the situation was quite different. Potential, and actual, competition triggered an increased emphasis on improving productivity, both during the 1976–1978 administrative deregulation and in the first years following formal deregulation. For the former trunk and local service airlines combined, productivity grew at an average annual rate of 2.8 percent between 1970 and 1975 but increased to an annual rate of 5.1 percent between 1976 and 1980.[5]

A quick perspective on productivity developments can be gained by comparing unit costs of output with the prices airlines paid for their inputs.

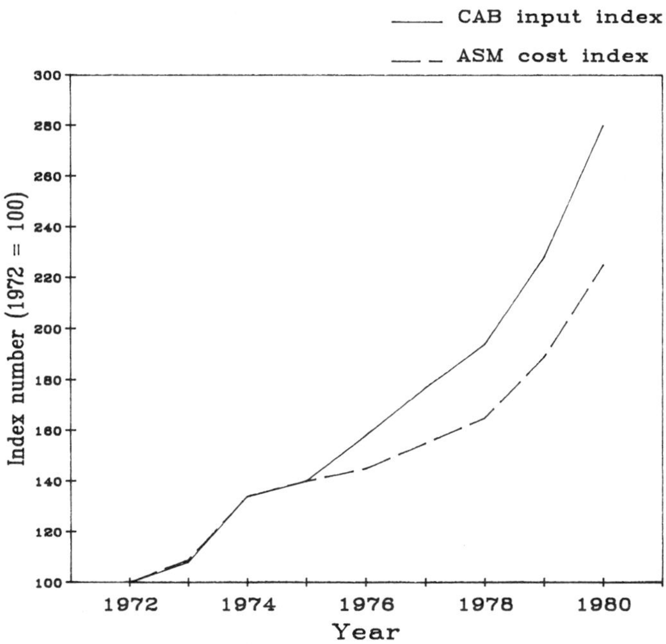

Figure 6.1 Trends in airline cost indexes, 1972–1980.

Index numbers for output and input cost levels for domestic operations of the trunk and local service airlines between 1972 and 1980 are shown in figure 6.1. Output costs are represented by the average expenditure per available seat mile (ASM). Input costs are represented by the airline industry's input price index developed by the CAB.[6]

Productivity, broadly defined and highly aggregated, can be considered to have improved when ASM unit costs grew less rapidly than the CAB input price index. As the figure demonstrates, by this measure the industry managed to improve its productivity during both the "boom" period of administrative deregulation from 1976 through 1978 when the airlines accommodated the largest traffic surge in the industry's modern history, and the contraction period following 1979 when fuel prices soared and recessions occurred. From 1976 to 1978 increases in input prices far outstripped average output costs, implying productivity gains as the airlines capitalized on traffic increases. Skyrocketing fuel prices during 1979 and 1980 are evident on the graph, as the weighted average of input prices tilts sharply upward during those years. Forced to cope with the simultaneous problems of high fuel prices, declining traffic, and accelerated obsolescence of the less fuel-efficient components of the aircraft fleet, the industry produced its output at much higher average cost.[7] But remarkably, even during this period of difficulties, the ASM unit cost did not rise as sharply as the prices paid by the airlines for their inputs.

In examining the postderegulation experience, it is useful to distinguish between two separate impacts of deregulation on productivity. The first is a one-time gain in productivity from redeploying factors of production that had been misallocated due to CAB regulatory policies. The second is any change that may have been fostered in the fundamental long-run ability of the airline industry to take advantage of technological change.

Examples of factor misallocation from CAB regulation abound. Indeed, a major part of the initial adjustment to deregulation was a redeployment of the factors of production away from regulation-induced service patterns toward patterns determined by market demand. In principle, these one-time productivity improvements should be distinguished from a potential change in the industry's ability to foster and take advantage of technological improvements. In practice, however, making this distinction is empirically difficult, especially with the short data series available on the deregulation experience. Usually both types of productivity changes have been lumped together and interpreted as a general change in the rate of productivity improvement.

The productivity analysis reported in this chapter differs from previous studies in three ways. First, it attempts (though only with limited success) to recognize the two separate aspects of deregulation's effect on productivity. Second, productivity change is disaggregated into four different components rather than focusing solely on total factor productivity. Finally, the productivity of the major jet carriers is compared with that of the lowest-cost carriers to assess the size of the productivity gap separating them and the progress of the majors in closing that gap.

Components of Productivity Change and Their Measurement

Four different measures of productivity performance were calculated on a carrier by carrier basis for 1978 and 1980: the ratio of available seat miles (ASMs) to, in turn, flight employees, fuel, and aircraft, and the ratio of available seat departures to ground employees. A simple comparison of percentage changes in these ratios across airlines is shown in table 6.1. Clearly most of the major airlines achieved aggregate productivity gains more or less in line with immediate historical precedent during 1979 and 1980, with the local service airlines actually doing even better.

Comparisons are conditioned, however, by differences in aircraft fleets and route networks.[8] To a considerable extent these differences in fleets

Table 6.1 Percent changes in productivity measures by carrier, 1978–1980

Carrier	Productivity measure: ASMs per gallon	ASMs per flight employee	Available seat departures per ground employee	ASMs per aircraft	Aggregate
Trunks					
American	7.07	−8.87	−8.99	−0.48	−0.32
Braniff	11.92	21.57	2.52	−5.43	9.40
Continental	*	*	*	*	*
Delta	11.93	−0.92	−4.75	7.14	5.22
Eastern	10.00	5.46	−7.38	12.33	5.31
Northwest	*	*	*	*	*
Pan Am	6.01	−7.83	−9.26	10.86	0.53
TWA	19.39	7.66	6.78	10.40	13.38
United	10.58	−0.47	−17.53	5.28	1.37
Western	11.64	−8.41	−14.02	2.97	1.12
Local service					
USAir	17.79	7.79	−3.43	29.06	12.24
Frontier	9.38	17.65	−13.44	23.04	9.38
Ozark	*	*	*	*	*
Piedmont	26.00	19.31	−15.83	58.21	18.37
Republic	12.86	8.06	−3.60	25.71	9.51
Texas Air	14.67	17.57	1.17	30.37	13.65

Source: Authors' calculations using data from CAB reports.
Notes: The aggregate column is calculated as the average percent improvement of each of the four components weighted by 1980 factor shares. The * denotes a strike, making the productivity measures for these years meaningless or difficult to interpret.

and networks can be attributed to past management decisions that were conditioned by the prior regulatory environment. Fleet and network configurations at the onset of deregulation thus must be taken into account when attempting to evaluate productivity performance during the early years of deregulation.[9]

In an attempt to evalute the impact of these differences, a simple linear regression model (see table 6.2) was estimated in which each productivity ratio was specified as a function of average aircraft size (seats per aircraft), average stage length, the percent of passengers departing for international destinations, and a dummy variable to distinguish between 1978 and 1980. By comparing the actual value an airline achieved with the value predicted for that airline by the regression function (i.e., examining the regression residual), the individual airline's performance can be compared to what might be expected for a "typical" established airline operating with the

Table 6.2 Adjustment equations for productivity measures

Explanatory variables	Dependent variables: ASMs per gallon	ASMs per flight employee	Available seat departures per ground employee	Million ASMs per aircraft
Constant	28.01	2,201,000	6,613	−47.48
	(11.62)	(5.60)	(12.16)	(2.32)
Aircraft size	0.0278	15,090	13.38	1.369
	(0.93)	(3.11)	(1.99)	(5.39)
Stage length	0.0081	105.6	−6.579	0.0449
	(1.96)	(0.16)	(7.08)	(1.28)
Percent International	−0.0764	2.324	8.88	0.6668
	(1.31)	(0.25)	(0.68)	(1.35)
1980 dummy	3.527	107,000	−40.4	−11.23
	(3.52)	(0.66)	(0.18)	(1.32)
R^2	0.69	0.78	0.86	0.94

Note: t-statistics are in parentheses. There are 24 degrees of freedom in each equation.

same route and fleet characteristics.[10] Changes over time in these regression residuals would denote improvement or deterioration in a particular carrier's productivity after controlling for route and fleet characteristics. To the extent that average stage length or aircraft size were modified because of the increased range of managerial choices made possible by deregulation, these elements of productivity change would be reflected in their corresponding regression coefficients.

Fuel Productivity

Coefficients of the equation for fuel productivity as measured by ASMs per gallon are shown in the first column of table 6.2. As would be expected, ASMs per gallon increase significantly with increasing stage length. Take-off, climb, and landing are more fuel-intensive portions of flights than level cruising, so short flights, with relatively little time spent in the cruise portion, typically yield fewer ASMs per gallon than do long flights. Obviously any increase in stage length resulting from deregulation's route freedoms should have yielded an improvement in this productivity measure. By contrast, aircraft size had a statistically insignificant, though positive, effect on fuel productivity, apparently reflecting the fact that fuel efficient aircraft come in many sizes.

The attention given to reducing fuel consumption in all phases of flight in 1979 and 1980 can be seen in the significant positive effect of the 1980 dummy variable. The dramatic fuel price increases that began in mid-1979 had an enormous effect on airline operations.[11] The airlines grounded the less fuel-efficient aircraft (or in some cases flew them much more selectively), flew more slowly, and directed more maintenance toward improving fuel consumption.

This improvement can also be seen in the universal advance made by major airlines in the ASMs they realized per gallon between 1978 and 1980, as reported in the first column of table 6.1. Some of these gains are attributable to increased stage length and can be considered a one-time productivity gain made possible by deregulation through redeploying aircraft away from short-haul multistop routes for which they were poorly suited. Some of the gains are also the result of factor substitution. Flying more slowly, for example, substitutes flight crew time for fuel. Similarly, directing more maintenance attention to fuel saving substitutes maintenance labor for fuel.

Labor Productivity

Measuring labor productivity is complicated by differing labor practices across the airlines and the range of business activities in which airline companies engage. Flight employees are reasonably easy to define and include pilots, copilots, flight engineers, and cabin crews. Creating a reasonably homogeneous measure of airline ground employees is rather more difficult. For this analysis, airline ground employees were defined to include all other (nonflight) airline workers except: (1) employees not primarily involved in passenger air transportation such as air freight or cargo handlers, hotel workers, and restaurant personnel, and (2) maintenance workers. Maintenance workers were excluded, even though they obviously are an integral part of airline operations, because airline maintenance practices vary widely, with some carriers contracting out much of their maintenance to others while some carriers do all or most of their maintenance "in house." Since maintenance is labor intensive, these differences in subcontracting practices could seriously distort the measurement of individual airlines' labor productivity were maintenance employees included.[12]

ASMs were used as the output measure for flight employees because the number of flight employees is mainly a function of aircraft miles and aircraft size. However, many nonmaintenance ground employees, such as ticket agents and aircraft handlers, perform tasks more closely related to departures and arrivals than to the enroute portion of the trip. Thus ground employee output was measured in terms of total available seats departed rather than seat miles flown.

The coefficients for the flight employee productivity equation are shown in the second column of table 6.2. The most important factor in explaining the variation among the established carriers is average aircraft size. A larger aircraft can generate more ASMs without a proportionate increase in flight crew since the required number of cockpit crew members is either two or three for the jet aircraft used by these carriers. For example, a 270-seat DC-10 can generate 80 percent more ASMs on the same length flight than a 150-seat B-727-200, yet both have three crewmembers in the cockpit. Similarly a DC-9-80 (later called a MD-80) can seat about 20 percent more than a DC-9-30, yet both have two crewmembers in the cockpit. The number of cabin crew, however, is roughly proportional to the size of the aircraft since FAA regulations require a minimum of one flight attendant for each 50 seats or fraction thereof.

As the coefficients in the table 6.2 indicate, once the effect of aircraft size was taken into account, neither stage length nor the percent of international enplanements has a significant impact on ASMs per flight employee. The insignificant effect of stage length is somewhat surprising since on longer flights aircraft are able to achieve higher average speeds, which should contribute to more ASMs per hour of flight time. The small and insignificant effect suggests that any impact from higher speed is overwhelmed by differences in flight crew utilization, work rules, or other constraints. For example, carriers with shorter average stage lengths may well be able to schedule their crews to fly slightly more hours per day and thus largely offset any effects of higher speeds on longer flights. Part of the effect of speed may also be captured in the aircraft size coefficient since carriers with longer than average stage lengths tend to have larger than average aircraft. Similar considerations may have biased the international variable's coefficient downward as well.

The low significance of the 1980 dummy suggests that deregulation improved flight employee productivity very little. The effect that was observable, though, was apparently positive. Nevertheless, as table 6.1 indicates, the trunks overall did not significantly improve this measure of productivity between 1978 and 1980.

The coefficients for the ground employee productivity equation are reported in the third column of table 6.2. Average aircraft size has a significant positive effect. Some of the ground employees' tasks are apparently more closely related to aircraft departures than seat (or passenger) departures, suggesting that there may be some scale economies to handling larger aircraft, once other variables (particularly average stage length) are controlled.

Longer average stage lengths are very significantly associated with poorer productivity per ground employee. Longer flights are more likely to involve vacation travel or overnight business trips so that a higher proportion of passengers check baggage. Longer fights also involve more refueling and restocking of the galley, whereas on shorter flights such duties may not be needed at each stop. Finally, an airline with a higher proportion of longer flights may have difficulty keeping ground crew fully utilized given collective bargaining or other constraints on the use of part-time labor and split shifts. Of course, since longer stage lengths and larger planes tend to go together, any scale economies of larger planes in utilizing ground employees may be outweighed by the greater need for such employees on the longer trips typically made by the larger aircraft.

The basic data on changes in available seats per ground employee between 1978 and 1980 are shown in the third column of table 6.1. Ten of the 13 carriers for which it was possible to calculate a change showed deterioration in this productivity measure. That same deterioration is also evidenced by the negative coefficient on the 1980 dummy in the adjustment equation; thus, after controlling for stage length and aircraft size, ground employee productivity was less in 1980 than before deregulation (though not significantly so).

Such widespread worsening of ground employee productivity is not necessarily surprising during the initial adaptation to deregulation. As reported in chapter 5, the average number of carriers serving each point was increasing and the average number of daily departures in secondary cities was dropping for almost all carriers. At these secondary cities, however, the carriers may not have been able to reduce the size of the ground crew proportionately to the reduction in departures (e.g., because of minimum crew requirements to handle an aircraft and constraints on part-time labor). Similarly, some of the local service airlines, who did relatively poorly on this productivity measure between 1978 and 1980 (as shown in table 6.1), may have built up their ground capabilities at some of their new airports more rapidly than their departures.

Aircraft Capital Productivity

Aircraft are the largest component of airline capital, and it is on aircraft acquisition and utilization that CAB economic regulation may have had one of its largest adverse effects. As discussed earlier, the CAB's encouragement of service competition to the exclusion of fare competition had predictable results of inducing low seating densities, a concentration of departures at the peak travel hours of the day, and a reduction in aircraft utilization. By contrast, the traffic boom of the late 1970s, coupled with the airlines' newly acquired fare and route freedoms, encouraged the airlines to squeeze more output from their existing fleets by adding extra rows of seats and flying the aircraft more hours per day.[13]

The coefficients for the productivity equation for aircraft are shown in the final right hand column of table 6.2. As expected, a significant positive coefficient was found for aircraft size, but stage length and international operations did not have significant separate effects. Once these variable were taken into account, aircraft productivity seemed somewhat lower after deregulation, as evidenced by the negative coefficient on the 1980 dummy. Nevertheless, as shown in table 6.1, ASM's per aircraft improved markedly between 1978 and 1980 for virtually every established carrier, although apparently mainly because of increases in aircraft size. Only American and Braniff failed to improve, although American's decline was quite small. Braniff apparently suffered from excess capacity in 1980.

Interpretation of changes in aircraft productivity between 1978 and 1980 is greatly complicated by the rapid run-up in fuel prices in 1979 and 1980 which made the vintage of a carrier's aircraft very important by rendering older fuel inefficient aircraft economically obsolete.[14] While some carriers quickly scrapped or sold their fuel-inefficient aircraft, others continued to use them sparingly on carefully selected routes where they apparently could still generate more revenue than their operating costs. Accordingly, as a productivity measure, the ratio of ASMs per aircraft will be biased downward for those carriers who continued to make limited use of these older aircraft in comparison to those carriers who either had few to begin with or disposed of them quickly.

Overall Performances

The four components of productivity can be aggregated to provide a measure of overall airline performance. Such aggregates for the basic performance data are shown in the final column of table 6.1. Each component was weighted by the factor share in 1980 for trunk airlines in domestic service. The factor shares, as measured by expenditures, varied between 1978 and 1980 largely in response to the dramatic change in fuel prices. The percent improvement in productivity appears slightly higher when weighted with 1980 factor shares than with 1978 factor shares because of the greater emphasis given to fuel productivity improvements. The pattern of improvements across carriers, however, is essentially the same with either set of weights. Of course these weights are admittedly arbitrary, but any other set of weights would almost surely be equally or more so. The aggregate productivity measures presented in table 6.1 should be regarded as useful and informative, but neither more nor less definitive than those derived from more complex weighting schemes or other methods.[15] As already noted, these aggregate productivity measures seem in line with those of the early 1970s for the trunks and somewhat better than those for the local service carriers.

Table 6.3 presents adjusted performance indexes, defined as the percentage difference between the value actually observed for the carrier and the value predicted by the regression equations for a carrier with the same average aircraft size and average stage length. In other words, these indexes

Table 6.3 Comparison of carrier productivity performance, 1980

	Adjusted performance index				
Carrier	ASMs per gallon	ASMs per flight employee	Available seat departures per ground employee	ASMs per aircraft	Aggregate
Trunks					
American	−9.41	−6.20	6.40	−3.59	−4.43
Braniff	−1.32	14.91	20.29	−6.25	6.08
Continental	*	*	*	*	*
Delta	−1.93	−5.48	−9.72	11.75	−2.90
Eastern	0.25	−0.88	−5.02	3.41	−0.84
Northwest	−8.81	13.25	11.56	−17.74	−1.15
Pan Am	−0.66	−8.46	5.52	−6.25	−0.61
TWA	1.68	−4.92	−11.30	−15.33	−4.43
United	0.49	−0.04	2.38	−0.15	0.78
Western	10.53	−11.64	6.79	11.22	5.94
Local Service					
USAir	−7.26	−3.98	−10.25	1.03	−6.51
Frontier	12.98	1.22	−2.51	−1.57	5.66
Ozark	*	*	*	*	*
Piedmont	−0.71	0.21	−8.65	0.52	−2.32
Republic	−2.66	−10.17	13.07	8.99	1.12
Texas Air	8.34	25.64	−8.28	25.90	9.22

Note: The adjusted performance index is the percentage difference between the value observed for the carrier and the value predicted by the adjustment equation using the 1980 route and fleet characteristics of the carrier. The aggregate column is calculated as the average percent difference for each of the four components weighted by the 1980 factor shares. The * denotes a strike, making the productivity measures for these years meaningless or difficult to interpret.

are the regression residual expressed as a percentage of the predicted value provided by the equations reported in table 6.2. The aggregate index in the table (far right column) is calculated as the average percent difference from the predicted values weighted by the 1980 factor shares.

The local service carriers recorded impressive improvements in aggregate productivity between 1978 and 1980 (table 6.1) and also performed well on the standardized relative productivity measure for 1980 (table 6.3). In large part their good performance stemmed from three factors. First, the locals continued their transition from prop-driven to jet aircraft. Second, they greatly reduced their service to very small communities for which their aircraft were poorly suited. Third, they used deregulation's route freedoms to rationalize their route networks and, in particular, to select routes that better fitted their aircraft fleets. Each of these factors, and particularly the latter two, represented one-time improvements from factor redeployment made possible by the relaxation of regulatory route restrictons.[16]

All of the trunks except American improved their aggregate productivity between 1978 and 1980 but fared less well than the local service carriers in 1980 in relative productivity performance. American, interestingly, was also one of the two relatively poorest trunk performers in 1980. On the other hand, American's absolute decline in productivity from 1978 to 1980 was so small as to be inconsequential. The productivity gains of Pan Am, United, and Western were also quite small, even though their adjusted relative performances were either very good, as in the case of Western, or essentially average, as for United and Pan Am.

Among the trunk carriers TWA had by far the greatest improvement in overall productivity, yet remained well below the aggregate productivity level that would be predicted for a carrier with its fleet and route characteristics. TWA entered deregulation with two serious problems. First, it had an older fleet with a high proportion of fuel-inefficient aircraft—a problem made more acute by the increase in fuel prices beginning in mid-1979. Second, its route network was much more linear than hub and spoke in nature—perhaps a carryover from the early days of commercial aviation when the range of aircraft was quite limited. Moreover, to the extent TWA did have a hub at the beginning of deregulation, it was in Chicago where United and American were dominant and expansion was limited by airport constraints. TWA made considerable progress in improving its operations between 1978 and 1980 and shifted its primary hub to St. Louis but, as the 1980 adjusted performance index shows, nevertheless remained less productive than the industry norm.

Productivity Changes in Expansion and Contraction

Productivity improvements expected by deregulation's proponents were largely fulfilled during the boom period following the first relaxations of fare and route regulation (between 1977 and 1979).[17] But the record subsequently (post-1979) became clouded as fuel prices rose, passenger traffic declined, and airline finances deteriorated.

As discussed in more detail later in this chapter, declining traffic and output after 1979 led to a series of employee layoffs, which occurred abruptly at a few (particularly those threatened with bankruptcy), sporadically at some, and gradually at others. Some airlines in fact delayed or avoided layoffs because of previously high productivity, no-layoff personnel practices, continued growth during the overall industry downturn, or a combination of these factors. The period from late 1979 through 1980 was thus one in which some carriers were facing contractions in output while others were still growing. Making productivity gains during expansion tends to be relatively easy if there is slack capacity in either aircraft or personnel. On the other hand, contracting output puts downward pressure on productivity by creating slack capacity and induces declines in labor productivity unless and until layoffs catch up with the contraction. One possible offsetting positive effect of lowered output on labor productivity, as discussed later in this chapter, is the potential for negotiated work rule givebacks during periods of financial difficulties.

Figure 6.2 plots the changes in aggregate productivity between 1979 and

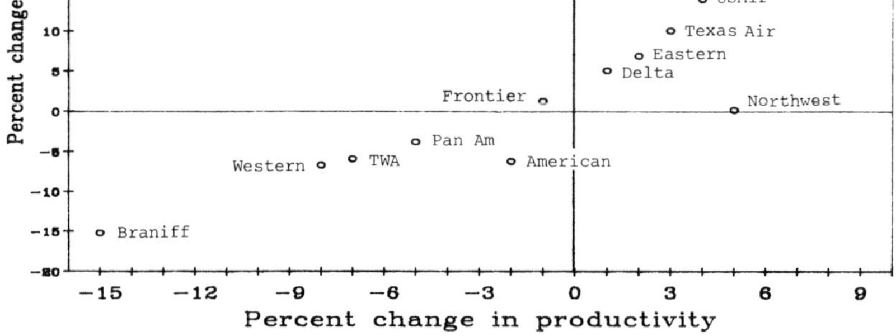

Figure 6.2 Changes in ASMs and aggregate productivity, 1979–1980.

1980 against the change in ASMs during the same period for individual trunk and local service airlines.[18] In the figure the upper right-hand quadrant represents both increasing output and increasing productivity while the lower left-hand quadrant represents declining output and declining productivity.

With the single exception of Frontier (where both productivity and output changes were quite small) all those carriers that increased output also increased aggregate productivity whereas all those carriers that decreased output also suffered decreased productivity. The period represented in the figure is quite short, however, and was at the onset of a recession that proved to be deeper and longer than expected. Still, the figure suggests how difficult it may be for airlines to improve productivity while also cutting output. Conversely, though, it also suggests that more productivity improvements can be expected in the longer run when and if the industry resumes something akin to its historical trends in output growth.

Comparing the Established Carriers and the New Entrants

The equations reported in table 6.2 can also be used to examine the gap in productivity in 1980 between the established carriers and their new competitors. In table 6.4 the highest adjusted productivity index achieved by an established carrier for each component of productivity and for aggregate productivity is compared with the performance of Southwest Airlines, taken as representative of the efficiencies achievable by the lower cost and newer carriers.[19]

Southwest's productivity achievements are well above the best of the established carriers for all four components and in the aggregate. Part of the difference of course stems from differences in the service Southwest provides and differences in route networks not fully captured by the adjust-

Table 6.4 Comparison of the productivity of best established carrier and Southwest Airlines (1980 performance)

Measure	Productivity index: "All-star" or best established carrier	Productivity index: Southwest Airlines
Aggregate productivity	9.22	51.92
ASMs per flight employee	25.64	43.14
Available seats per ground employee	20.29	91.58
ASMs per gallon	12.98	34.68
ASMs per aircraft	25.90	54.72

Source: Author's estimates based on CAB data, as described in text.

ment equations. For example, Southwest's passengers are reportedly not able to board their flights in quite as leisurely a manner as are passengers on many established carriers. Southwest offers only coach service, and it neither interlines tickets nor participates in interline baggage transfers.

These and other differences notwithstanding, Southwest's productivity advantage is so great that much of its demonstrated efficiency must be attributable to company-specific practices—some of which might be transferable to other airlines. Indeed, the existence of any continuing gap between the established carriers' best efforts and the new entrants suggests further gains can be achieved by the older carriers as they better utilize the opportunities unleashed by deregulation. Indeed, the best productivity standards should become controlling in a competitive deregulated environment.[20]

The Terms of Employment

Reflecting the major carrier's concern about the continuing productivity and cost differences between themselves and the most efficient new entrants, union labor contracts settled from 1982 through 1984 gave employees far smaller raises than had been the practice under CAB regulation and in some cases even involved wage cuts (or givebacks). The average annual increase in compensation per employee of the major carriers was 3.8 percent above the consumer price index (CPI) between 1972 and 1978 but fell to one percent below the CPI from 1979 through 1982. The work rules contained in post-1979 labor contracts have also been less restrictive, often permitting assignment of employees to a broader variety of tasks and more working hours per month.

To be sure, these settlements came during a recession with record financial losses by the airline industry. Under such circumstances labor agreements are frequently less favorable toward employees. Nevertheless, deregulation has seemingly altered, perhaps permanently, the nature of labor relations in the airline industry. This change has been created by a composite of different management responses to the new competitive realities. These can be classified into five basic categories:

1. Maintaining the status quo, making no major changes in approach to labor relations.
2. Seeking concessions or givebacks in contract negotiations.
3. Selling the airline to the employees, by trading equity in the company for wage and work rule concessions.

4. Starting a nonunion airline subsidiary.
5. Negating the existing labor contract as part of a bankruptcy proceeding.

Each of these approaches is discussed in turn.

Maintaining the Status Quo

Only two carriers, USAir and Piedmont, did not make major changes in their approach to labor relations after deregulation. Both started as local service airlines and both expanded, and prospered, under deregulation.

USAir and Piedmont entered deregulation with a somewhat better strategic positioning than most other established carriers. Both had rationalized their route structures to a considerable extent even under regulation. As a consequence USAir was receiving no subsidy by the end of regulation and Piedmont was less dependent on subsidy than most other local service airlines. Like other local service airlines, both mainly served short-haul routes where fare markups under regulation were modest. Most of their routes were therefore not attractive candidates for entry. Finally, Piedmont, unlike the trunk airlines operating B-737s, had convinced its pilots long before deregulation began that only two rather than three crewmembers were needed in the cockpits of two-engine planes like the B-737. Taken together, these factors permitted these two airlines to pursue relatively consistent and conventional labor relation practices after deregulation.

Seeking Concessions

By far the most common response among the established carriers was to seek contract concessions on work rules and wages. Among the airlines negotiating such concessions were American, United, TWA, Delta, Northwest, and Ozark. These carriers were generally among the most financially secure in the industry. (The only partial exception was TWA which, though financially weak itself, was then owned by a profitable parent company.) These carriers had also all experienced increased competition after deregulation, often in markets they had previously dominated.

Illustrative of these agreements was that signed by American Airlines in March 1983 with the Transport Workers Union (TWU). This pact not only broke sharply with past practices but set a pattern for many others in the airline industry.[21] The settlement had four important elements, two that favored employees and two that favored management. Union members on the payroll on the date of the settlement received both lifetime job security and small increases in pay and benefits (at a time when many other airlines were seeking actual wage reductions). In exchange, management received work rule changes that allowed much more flexibility in utilizing workers, including the right to hire part-time employees. In addition newly hired workers could be paid on a lower scale than previously hired employees, thus preserving past contract gains for the current union membership while permitting the company to lower its labor costs over the longer run. Of course such a wage structure could also raise potential problems in the long run because of friction arising between workers performing the same task side by side but for substantially different pay.

Even before American had signed this landmark agreement, United Airlines achieved a major postderegulation contractual breakthrough when, in 1981, its pilots agreed to eliminate flight engineers (a third man in the cockpit) on B-737s in exchange for a guarantee against being furloughed. United followed this in June 1984 with a contract with the International Association of Machinists (IAM) patterned after American's settlement with the TWU.[22] In exchange for a modest pay increase United achieved more flexible work rules and the right to start newly hired workers at rates ranging from 27 to 53 percent below the then current levels. Among IAM members only food service workers received employment guarantees in exchange for these concessions.

Delta Airlines is unusual among the established carriers in that the majority of its employees have never been unionized. Delta has also been known for its relatively high productivity and amicable labor relations. It is therefore indicative of the depth of change in the industry that Delta after deregulation sought and received concessions, albeit modest ones, from its employees. Delta delayed general pay increases in 1983, and the vast majority of its employees took a voluntary temporary wage reduction to purchase Delta's first B-767 aircraft.[23] Delta also adopted a dual wage structure by lowering the wage level at which new employees started.

Northwest Airlines, unlike Delta, had a history of labor confrontations and antagonisms. But Northwest, like Delta, seemingly did not seek, and did not achieve, major concessions after deregulation. In the case of its pilots, for example, work rules were changed in 1983 to increase pilot hours from 75 to 83 per month and wages were frozen for six months. But the pilots' contract called for raises of 7.5 percent in 1984, 6.5 percent in 1985, and 3 percent in 1986, rather generous by the standards of the industry at that time.[24]

Selling the Airline to the Employees

Four major prederegulation carriers—Pan American, Eastern, Western, and Republic—have traded equity for wage and work rule concessions.

These companies shared the characteristics of being in severe financial peril when the deals were struck and of requiring substantial cost reductions to remain in business.[25]

Pan American was the first of the major carriers to face serious financial difficulties following deregulation and the first to trade equity for labor concessions. In exchange for 10 percent ownership in the company, Pan Am's unions accepted substantial work rule changes and took a 10 percent wage cut in addition to forgoing wage increases already in their contracts.[26] Half (5 percent) of these wage cuts were restored in 1983 and the other half in 1984. Contracts were also signed tying future wage increases to the company's profitability.

Eastern Airlines agreed to a surprisingly generous settlement in early 1983 with the IAM, calling for a 32 percent wage and benefit increase over three years with no substantial work rule changes.[27] However, as Eastern's financial position continued to deteriorate through 1983, Eastern and its major unions developed what they called the 1984 Wage Investment Program. In addition to productivity increases, Eastern's employees agreed to invest 18 percent (for flight attendants and machinists) and 22 percent (for pilots) of their wages in exchange for stock representing 25 percent ownership in the company and representation on the board of directors.[28] Subsequently Eastern's unions made several public suggestions that they would like to achieve full control of the airline, with the apparent intent of introducing new management; this was preempted in 1986 when Eastern's board agreed to sell the airline to Texas Air Corporation.

Western Airlines in 1983 reduced labor costs through a Partnership Plan that involved three components: (1) an employee stock plan under which employees eventually owned 7.8 million shares of common stock (about 32 percent of the company's total), (2) a profit-sharing plan that distributed to employees 15 percent of the first $25 million of any pretax (operating) profits and 20 percent of such profits in excess of $25 million, and (3) labor designation of two nominees for election to Western's board of directors. In exchange for this program, Western received work rule concessions and wage cuts ranging from 10 percent to about 18 percent and valued in total at $41.6 million.[29]

Republic Airlines in July 1984 reached agreement with its five unions to grant the employees 5.5 million shares of common stock (15.3 percent of the company) in exchange for continuation through 1986 of a 15 percent wage cut that began in 1983 and work rule changes estimated to improve productivity by 8 percent.[30] The employees also obtained 3 million warrants for Republic's common stock exercisable at $10 per share (the stock sold for

$3.75 at the time of the agreement) and $100 million worth of new stock with priority over common stock in the event of liquidation.[31] The unions also received one seat on Republic's board of directors.

Starting a Nonunion Airline

Two airlines, Texas International (now part of Texas Air Corp.) and Frontier, have experimented with startups of their own low cost nonunion airline subsidiaries, New York Air and Frontier Horizon. Although these subsidiaries were set up to avoid direct competition with the parent companies, they nevertheless posed at least an indirect threat to the unionized workforces of the parents; if these unions were unwilling to reduce costs, resources could be shifted to the nonunion subsidiary.

Texas International started nonunion New York Air shortly after the beginning of deregulation, along eastern seaboard routes far removed from Texas International's traditional markets. Nevertheless, Texas International's unions tried unsuccessfully in court to block the formation of New York Air and for a considerable period of time picketed New York Air operations.

Frontier Horizon began operations in January 1984 serving long-haul, high-density markets out of Frontier's Denver hub. Operations began by using B-727-100 aircraft and nonunion personnel; the goal was to achieve operating costs per available seat mile one third less than the parent.[32] Frontier Horizon's intended markets, however, were drawn from those not served by Frontier Airlines' flights.

In late January 1984 Frontier reached agreement with its pilots for work rule changes, an 8.1 percent wage cut, and elimination of any restoration of earlier wage cuts.[33] Taken together, these concessions amounted to a 20 percent reduction in pilot labor costs. In addition new pilots were started at 65 percent of the then current minimum union wage rate. In exchange Frontier Horizon was to get approval from Frontier's unionized pilots before expanding into any new markets. Frontier reached agreements calling for similar wage and work rule concessions with its flight attendants and its customer service and clerical workers later in 1984. These arrangements became somewhat irrelevant in 1985 when People Express acquired Frontier and then, shortly thereafter in 1986, when People Express (and Frontier) were acquired by Texas Air Corp.

Filing Bankruptcy

Two former trunk airlines, Braniff and Continental, have declared bankruptcy since deregulation, Braniff in 1982 and Continental in 1983. Both have resumed operations since, Braniff on a limited scale and Continental on a network larger than before its bankruptcy.

In addition to restructuring their debt through bankruptcy, both airlines have escaped the labor contracts under which they operated prior to bankruptcy, and as a result have sharply reduced their labor costs as nonunion operators. Continental's right to do this was challenged vigorously, but unsuccessfully, by its unions in the courts.

Employment Levels

The net effect of deregulation on airline employment is the combined result of deregulation's impacts on traffic, on productivity, and on the mix of factors used in producing airline output. As discussed briefly in chapter 3 (and in more detail in the next chapter), deregulation increased airline traffic (primarily because of the spread of discount fares to price-sensitive travelers). However, as seen earlier in this chapter, airline productivity may also have improved with deregulation so that airlines needed less labor to produce a given output. On the other hand, the changes in work rules and wage rates discussed earlier made labor relatively less expensive; thus any incentives the airlines might have had to shift away from labor were dampened. In addition the fuel price increases of 1979 caused the airlines to substitute labor and capital for fuel through flying more slowly and increasing certain types of maintenance.

The so-called employee protection program of the Deregulation Act, as contained in Section 43, embodies three major provisions, each of which applies to people employed by certificated carriers for at least four years prior to passage of the act.[34] In the first of these, employees who lose their jobs because of deregulation become, under certain circumstances, eligible for monthly assistance payments from the government for up to six years. The second provides that employees who lose their jobs because of deregulation and relocate to obtain other employment may receive relocation assistance payments. The third and final Section 43 provision holds that employees laid off by one certificated carrier have the right of first hire with other certificated carriers expanding their labor force. This provision, like the other two, applies only to carriers certificated prior to the act, as newly certificated carriers and their employees were not included in the program. Apparently, in these labor matters, as with many other issues (see chapter 4), not too much was expected of new carriers.

In 1982, at the bottom of that year's business recession, airline unions began pushing aggressively for the government to act on Section 43 provisions, particularly to provide some assistance payments. These initiatives were triggered by sharp job losses; between the third quarter of 1979 and the third quarter of 1982, the twelve largest airlines lost 43,000 full-time jobs (about 14 percent of their work force).

As for the obvious question of what caused these job losses deregulation is clearly only one possible explanation. As noted in chapter 3, the economic environment in which the airlines operated during the first five post-deregulation years was also greatly influenced by events unrelated to deregulation—two back-to-back recessions and dramatic increases in fuel prices and interest costs. Beyond these events, the industry was also subject to sharp and uneven reductions in air traffic control capacity following the PATCO strike and the subsequent dismissal of striking air traffic controllers.

To help sort out the influence of these various factors, econometric models of airline employment for the twelve major airlines were estimated using quarterly data for the period 1970 through 1982.[35] The models were similar to those used in the financial and capacity analyses of chapter 3 (and as described in appendix B) and were designed to isolate the effects of recession, fuel price increases, the PATCO strike, and several other (relatively minor) external factors from those attributable to deregulation. As in chapter 3, a fundamental assumption was that airlines plan capacity, roughly six months in advance.[36] The regression results are shown in table 6.5.

Table 6.5 Regression results for the employment model, major carriers, 1970–1982

Variable		Coefficient	*t*-statistic
Constant		270,167.1	20.94
RPMs** (thousands)		0.0009	3.61
Foreign RPMs** (thousands)		−0.2378	0.48
Unemployment rate** (percent)		−4,756.1	4.37
Second-quarter dummy		8,766.5	3.74
Third-quarter dummy		9,049.2	3.71
Fourth-quarter dummy		5,420.6	3.38
PATCO*		−20,482.0	4.17
Deregulation route freedom dummy		6,803.1	1.54
R^2	0.89		
Durbin-Watson statistic	2.12		
Cochrane-Orcutt rho	0.58		

Note: The ** denotes variable lagged two quarters; the * denotes a variable lagged one quarter.

The dependent variable is quarterly full-time employment. The employment data encompass all full-time employees, including those involved in international operations. Since the Deregulation Act applies only to domestic operations, data on domestic full-time employment would be preferable, but these figures are not available.

The coefficient on the first independent variable, domestic revenue passenger miles (designated in the table as "RPMs" and lagged two quarters to be consistent with the capacity adjustment assumption), is positive and statistically significant.

The number of RPMs in international service was included as a second independent variable to avoid attribution of changes in employment in support of international service to domestic deregulation. However, the coefficient for this variable, designated "Foreign RPMs" in the table, was not statistically significant.

The national unemployment rate, the third independent variable, also has a two-quarter lag and was included to examine the hypothesis that airline managers look to economic conditions beyond those in the airline industry when making future plans. This variable, as expected, has a negative sign indicating that employment in the airline industry drops when the national unemployment rate goes up.

Three dummy variables corresponding to the second, third, and fourth quarters were included to account for seasonal variation in full-time employment patterns.

A PATCO variable was included to account for the employment effects of the strike and subsequent dismissal of some controllers. The percentage reduction in flights enforced at the 22 largest U.S. airports because of the strike was normalized to 1.00 for the fourth quarter of 1981, the quarter when the effects of the air traffic control restrictions were the most severe. As the large negative and statistically significant coefficient indicates, the PATCO strike and its aftermath had a major effect on employment among the major airlines. This variable was lagged one quarter instead of two because shortly after the strike the FAA announced a schedule for restoring air traffic control capacity, thus giving the airlines an early indication of restrictions to be in effect in future quarters.

A dummy variable to account for deregulation's route freedoms took on the value of zero prior to the first quarter of 1979 and one thereafter. The positive sign for the coefficient indicates that on net, deregulation's freedoms apparently resulted in an increase in employment, although the effect is not large and the coefficient is of little statistical significance.

The employment model, in combination with the demand model for

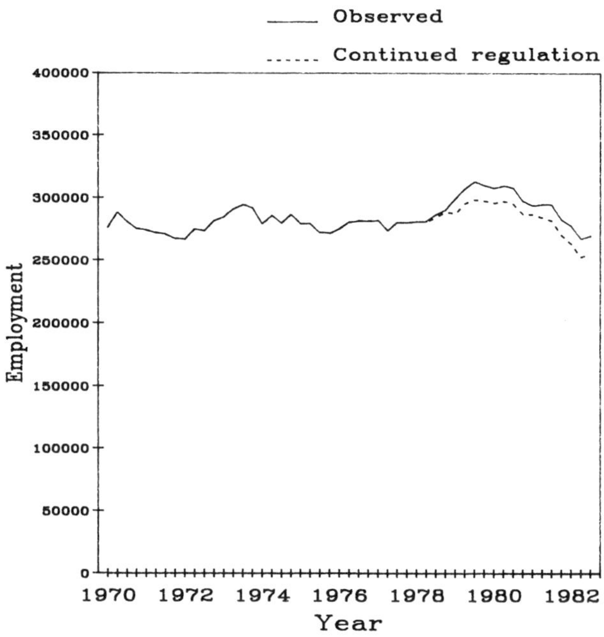

Figure 6.3 Simulation of major airlines employment: actual vs. continued regulation, 1970–1982. (Source: Estimated from regression results given in table 6.5.)

revenue passenger miles presented in chapter 3 and appendix B, can be used to simulate the effects of deregulation on airline employment. Specifically, the revenue passenger miles model can be used to estimate the RPMs that would have occurred in the absence of deregulation, under the assumption that the average fare per mile would have continued to have had the same relationship to airline costs per mile that prevailed from 1970 through 1977. The resulting estimate of "regulated RPMs" was then used in the employment model (with the deregulation route freedom dummy set at zero) to estimate what employment would have been with continued regulation.[37]

The results are shown in figure 6.3. The dashed line represents the estimate of what aggregate employment would have been under continued regulation. The solid line is the actual level of full-time employment as reported to the CAB for these carriers. As can be seen, employment, as estimated, would have been lower among the major carriers in the absence of deregulation. Indeed, throughout the postderegulation period, according to the estimates, full-time employment among these carriers would have been about 3.7 percent lower had CAB regulation continued.

Table 6.6 Percent changes in RPMs and employment due to deregulation, 1979–1982, by airline

Airline	Percent change in RPMs	Percent change in employment
American	22.5	1.0
Braniff	22.2	7.8
Continental	29.2	3.4
Delta	20.3	0.7
Eastern	24.0	1.6
Northwest	3.8	13.5
Pan Am	15.1	8.2
Republic	26.6	19.6
TWA	23.6	0.1
United	21.7	2.1
USAir	7.5	4.2
Western	19.0	4.9
All majors	13.2	3.7

Source: Estimated from the employment and RPM regression models, as described in the text, table 6.5, and appendix B.

Table 6.6 presents estimates of the differences in employment and RPMs due to deregulation for each of the twelve major carriers over the period from 1979 to 1982. These estimates are based on separate application of the employment and RPM models to each of the carriers. Even accounting for the uncertainty surrounding these estimates, deregulation does not appear to have been a major cause of reduced employment for any of these carriers as of 1982.[38]

In short, without deregulation, job losses in the airline industry would have been even more severe in 1981 and 1982 than they actually were. Suggestive evidence in further confirmation of this basic conclusion has been provided by events subsequent to 1982. With recovery of the economy from 1983 to 1985, employment at the large established carriers rose by over 26,000 fulltime jobs, eliminating over half of the losses incurred earlier. Indeed, by 1985 trained airline personnel, particularly pilots, had become somewhat short in supply—and the commuter and new entrant jet carriers paying lower wages than the majors complained of losing pilots to the larger airlines. Similarly by 1985 there was increased talk of granting "amnesty" to the PATCO members who had been fired for illegally striking in 1981, as the need for additional experienced controllers was considered by many to be acute. Not surprisingly, trade union pressure for implementation of Section 43 relief also diminished as recovery and reemployment of airline personnel occurred.

Concluding Observations

The combination of a deregulated and openly competitive environment and the emergence of low-cost new entrant jet carriers has forced the established carriers to seek new ways to reduce costs. In addition to improving fuel and capital productivity, the airlines have also looked to the wages they pay and the productivity of their employees in their attempts to reduce costs. However, as of the early 1980s, the established airlines had not yet matched the productivity performance of their lowest-cost competitors.

The competitive pressures unleashed by deregulation have changed the nature of labor relations in the airline industry, perhaps permanently and quite fundamentally. Virtually all the major airlines have sought to cut costs through work rule changes and moderation of wage increases or, in some cases, actual decreases in wage rates. A strong trend toward dual wage structures with newly hired employees earning less than the established workers also emerged.

Of course productivity gains in the absence of much traffic growth could, in principle, lead to lower levels of employment with or without deregulation. After almost a decade of administrative and formal deregulation, however, the airlines' use of deregulation's fare and route freedoms had apparently stimulated enough traffic to absorb productivity gains and resulted in higher employment among the major carriers than would have been the case under continued regulation. This conclusion seems to be true in the aggregate, even ignoring employment gains among the new entrant carriers; it also seems to hold for each of the established major carriers. Typically the established major carriers employed about as many people in the early 1980s as they had in the early 1970s prior to deregulation and probably would have employed about 4 percent fewer in the early 1980s had deregulation not occurred.

The net effect of deregulation on labor seems clear: deregulation has apparently created new job opportunities, but at lower wages than would otherwise have been the case. Furthermore, because of deregulation, the industry's productivity, and particularly labor productivity, has probably been enhanced. These productivity gains may have come largely from a one-time redeployment of factors of production that were misallocated under regulation. Only a decade or two of experience will tell whether deregulation will continue to sustain high rates of airline productivity gain in the future.

7

The Effect on Travelers: Fares and Service

with John S. Strong

Prior to administrative deregulation in 1976, airline fares were generally constrained to two price and quality combinations, first class and coach. But beginning in 1976, the CAB, under chairman John Robson, adopted a new and more permissive position on discount fares. The first significant change was the approval of advanced booking charter service in October 1976 which allowed the advance purchase sale of charter flights without accompanying ground services.[1] The first major change for scheduled carriers was Texas International's "Peanuts" fare in February 1977, which gave 50 percent off-peak discounts, and soon after, American's "Super-Saver" fares, which initiated discounts in transcontinental markets.[2] In reviewing applications for new routes, the CAB also began to give preference to applicants willing to offer low fares. In April 1978 the CAB proposed to allow fare reductions or increases of up to 50 percent without Board approval.[3] The essentials of this proposal were put in place six months later by the Airline Deregulation Act, which gave trunk carriers the freedom to raise fares up to 5 percent above the Standard Industry Fare Level (SIFL) and all certificated carriers the ability to lower fares 50 percent below the SIFL without CAB approval. (The local service carriers even prior to formal deregulation had been allowed to charge 30 percent above SIFL because of the short-haul, and therefore ostensibly high-cost, character of their operations.) These provisions remained in effect until January 1, 1983, when CAB fare authority expired. Since then airlines have been able to freely enter or exit routes, to change fares quickly, and to offer a variety of price and service combinations.[4]

As a consequence, the average airline fares paid by consumers have declined since deregulation, both compared to consumer prices in general and to the fares that would have likely prevailed had regulation continued.[5] To be sure, airline fares did not decline in every market and some individual markets experienced fare increases, even when adjustments are made for inflation.[6] However, average fares have declined relative to general inflation and airline costs even in markets with relatively little direct competition. Moreover, though the increased use of discount fares has created much of this decline, even consumers unable to meet stringent discount fare restrictions have typically experienced relatively lower fares.[7] The only major

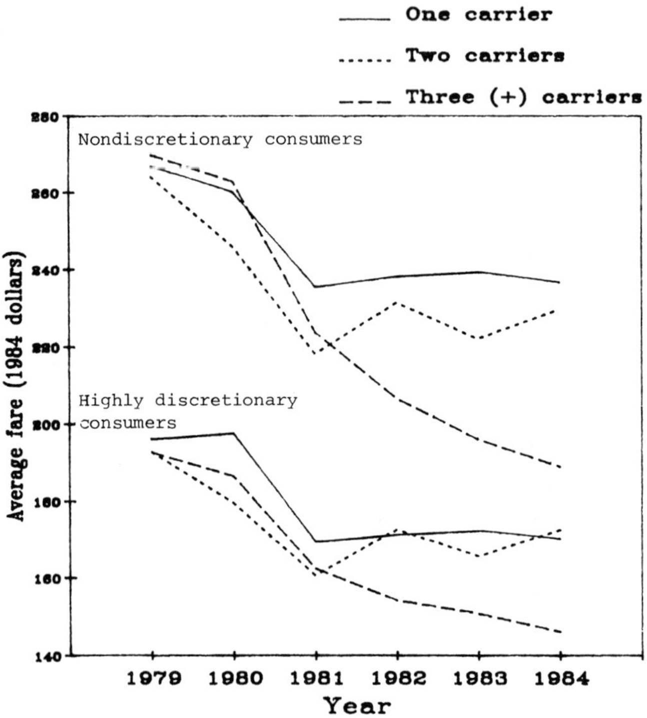

Figure 7.1 Fare changes by type of market and type of consumer, 1979–1984. (Source: See note 8.)

exception would be business travelers who demand first-class services but probably pay more since deregulation than before. Deregulation has thus lowered most fares for most travelers but not all fares for everyone.

Figure 7.1 shows changes in average fare (adjusted for inflation using the Consumer Price Index [CPI]) for two types of traveler in three types of markets.[8] Nondiscretionary consumers are defined as those unable to use discount fares with either minimum stay requirements or requiring advanced purchase of seven days or more. As can be seen from the top three lines of the figure, average fares for such consumers have declined since deregulation in one-carrier, two-carrier, and three(+)-carrier markets, with greater declines in markets characterized by more competition. Similarly highly discretionary consumers, those defined as being able to meet the minimum stay, advanced purchase, and other requirements of the lowest discount fares, have also seen fares decline since deregulation. Here again, fare declines were greatest in the three(+)-carrier markets.

Sample and Analytic Procedures

To explore the impact of deregulation's fare freedoms on travelers, a stratified sample of city-pair markets was selected to study fare and service changes. On the basis of passenger volume data from the CAB's Origin and Destination Survey, city-pair markets were divided into three groups:[9]

1. The top 50 markets (highest density).
2. Markets ranked 51–200 in passenger volume (medium density).
3. Markets ranked 201–500 by passenger volume.

Data limitations reduced the sample to 43 of the top 50 markets and 139 of the 150 medium-density markets; a random sample of 150 city-pairs was drawn from the smallest three hundred markets. The sample markets accounted for 71 percent of domestic passengers in the fourth quarter of 1980.

By using a stratified sample and looking at a wide range of market types, fare and service differences could be uncovered that might remain hidden in analyses which use highly aggregate data.[10] A stratified sample also avoids the tendency to emphasize individual cases of large service or fare change.[11]

This sample does, though, largely omit smaller cities and towns served by commuter airlines. In these markets, as noted in chapter 4, the number of seat departures fell after deregulation, but the number of aircraft departures increased (see table 4.1). Commuter airline fare policies have been studied extensively elsewhere.[12] In essence, the finding has been that fares in commuter markets rose (in nominal terms) after deregulation but at a slower rate than the average increase in airline costs and at approximately the same rate as general inflation.

Changes in Fares: 1976–1984

Data on first-class, coach, and discount fares were taken from *Official Airline Guides* for 1976, 1981, and 1984. To control for seasonal influences, fares in effect on May 1 of each year were studied.[13] The 1976 fares were chosen to reflect pricing practices under regulation, since some 1977 and 1978 fares were influenced by the "administrative deregulation" undertaken by the CAB prior to passage of the Airline Deregulation Act. The 1981 fares illustrate fare policy in the early stages of deregulation, when fares were also strongly influenced by the sharp 1979–1980 rise in fuel prices and the 1980 recession. By contrast, the 1984 fares reflect a sustained period of falling fuel prices, low inflation, and economic recovery.

First Class

Since 1976 first-class passengers have faced higher fares in the overwhelming majority of markets. After correcting for general inflation (using the CPI), first-class fares appear to have increased by more than inflation in over three-fourths of all markets. The average real fare increase by this measure was 21 percent in the top 50 markets; 19 percent in markets ranked 51–200; and 26 percent in smaller markets.

An alternative way to restate 1976 fares in 1984 terms would be to inflate the 1976 fares by the change in airline input costs, as represented by changes in the CAB's Standard Industry Fare Level (SIFL) over the period. Using the SIFL as a cost index almost fully incorporates the impact of the extraordinary fuel price increase of 1979–1980 and was also the CAB's basis for determining fare increases under regulation.[14] Adjusting 1976 fares by the SIFL index thus also provides a reasonable measure of what fares were likely to have been under continued regulation.[15]

The SIFL adjustment offers a somewhat different perspective on changes in first-class fares than the CPI adjustment. Although 1984 fares were still higher in most markets, the average increases were relatively small. In the top 50 markets the mean increase was 2 percent, while medium and small markets experienced increases of 1 percent and 7 percent, respectively. Overall, it appears that first-class fares may have increased slightly compared to the fares that might have prevailed under continued regulation.

Coach Class

Under CAB regulation "*the* coach fare" was the standard price of air travel for most passengers. After deregulation, though, consumers faced a variety of "coach" fares, often varying with time of day or day of the week, but still without restrictions concerning advance purchase, minimum stay provisions, and the like. Thus the term "coach" came to refer to a variety of fares rather than the unambiguous single standard fare of the prederegulation period. To represent this range of postderegulation coach fares, the lowest unrestricted "Y" coach fare available on at least half the flights for a particularly city-pair in May 1984 was compared with the "Y" coach fare in effect in May 1976.

A comparison of these 1976 and 1984 coach fares after adjusting by the SIFL cost index, shows that coach fares were lower in 70 percent of the top 50 markets, with an average fare decrease of 9 percent. However, in medium-density markets 59 percent of the markets faced higher fares in 1984, with an average fare increase of 3 percent. Coach fares were most affected in smaller markets, where fares rose in 70 percent of the markets with an average increase of 6 percent in the price of a ticket.[16] In short, those traveling on unrestricted coach class fares in large markets have apparently experienced reductions, whereas those in medium and small markets have had increases.

Discount Fares

Perhaps the most striking change in fares since deregulation has been the proliferation of discounts. These discount fares have substantially reduced the importance of standard coach fares in many markets. The left portion of table 7.1 shows the percentage of markets within each group in which some type of discount fare was available in 1976, 1981, and 1984. Although discount fares were seldom found outside of the top 100 markets in 1976, discounts were offered in well over 80 percent of all markets served by certificated carriers by 1981. The rapid expansion of discount fares slowed between 1981 and 1984, as the economic recovery strengthened demand and reduced airlines' incentives to discount. At the same time consumers faced an almost explosive growth in the diversity of discount fares. In 1976 only five classes of discount fares were available, the most common being the "YN" night coach discount of 20 percent offered on some late evening flights. By contrast, the May 1, 1984, *Official Airline Guide* listed no fewer than seventeen types of discount fares, with a bewildering array of names, restrictions, and availabilities.

Along with this growth in the availability of discounts has come a sizable increase in the depth of discounting in all markets, particularly between 1976 and 1981, as shown in the right-hand columns of table 7.1. The table

Table 7.1 Availability and scope of discount fares, 1976, 1981, and 1984

	Percent of markets with discount fares			Average discount fare as percentage of coach fare		
Market rank[a]	1976	1981	1984	1976	1981	1984
Top 50	69	95	96	78	63	61
51–100	60	92	90	80	67	63
101–150	36	82	84	80	70	72
151–200	39	86	80	80	72	77
Smaller markets	30	81	72	80	74	76

Source: Calculated from data in the *Official Airline Guide*.
a. Markets ranked by fourth-quarter 1981 passenger volume. Due to unavailable or inconsistent data, the sample covers only 39 of the top 50 markets and 139 of the markets ranked 51–200.

Table 7.2 Average coach and discount fares in top 31 markets, first quarter 1981

City-pair	Standard Industry Fare Level (SIFL)	First-quarter average coach fare (ACF)	ACF as percent of SIFL (3 ÷ 2)	First-quarter average discount fare (ADF)	ADF as percent of SIFL (5 ÷ 2)
Boston–New York	51.92	49.93	.93	35.93	0.69
New York–Washington	55.55	52.98	.95	46.03	0.83
Chicago–New York	118.58	165.69	1.40	103.97	0.88
Miami–New York	158.09	116.84	.74	113.78	0.72
Los Angeles–San Francisco	81.54	55.73	.68	41.92	0.51
Los Angeles–New York	298.61	266.64	.89	180.54	0.60
Las Vegas–Los Angeles	56.94	52.23	.92	48.86	0.86
Detroit–New York	93.58	116.58	1.25	80.34	0.86
New York–San Francisco	310.97	310.42	1.00	184.81	0.59
New York–Pittsburgh	71.43	102.99	1.44	66.96	0.94
Cleveland–New York	82.57	109.02	1.32	64.58	0.78
Chicago–Los Angeles	225.81	238.55	1.06	162.69	0.72
Buffalo–New York	65.72	95.14	1.45	60.60	0.92
Boston–Washington	82.02	101.66	1.24	64.68	0.79
Chicago–Detroit	58.61	71.76	1.22	50.10	0.85
Chicago–Miami	168.18	145.18	.86	130.92	0.77
Chicago–Minneapolis	73.52	98.77	1.34	66.38	0.90
San Francisco–Seattle	113.38	114.64	1.01	82.52	0.73
Chicago–St. Louis	61.12	71.99	1.18	48.15	0.79
Chicago–Philadelphia	113.06	161.50	1.43	107.17	0.95
Los Angeles–Seattle	143.86	137.62	.96	95.90	0.67
Atlanta–New York	122.19	140.43	1.15	98.00	0.80
Boston–Philadelphia	64.46	82.01	1.27	54.60	0.85

Table 7.2 (continued)

City-pair	Standard Industry Fare Level (SIFL)	First-quarter average coach fare (ACF)	ACF as percent of SIFL (3 ÷ 2)	First-quarter average discount fare (ADF)	ADF as percent of SIFL (5 ÷ 2)
New York–Rochester	60.56	86.01	1.42	53.85	0.89
Chicago–Washington	104.77	135.46	1.29	84.22	0.80
Chicago–San Francisco	237.45	245.47	1.03	171.87	0.72
Chicago–Cleveland	68.78	79.96	1.16	55.86	0.81
Dallas–Houston	58.99	35.30	.60	27.68	0.47
New York–Syracuse	52.90	69.97	1.32	46.98	0.89
Boston–Chicago	133.34	191.26	1.43	108.79	0.82
Los Angeles–San Diego	40.64	34.89	.86	26.49	0.65

Source: Calculated from data from March 1, 1981, *Official Airline Guide*. SIFL data provided by CAB.

also shows that travelers in the top 100 markets faced significantly deeper discounts (in addition to greater availability) than travelers in the medium and small markets.

The extent of fare discounting in the 31 largest markets is shown in detail in table 7.2. The greater the depth of discount fares (column 6), the greater was the competitive pressure on carriers to reduce their standard coach fare (column 4). (The rank correlation coefficient between the average coach fare as a percent of SIFL and the average discount fare is 0.812.) The influence of discounts on coach fares is less evident in smaller markets, although coach fares have fallen in many medium-density markets following the introduction of reduced discount fares (e.g., in markets linking the midwest with Florida).

The other striking aspect of table 7.2 is the apparent impact of airport capacity restrictions and slot allocations on fares. With the exception of the Florida and transcontinental markets, coach fares for those flights involving a slot-controlled airport are consistently above the SIFL, with correspondingly less discounting as well.[17]

The wider availability and increasingly large savings due to discount fares resulted in discount fare tickets becoming the dominant form of travel in many markets. The extent of discount fare travel can be analyzed using the CAB's Origin and Destination Survey, which provides data on passenger volume by carrier and fare class for most major airline markets in the United States. The use of discount fares for airline markets as a whole has jumped from 15 percent in 1976 to 55 percent in 1981 to over 65 percent in 1983. As shown in figure 7.2, in the top 50 markets just over 20 percent of travelers used discount fares in 1976; by 1981 three-fourths were flying on discount. While the growth in discount passengers in the top 50 markets began prior to formal deregulation, most other airline markets experienced only modest growth in discount travelers before 1979.

In the early stages of deregulation airlines instituted a variety of capacity-controlled, market-segmenting discounts aimed at inducing the discretionary traveler to fly in a seat that would have otherwise flown empty.[18] Such fares involved restrictions designed to prevent their use by business travelers (e.g., advance-purchase and minimum-stay requirements) and to limit discount travel to off-peak periods. These fares typically applied to only a portion of the seats on any given flight. This market-segmenting fare structure contributed to record profit levels in 1978 and 1979 as reported in chapter 3.

After 1980, however, careful targeting of promotional fares began to break down in response to deteriorating economic conditions and in-

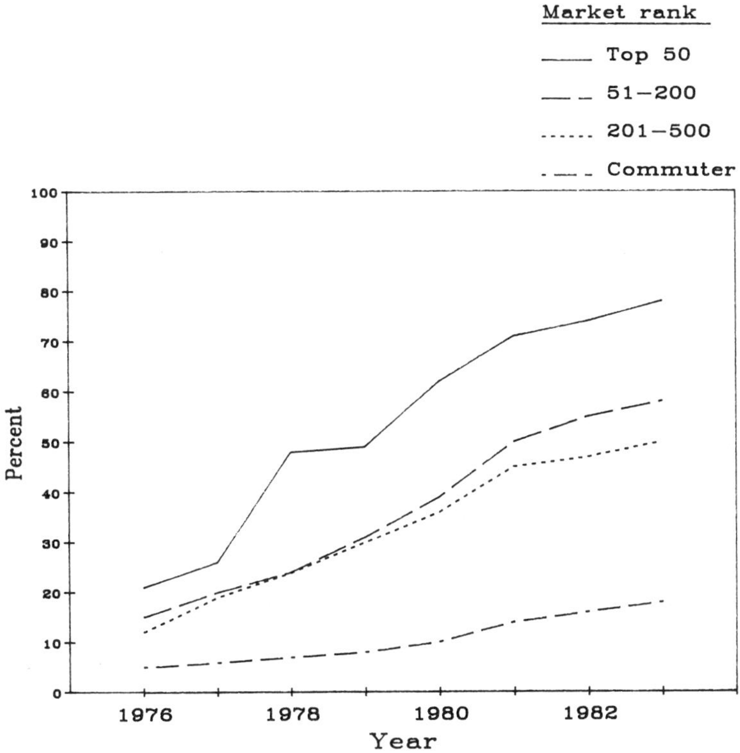

Figure 7.2 Travelers using discount fares by market rank, 1976–1983. (Source: Calculated from data in *Official Airline Guide*.)

creasing competitive pressures.[19] Airlines, in an attempt to sustain passenger volumes, especially eased discount fare restrictions in the severe economic recession of 1982. As a result more business travelers were able to use discount fares. With the onset of economic recovery in 1983, though, the airlines once again attempted to bar discounted business travel by reinstituting more restrictions on the use of such fares.

Whether fares based on market segmentation will persist over time remains an open question.[20] The airline industry's sensitivity to national economic conditions suggests, though, that discount fares are likely to reappear or expand whenever excess capacity emerges from declines in traffic volume. Recurrent cycles in the use of discount fares may also result from long lead times on aircraft orders, as equipment and capacity adjustments in particular markets may lag behind changes in market conditions. Discounting, then, will likely remain a key feature of airline pricing, although its extent and duration in individual markets may vary with economic conditions.

Considerable restructuring may also occur in joint fare agreements between carriers. The expiration of the mandatory joint fare system on January 1, 1983, freed carriers from the past arrangement mandated by the CAB in which long-haul carriers subsidized short-haul feeder carriers and removed the guarantees of equal access to joint fares by all carriers.[21] Joint fare arrangements between carriers will likely be determined in the future by the value to the long-haul carrier of the feed the short-haul route can provide.[22] Given the large volume of passengers from small communities that connect at the major hubs, it is not surprising that the dominant carriers in each hub have competed strongly for these passengers, especially since 1985, through marketing alliances with commuter carriers.

In general, market power still seems important in pricing policy. Markets served by more than two carriers often offer a greater variety of discount fares than do markets dominated by one or two carriers. Similarly markets that have experienced entry are also characterized by greater discounting, even including short-haul markets experiencing new or more intense competition from commuter airlines.[23] Discount fares have been most prevalent, however, in long-haul markets, apparently due to greater concentrations of discretionary travelers and the surplus of wide-bodied aircraft capacity suitable for these routes.

Changes in Service Patterns: 1976–1984

Service patterns in the wake of deregulation have been strongly influenced by the various route strategies adopted by the airlines. These strategies were discussed for the new entrant airlines in chapter 4 and for the established carriers in chapter 5. After experimentation with a variety of management approaches to route structure development in the first three years of deregulation, most major airlines have since emphasized hub and spoke network strategies. This approach has led to the expansion of previous hubs as well as development of new ones.

For travelers living near these new or expanded hubs, the available service options have grown rapidly. In addition cities linked to these hubs generally have seen increased frequencies to the hub, often with faster connecting times and a wider choice of final destinations. However, some airlines have scaled back the volume of hub service at several major airports due to increased passenger delays.[24] These delays stem in part from carriers building their hubs beyond peak airport capacity. And of course not every

Table 7.3 Service changes in selected markets, 1976–1981, 1981–1984

	More flights	Same number of flights	Fewer flights
1976–1981			
Top 50 markets	12 (28%)	7 (16%)	24 (56%)
Markets 51–200	85 (61%)	10 (7%)	44 (32%)
Markets 201–500	66 (44%)	10 (7%)	74 (49%)
1981–1984			
Top 50 markets	26 (60%)	3 (7%)	14 (33%)
Markets 51–200	43 (31%)	14 (10%)	82 (59%)
Markets 201–500	108 (72%)	12 (8%)	30 (20%)

Source: Calculated from data from *Official Airline Guide*.

city can be a hub or closely connected to a hub. Critics of deregulation have thus charged that service frequency and quality to medium and small nonhub cities has deteriorated since 1978.[25]

The same stratified sample was employed for the analysis of air service as for fares (except that data were compared from June of each year, instead of May). Between 1976 and 1984, service (as measured by flight frequency) improved across all market groups, with fewer than half of the markets receiving less service. Moreover smaller markets (those ranked between 200 and 500) saw the largest increases in service with over three-fourths receiving more flights. Rapid expansion by commuter airlines and increased hub development by former local service airlines probably explains much of the service gains in these smaller markets.

In table 7.3 service changes for the initial period of deregulation, 1976 through 1981, are contrasted with those for the 1981 to 1984 period. The 1976 to 1981 data reflect the effects of economic recession and the 1979 fuel price increases as well as deregulation. On the other hand, the 1981 to 1984 changes occurred during a strong economic expansion, although somewhat dampened by restrictions imposed in the wake of the air traffic controllers' strike of 1981.

In the early years of deregulation, from June 1976 to June 1981 (prior to the August PATCO strike), about half the markets experienced reductions in frequencies. The only markets to gain substantially were medium-sized, as the former trunk and local service airlines expanded rapidly in 1979 and 1980. Overall, though, the number of flights fell in only 142 of 332 markets, with the average decrease of five flights in these 142 markets being offset in the aggregate by an average increase of four flights in the 190 markets where service increased.

Between June 1981 and June 1984 these initial trends were reversed, with significant expansion in large and small markets and accompanying reductions in medium-sized markets. Increased volumes of vacation and business travel in the densest markets, the extensive development of hub feeder systems, and new entry in the smaller cities all contributed to these new trends. In the medium markets the reductions in flights from 1981 to 1984 may indicate a pullback from the initial expansion in such markets, as well as the effect of financial problems at several carriers emphasizing such routes.

Overall, service patterns appear to have improved since deregulation. Although cyclical and seasonal variations remain pronounced, the number of flights has increased or remained the same in roughly two-thirds of all markets, with no market group showing overall decreases in frequencies.

The service offered air travelers has changed in at least two other important ways as well. First, the average number of carriers serving each airport has increased 31 percent at large hubs, 51 percent at medium hubs, 42 percent at small hubs, and 15 percent at nonhubs. More carriers serving each airport means a greater variety of service offerings for travelers and more competitive checks on the actions of each carrier. The modest increase at nonhubs indicates that even for these small communities, fewer are "captive" to a single carrier since deregulation.

A second change, as can be seen in figure 7.3, is a marked shift away

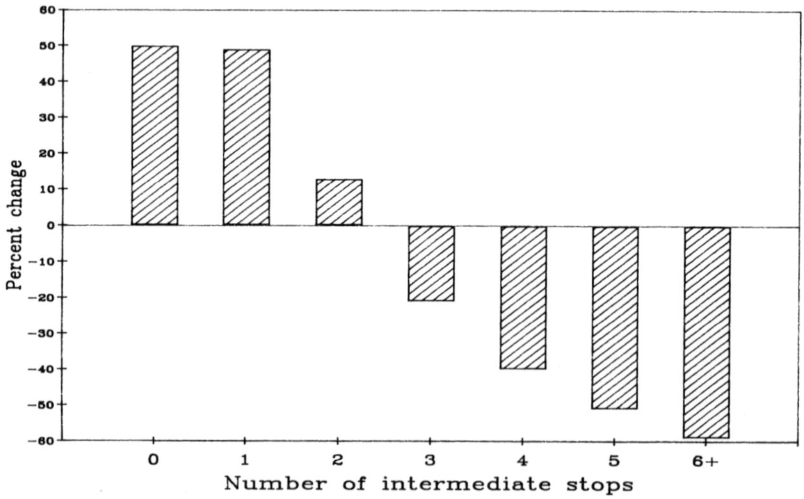

Figure 7.3 Percent change in monthly flights by number of stops per flight, December 1983 vs. December 1978. (Source: *CAB Report on Airline Service, Fares, Traffic, Load Factors, and Market Shares,* issue 29.)

from multistop flights toward more direct nonstop and one-stop flights. A decline in flights with three or more intermediate stops has resulted from the replacement of LSAs' jet aircraft with commuter airline turboprops in small community service. To some extent an increase in one-stop flights may have been an accompaniment to the hub strengthening described in chapter 5; one-stop flights with the hub as the intermediate stop are building blocks from which hub and spoke route networks are developed.

Differential Impacts on Business and Leisure Travelers

The business traveler's high value of time and limited schedule flexibility place a premium on early morning and late afternoon flights, and the availability of last minute reservations. In addition the tax treatment of business travel expenses can lower the effective fare by the corporate tax rate. Thus business travelers are generally deemed to place an emphasis on flight frequency and timing, with price, although not unimportant, playing a decidedly secondary role in their choice of flight. On the other hand, leisure travelers are thought to have more flexibility in their schedules and therefore are better able to take advantage of low fares. Air fares are not only often a large part of vacation expense but are also usually not tax deductible; leisure travelers thus seem more willing to fly in off-peak periods and to accept lower levels of service in exchange for lower fares.

These differences can result in higher costs of serving business travelers, for example, because they may need to make reservations on short notice and they are permitted to cancel such reservations without penalty. The need for flexibility in reservations requires airlines to provide greater capacity (more seats). The business traveler also places great emphasis on peak-hour departure times for business trips. These scheduling needs may limit an airline's ability to utilize its fleet intensively, again implying a greater capacity requirement and higher costs.

It is hardly surprising therefore that some carriers apparently used their fare freedom under deregulation to raise fares in business markets. A sample of fares in 50 business and 25 leisure markets was selected and analyzed for May 1980 and May 1984.[26] The average fare paid in each market was compared to the estimated fare under regulation as calculated from the SIFL formula. In the business markets the 1980 average fare was 28 percent higher than the SIFL formula; the sample of leisure markets showed only a 1 percent markup over the SIFL. By 1984 average fares were 12 percent above SIFL in the business markets, while fares in leisure markets were roughly 7 percent below SIFL. Although part of this difference is due to the higher proportion of discount passengers in leisure markets, the unrestricted fares in business markets were approximately 11 percent higher than unrestricted fares in leisure markets.[27]

These and other differences in the extent to which different airline markets have enjoyed lower fares from deregulation have elicited widespread complaints about the "inequities" of deregulation. Illustrative examples of these fare inequities have indeed become part of the folklore. One favorite citation is that it has sometimes been cheaper to fly from a major city in, for example, Ohio to the West Coast via New York than to proceed directly. Or, a considerable outrage can often be generated by noting that it may be cheaper to fly coast to coast between two major cities than to fly from one coastal city to an interior point, even though the trip is much shorter in the latter case. Similarly some enterprising travelers have taken a certain glee in pointing out that they have flown to a high-fare interior city at the same low cost as going coast to coast by simply booking themselves on a one-stop coast to coast flight where that one stop is at their interior destination and then simply departing the plane when it arrived at the inland city (presumably shouldering their own carryon luggage).[28]

Some critics have even suggested that such inequities build a case for restoring regulation. However, the essential issue is the level of fares relative to some standardized measure of costs (or fares) before and after deregulation. On inspection, the highest fares since deregulation are usually little or no higher relative to appropriate measures of standardized fares or costs than prior to deregulation. The so-called inequities arise not so much because some fares are marked up more after deregulation but because only some fares have been marked down substantially after deregulation, markdowns that were mostly not available anywhere under regulation. Deregulation has thus typically not made many people pay more than they would otherwise have paid but has simply permitted some to realize greater, perhaps even exceptional, bargains.

Deregulation and Business Aviation

The 1970s were a decade of rapid and sustained growth for corporate aviation. Sales of business aircraft rose steadily from 1970 to 1982, with an average annual increase in sales of 22 percent for turboprops and 28 percent for private jets. In 1975, 479 of the *Fortune* 1000 companies operated 1489 aircraft; by 1982, 542 firms were operating 2018 planes. Members of the business aviation community generally attributed this

Table 7.4 Business aircraft destinations, 1970 and 1982 (percent of total)

	1970	1982
Nonairline airports	25	43
Air carrier airports	39	32
Connecting with air carriers	36	25
Total	100	100

Source: *Business and Commercial Aviation.*

sustained growth to two major influences: changes in the location of manufacturing activity and the advent of airline deregulation.

The decentralization of manufacturing activity seems likely to have been a major factor in the growth of corporate aviation. In addition increased natural resource exploration and development may have resulted in an increased need for corporate access to remote areas not served by commercial air carriers. Over the 1970 to 1982 period, business aircraft destinations to nonairline airports rose markedly, as shown in table 7.4.

The effects of deregulation on corporate aviation are less clear. Many analysts believed corporate aviation would benefit from deregulation because of predicted reductions in service to small communities. John Olcott, editor of *Business and Commercial Aviation* magazine, wrote at the time:

> Airline deregulation, rising fuel prices, and jumbo jets will force scheduled air carriers into long-haul, high-density routes, leaving general aviation as the primary means of efficient transportation between a vast network of locations and city-pairs.[29]

What Olcott and others did not anticipate was the expansion of commuter air carriers and their ability to provide replacement service for major airlines pulling out of smaller markets. Deregulation also contributed to the rapid growth of the commuter industry by raising aircraft size limitations and extending eligibility for federal subsidies and equipment loan guarantees. As discussed in chapter 4, the commuter carriers were able to provide adequate capacity in most cases where service terminations occurred, often with increased frequencies and sometimes even with more seats.

Overall, the expected postderegulation boom in business aviation failed to materialize. The 1981–1982 recession severely curtailed the industry's long-run growth trend, with new orders markedly down after 1982. There is also little evidence of more intensive use of corporate aircraft following deregulation. Average fleet sizes of companies had declined slightly by 1985, while utilization levels had not changed from prederegulation levels. Thus sales volume and utilization data suggest that airline deregulation has had little observable impact on corporate aviation.

Conclusions

Deregulation's effect on fares has varied with the type of ticket and the size of the market. First-class fares are relatively higher in most markets, although increases generally have been small (on the order of 2 percent). Unrestricted coach fares have decreased slightly in the largest and most dense markets, while average coach fares in medium and small markets have risen about 3 and 6 percent, respectively.[30] More important, since deregulation discount fares have become available in over 80 percent of all markets, and well over 60 percent of all passengers were flying on discount fares by 1984, with these discounts ranging upward to 50 percent or more. Prior to 1976 discount fares were rarely available outside the largest markets and were seldom deeper than a 20 percent reduction. Discounting also has increased pressures to reduce standard coach fares in the largest markets.

These fare reductions, however, may not have benefited all travelers equally, and indeed, some travelers may even be worse off following deregulation. Leisure travelers in the largest markets and travelers in markets served by the low-fare new entrants have probably been the clearest winners from deregulation. The former have been able to take advantage of the widest array of discount fares with the largest fare reductions and the latter have had the lowest unrestricted fares. On the other hand, trips involving a commuter airline leg connecting to a jet flight in a relatively short- to medium-haul, low-density market may well face slightly higher coach fares and higher commuter fares from the loss of the short-haul cross subsidy realized under CAB joint fare practices.

Service has either improved or held constant in most markets since deregulation. The development of hub systems has meant increased frequencies in most markets, with smaller markets receiving the largest gains. The evidence also suggests that under deregulation business travelers have benefited more from service improvements than from fare reductions, while leisure travelers have been more direct beneficiaries of lower fares.[31] As one consequence of continued or improved scheduled service to business travelers, private corporate flying has not boomed since deregulation, as some observers had expected.

Overall, the variety of price and service combinations available to travelers has greatly expanded. Deregulation has also brought promotional pricing, seasonal sales, and other types of discounting—practices long prevalent in the rest of the economy but previously unavailable to the air traveler due to regulatory constraints.

8

Changes in Distribution Channels and the Travel Agency Business

with Marni Clippinger and John S. Strong

Getting there may still be half the fun, but finding the lowest priced ticket these days demands the guile of a currency speculator and the stamina of a Himalayan Sherpa.

—Editorial,
The New York Times[1]

The ever-changing array of fares, schedules, service terminations, route entries, and entirely new airlines that came in the wake of deregulation threw increasing numbers of confused consumers into the arms of travel agents, the official interpreters of the mysteries of air travel. Travel agents responded to this surge in demand by increasing their numbers, introducing new technology, and—when given the chance by the CAB in 1980—raising their commission rates. Between 1977 and 1985 the number of accredited domestic travel agents in the United States rose from 13,000 to over 27,000. Travel agent commissions paid by the U.S. major carriers on domestic flights increased from $527 million in 1977 to slightly more than $3.1 billion in 1985.[2] The share of tickets written by travel agents rose steadily following deregulation. In 1985 tickets purchased through travel agencies represented about 74 percent of air carrier revenues.[3]

By the mid-1980s the travel agent distribution system had also come under unprecedented scrutiny. The travel agents' so-called conference system (which some characterized as a cartel) had been challenged by the loss of exclusive distribution rights in 1982, by the withdrawal of antitrust immunity in 1985, and by investigations into built-in biases of the two airline computer reservation systems (American Airlines' SABRE and United Airlines' APOLLO) most widely used by the agents. This confused, almost disorderly state of affairs was not just a product of deregulation but also had its roots in the history of air travel distribution services, augmented by judicial and administrative actions that have occurred since deregulation.

History

Prior to 1940 airlines entrusted the task of selling tickets to virtually anyone who had contact with the traveling public, including barbershop proprietors, taxi drivers, and bell captains.[4] To counter the problems that accompanied this haphazard distribution system, the Air Traffic Conference (ATC) was created in 1945 as a division of the Air Transport Association of America. The first agents were appointed by individual carriers to represent them, but that relationship changed over time with the introduction of standard ticket stock and the Area Settlement Plan, an ATC agreement that established a central location for airlines and travel agents to exchange funds from interlining or substitute flights. These changes expedited the settlement of accounts between agents and carriers. ATC agents have thus come to serve as industry agents, representing all ATC member airlines. The roughly 27,000 ATC accredited agency locations in 1985 represented 33 member airlines. Shortly after the formation of the ATC, the International Air Transport Association (IATA) implemented a similar program, standardizing the selection and qualification of agents representing international air carriers. As of 1985 there were approximately 36,000 IATA accredited agents worldwide. The IATA and ATC programs are similar in many respects and contain many basic provisions that are substantially identical.

With the aim of "professionalizing" the marketing of air transportation services, the ATC Passenger Sales Agency Program was, and continues to be, built on agreements adopted by member airlines concerning the methods by and conditions under which accredited agents may sell airline tickets. Although these agreements have been subject to review and modification over the years, the exclusivity provisions (which prohibit the use of non-ATC accredited travel agents by member airlines) were at the heart of the conference system. Exclusivity effectively restricted the right to sell airline tickets to accredited travel agents and to the airlines themselves. The conference agreements also established standards for agent accreditation in several categories, including business practices, financial requirements, personnel training, and agency location. One of these provisions is the so-called "20 percent rule," which stipulates that an agent must do less than 20 percent of its annual air transportation business with itself or other businesses under its control or under common control with an agent.[5] This provision effectively prevented corporations from entering into ticket distribution for their own business-related travel.

Until 1979 business travel departments were also not eligible to receive commissions or rebates from airlines on ticket sales. In that year, however, a CAB ruling made it possible for corporations to establish "in-plant" travel agency locations, thus providing a sort of hybrid between a business travel department and an ATC travel agency. Under such an arrangement an ATC agent could locate an agency within a corporation and staff it with non-ATC-accredited personnel. Carriers paid the overseeing agent 3 percent on these in-house ticket sales, in contrast to the 7 percent general commission in effect at the time. The agent then paid the corporation 85 to 90 percent of that commission as reimbursement to cover the cost of operating the travel department. The parent travel agency assumed liability for the ticket stock, and the firm provided reservation and ticketing services. However, no one seemed to be particularly pleased with these arrangements, other than those travel agents who had not previously collected any commissions on in-house sales (e.g., in cases where the firms previously had dealt directly with the airlines). The airlines were now obligated to pay 3 percent commissions on sales that, in some cases, once came their way at no charge; firms maintained they should be able to collect commissions without a travel agent intermediary; travel agents bemoaned the fact that their commissions on in-plant sales were less than standard commissions. Nevertheless, the number of in-plant travel agent locations had risen to approximately 400 by early 1984.

The airlines and the ATC were able to develop their joint accreditation process because the Civil Aeronautics Board exempted the airlines from antitrust laws that would have otherwise applied. However, in September 1979 the CAB initiated an investigation of the air transportation marketing and distribution system to "determine how competition can best be introduced into the entire marketing system." The investigative order charged that

> the means by which, and the locations from which, the retailers may compete for sales with the suppliers are limited, and the classes of consumers with which the retailers may do business are circumscribed. The result is little or no competition on price at any level, and carefully controlled competition between suppliers and retailers. Competition among retailers is therefore largely confined to providing services, which consumers may not necessarily want or need.

While this investigation was being conducted, the CAB voted in 1980 to eliminate fixed industrywide commissions, necessitating individual negotiations between carriers and agents.[6] United Airlines then proposed a new rate structure, hoping to improve on the relatively high commission per ticket that it traditionally paid under the established fixed percentage formula. (United's commissions were higher because of its longer than average haul length, an arrangement that corresponded with the higher than average fare markups on long hauls that existed under regulation.) Travel agents vigorously opposed United's proposed flat rate of $8.50 on all tickets, and United soon withdrew its proposal.

Following the deregulation of sales commissions, and almost certainly contrary to the CAB's expectations, the average commission rose steadily.[7] On domestic ticket sales the average industry commission to travel agents rose from 8.3 percent in 1977 to 9.6 percent in 1985, with the highest rates paid for tour sales and the lowest for point to point ticketing. The rapid increase in commission costs relative to passenger revenues was due in part to the increasing proportion of tickets sold by travel agents. Another factor was the extension of volume "overrides," usually in the form of additional payments from an airline to a travel agency of up to 5 percent of the ticket price when agency sales of that airline's tickets exceeded a certain volume. By structuring overrides to be paid based on the share of an agency's tickets issued for an airline, an airline can provide an incentive for the agency to shift passengers away from competing airlines to the airline paying the overrides. Such incentives could be particularly useful for a carrier trying to establish a new hub in an area or seeking to become dominant in an existing hub. According to ATC estimates the percentage of agents' tickets benefiting from these overrides grew from 38 percent in 1977 to 60 percent in 1985, with the share of international sales even higher (roughly 80 percent).[8] As an accompaniment total airline ticket sales by travel agents increased from $3.6 billion in 1972 to over $32 billion in 1985.[9]

A CAB ruling in October 1981 permitted carriers to negotiate rebates, commissions, or bulk discounts directly with any firms providing ticketing services, instead of channeling such commissions through a travel agent. The anticipated revolutionary impact of this ruling did not materialize. Instead of offering discounts to businesses equivalent to standard agency commissions, the airlines did nothing, preferring to continue paying 3 percent commissions on in-plant ticket sales to paying commissions of up to 10 percent (or offering equivalent discounts) on direct sales to businesses. As long as the exclusivity agreements between ATC members continued to be protected by antitrust immunity, there was little reason to expect the carriers to encourage additional entry.

In the wake of this ongoing administrative deregulation of travel agent activities, the CAB's Competitive Marketing Investigation, begun in 1979, was completed in 1982. The CAB's administrative law judge, Ronnie A. Yoder, held that the travel agent exclusivity provisions should remain virtually intact and that antitrust immunity be continued for ticket sales agreements. Despite Yoder's recommendation, the CAB voted 3–2 to eliminate exclusivity over a two-year phase-in period. The CAB did, though, grant continued antitrust immunity during the transition period ending on December 31, 1984, and antitrust immunity without time limit was continued for the Area Settlement Plan. Business travel departments also were precluded from entry as accredited agents until 1985. The then CAB Chairman Daniel MacKinnon attempted to downplay the significance of the decision, noting that the action did not require the airlines to license outlets other than travel agents to sell their tickets; the decision only made it possible if they so wished. Nevertheless, the American Society of Travel Agents (ASTA), the industry trade association, launched an intensive lobbying effort in Washington, contending that the loss of exclusivity would lead to fragmentation, the dissolution of interline agreements, and higher ticket prices. However, the 1984 elections and a heavy congressional agenda precluded legislative action on the CAB decision.

Although changes in ticket distribution had not been as great as some hoped (or feared) by 1985, a few attempts were made at entry. The number of business travel departments continued to grow, and many more large corporations hosted in-house travel agencies with the end of exclusivity agreements in 1985. A few large firms were also successful in negotiating price discounts for advance purchases of blocks of tickets (on the routes used most by a corporation's executives). As a variation on this same theme a corporation could sell seats to the public for "regularly scheduled" flights made by its private corporate aircraft between the corporation's principal business locations, perhaps ultimately (as in the case of Kimberly-Clark with Midwest Express) actually entering into certificated airline service.

A most notable attempt at entry into airline ticket distribution was also made by Ticketron, whose main business was retailing tickets for sporting and entertainment events. Ticketron had some prior experience in selling airline tickets for World Airways (an arrangement that was permitted because World was not a member of the ATC). The CAB granted Ticketron the right to act as a retailer selling point to point tickets, although it was not permitted to offer travel agent services, tours, and other similar products. However, no airline had entered into an agreement with Ticketron as of 1985, with the stated reason being that any sales through the ticket agency would have mostly come to the airlines directly, thereby avoiding unnecessary commissions. Another plausible explanation is that carriers felt that any benefits Ticketron might provide would be outweighed by the damage (traffic diversion) that would result from incurring the wrath of travel agents.

Technological Change and the Bias Issue

Competitive pressures on entry and distribution are not the only aspects of airline marketing and distribution to be modified over the years. The proliferation of fare and schedule changes under deregulation resulted in a growing need for sophisticated information and data management services by travel agents. At the same time advances in computer technology yielded integrated systems capable of updating information on an ongoing basis and rapid processing of orders. *Business Week* estimated that 82 percent of all travel agents were automated by 1983, up from only 15 percent in 1979.[10]

In the early days of automated reservation and ticketing systems, direct access to each carrier's computer system was available only through the carrier's own ticket offices. In the mid-1970s an attempt was made by the travel agent industry to create a single, industrywide reservation system, the Joint Industry Computerized Reservation System. Shortly before this system was to become available, United opened subscriptions to its APOLLO system to travel agents, and American immediately followed suit with its SABRE system. Plans for the industrywide system were disbanded, and a competitive war began with each carrier that had a system scrambling to sign travel agents on to its system. A subsequent plan by the travel industry, in conjunction with 10 airlines and American Express, to develop an unbiased universal reservation system was abandoned in 1978, ostensibly because of carrier fears of antitrust action.[11] Despite other attempts to develop unbiased reservation systems, the carrier-hosted systems achieved large market shares. By 1981 American's SABRE system claimed 41 percent of total automated agency subscriptions, with United's APOLLO close behind with 39 percent and TWA's PARS garnering 15 percent.[12] Similarly SABRE system collected 43 percent of 1983 computerized reservation system revenues, with APOLLO gathering 27 percent and PARS 10 percent.[13] These market shares were seemingly changed very little by deregulation.[14]

The airlines' operation of computer reservation systems has evoked strong criticism and raised charges of bias.[15] The major complaint has been that the systems were programmed to display the flights of the host carriers before competitors' flights, even though a competitor may have services more closely matching the customer's needs. Other complaints included charging system listing fees based on the degree of competition with the host carrier, delaying the entry of route and fare changes by competitors, and requiring "net ticketing agreements" that compensated the larger host carriers for tickets written for smaller airlines. American and United defended these practices, saying that they developed and paid for the reservation system to better market their own airlines; any extra bookings resulting from bias help defray some of the system development and operating costs and were thus necessary to offering the service to agents at reasonable rates.

The development of multiple hubs in the nation's air system has also allegedly created opportunities for using the reservation systems to suppress competition, especially from new hubs that expand the network of possible connecting flights. As one CAB report noted:

> The inability or refusal to show additional connecting points results in an extreme form of bias—suppression of all connecting flights that might be available over nonselected hubs, even if those connections are superior from the point of view of consumers.[16]

The extent to which biases favoring the host carriers have actually affected travel agent recommendations remains an open issue. It has been estimated that between 70 and 90 percent of all computer reservation system bookings are made from the first screen displayed to the agent, and nearly half from the first line of the first screen.[17] Nevertheless, many agents contend that they circumvent or work around the biases. Problems of information updating and reliability are more difficult to eliminate, however, so a host carrier may still enjoy at least some additional influence over an agent using its system.

The debate over reservation system bias resulted in congressional hearings in late 1982, as well as a preliminary investigation of anticompetitive practices by the antitrust division of the Department of Justice. The CAB launched its own investigation in September 1983 to determine whether, and to what extent, it should regulate reservation systems. The CAB issued rules concerning computerized reservation systems on August 10, 1984. The administrative order mandated that system vendors must offer a primary terminal display that ranks flights based on fare and service factors rather than carrier identity. Displays of connecting flights must be based on "objective" criteria, requiring consideration of multiple hubs when constructing connecting flights. These new rules became effective in late 1984 and were transferred to the Department of Transportation for enforcement upon the CAB's sunset on January 1, 1985.

The ruling requiring unbiased primary displays did not produce the results many had desired. The major vendors, United and American, quickly developed secondary displays that retained much of the previous bias and that were easily accessible by travel agents. Moreover both systems eventually also developed "lock-in" features that allowed a travel agency manager to make only "secondary" displays available to agents. Not surprisingly, there were more congressional hearings in March 1985. Subsequently the computer reservation system vendors agreed to eliminate the biased secondary screens and offer only displays based on objective criteria.

Even then the computer reservation system bias issue did not fully subside. As discussed in chapter 4, the reservation systems almost inherently retained a bias in favor of online connections over interline connections. Although the major vendors defended this practice in the March 1985 hearings before the Senate Commerce Committee as reflecting the preferences of consumers, this feature of the reservation systems has aided the carriers in their efforts to build hub and spoke connecting systems (as described in chapter 5).

The remaining potential for subtle bias in carrier-owned systems is also substantial. For example, in June 1986, Delta filed a complaint with the Department of Transportation alleging that American Airlines obtained higher display ranking for some of its flights in SABRE by reducing the scheduled flying time without a correponding reduction in actual flying time (i.e., without a change in operations).[18] Whether or not Delta's specific allegation is correct, the possibility of such manipulation is cause for concern among competing carriers who rely on the dominant computer reservations systems for a substantial part of their bookings. The bias need not divert a high proportion of passengers for its revenue impact to be important. As Delta alleges in its complaint, a bias that diverts only one passenger per month with a $200 round-trip flight for each SABRE computer terminal would gain American Airlines, and cost American's competitors, $120 million per year. Moreover, since the cost of operating a jet flight is not highly dependent on a small change in the number of passengers on that flight, such a revenue gain is likely to translate almost entirely into higher profits.

Even in the absence of regulatory rulings to curb possible abuses, the changing economics and technology of computerized reservation systems may force changes. The high research and development costs, scale economies, and learning curves that characterized development of early computer reservation systems may have been largely eroded, and significant potential competition could develop. For example, Dun and Bradstreet developed a personal computer version of the *Official Airline Guide* and began marketing the product in 1983. Other large information services and computer companies have worked on similar systems. Developments in videotext technology are also looking increasingly promising for entirely new forms of distribution. Pilot programs have been tested (e.g., at Warner-Amex) using interactive cable television systems to enable consumers to make airline and hotel reservations at home. As of 1985, though it was still necessary to either pick up tickets or receive them by mail, the entire ticketing transaction could otherwise be completed in one's own study or living room, if equipped with a personal computer and communication modem.

Nevertheless, substantial overhead and training costs have apparently precluded most travel agents from maintaining or accessing more than one reservation system. Thus SABRE and APOLLO will probably maintain a strong market position, even as the growing number of alternative systems will likely force APOLLO and SABRE to temper any biases and moderate any discriminatory practices. Pressure to do so may also come increasingly from travelers. For example, business travel departments could use the electronic edition of the *Official Airline Guide* to check on availability and fares, and then use this information to request specific reservations from travel agents. Moreover, as American and United move toward the completion of their desired route networks, the benefits of some forms of bias may no longer be as important to their development strategies.

Overall, technological change has been the principal competitive force behind recent developments in air travel marketing and distribution. According to a 1981 Louis Harris survey, 80 percent of automated travel agencies reported increases in sales volume since computer terminals were installed; at the same time the average productivity of automated agencies had increased 42 percent.[19] To be sure, the capacity to update continually fare and schedule information has had much to do with travel agents' ability to double their market share since deregulation. The question is whether future technological changes might reverse, or at least endanger, those gains. Specifically, improved technology permitted a decentralization of the airline ticketing function from the airlines to the travel agents; an extension of those same technological trends might permit a further decentralization from the agents directly to the traveling public.

Implications for Industry Strategy and Structure

In assessing the potential effect of technological and regulatory change on the structure of the air travel distribution activity, it is useful to think about the three particular functions or services a travel agency provides.[20] First, the agent supplies information of various sorts to the consumer. Second, the agent sells a variety of products, services, and information, often bundling these items in ways that create value to customers, such as vacation tours or fly/drive packages. Finally, the agent provides a clerical function, writing tickets and handling payment transactions. Deregulation has essentially separated or ensured the unbundling of these three activities, while technology has reduced both the cost of obtaining current information and the expense of the associated clerical services. At the same time the removal of administrative entry barriers has engendered growing competition in all three activities. The decreasing costs of entry into the clerical and information activities has placed persistent pressure on existing travel agencies to control costs in order to maintain operating margins. Moreover, to the extent more large firms begin to negotiate directly with the airlines for discounted ticket purchases, travel agents may lose a sizable portion of the sales function as well.

A final threat to the sales activities of agents has come from the airlines themselves. A variety of new direct marketing incentives have been developed, most notably the frequent-flyer programs now offered by virtually every major airline. These programs generally involve free first-class upgrades, free tickets, and other inducements to build up mileage on one airline. By developing a form of brand loyalty directly with passengers, the airlines may have weakened the intermediary role of travel agencies.

What effects will all of these changes have on travel agencies? Increases in the late 1970s and early 1980s in both the number of travel agents and the commissions paid were obviously to some extent a result of the confusion wrought by deregulation. Nevertheless, the increasing costs of traditional travel agent systems suggest that new players and channels should emerge—or at least be objects of experimentation. Direct negotiations with business travel departments to reflect quantity discounts and lower commission rates have already happened. Bulk discounts to other kinds of transportation retailers have also apparently occurred in some instances. For example, vacation packagers are the major purchasers of bulk discount tickets, which they usually purchase by chartering a flight. These ticket retailers have increasingly negotiated the price of blocks of seats on regularly scheduled flights directly with the airlines and assumed the risk of selling them. The price of the seats to travelers is determined by ticket availability and demand, in a manner similar to the ticket agencies that often sell theater or sporting event seats. Peak and off-peak pricing have also become more prevalent, as well as "marginal" pricing in which retailers reduce prices to sell any remaining tickets (in a manner similar to that of European charter operators). Since the airlines bear the risk of unsold seats only until sold to retailers, the inventory risks are divided between the carriers and retailers.

These market, technological, and regulatory changes strongly suggest that the travel agent industry could be radically transformed. Many analysts contend that drastic consolidation is inevitable, with the number of agencies falling by 50 percent or more. This view argues that technological advances entail large capital investments with incumbent increases in fixed costs, thereby requiring offsetting increases in minimum volume. Technological change may produce sizable economies in labor, space, and other factors as well. Larger agencies also tend to have a greater percentage of corporate accounts, while benefiting from commission overrides more frequently than smaller agencies. As a result the larger agencies also have strong bargaining power with airlines concerning rebates, bulk sales, and the like. However, the basic costs of the underlying computer and communications technologies have also steadily decreased, with an accompanying emphasis on decentralization of information services. Thus, though some consolidation may occur, the underlying technological trends and economics do not suggest that this outcome is inevitable.

Indeed, increased differentiation and specialization among travel agencies could well occur, with a variety of marketing techniques being tested such as direct mail campaigns, bartering of airline tickets in exchange for other tour packages, and joint promotions with hotels and auto leasing companies. Such proliferation of products, prices, and marketing techniques may require that the travel agent industry pulls back from its traditional general service orientation.

In a fashion similar to many other industries, different travel agencies may adopt different market strategies.[21] Some full-service agencies may develop on a national or regional scale. Some firms may achieve such a position through internal expansion, while others do so through geographic expansion via mergers or acquisitions or, alternatively, through franchise arrangements. Alternatively, some agencies may adopt "niche" strategies, specializing in the provision of particular products or services to particular travel groups. These areas of specialization might include business travel, last minute discount ticket selling, vacation travel, and tour planning and operation.

Conclusion

While travel agencies experienced unprecedented growth and profits in the initial years of airline deregulation, substantial competition has also emerged. In this context the travel agent industry will likely undergo a major transition, with individual firms attempting to identify and implement strategies appropriate to their positioning in this evolving industry structure. Indeed, the possibility cannot be ruled out that the travel agency, in its current mode of operation, will largely become extinct as technology permits a decentralization of the information dispensing and clerical functions to the household or office of the individual traveler. Only the more personalized aspects of the travel agents' advising function would seem relatively impervious to such developments, particularly for infrequent travelers. With or without continued antitrust immunity, the combination of rapid technological change and deregulation of the travel agents' principal revenue source, airline services, ensures that traditional marketing and distribution channels will be subject to increasing competitive pressures.

9

International Consequences

by Ivor P. Morgan

The history of modern international commercial aviation started with a world conference on the future of the industry held in Chicago in October 1944.[1] Discussion at Chicago focused on several so-called "freedoms of the air" (five in number at the time of the Chicago Conference and a sixth added at a later date):

1. The right to use the airspace of another country without landing.
2. The right to land for servicing or noncommercial purposes.
3. The right to discharge passengers and cargo from the home country in the foreign country.
4. The right to pick up passengers and cargo in a foreign country bound for the home country.
5. The right to pick up passengers and cargo in a foreign country and convey them to yet another country.
6. The right (in reality a combination of the third and fourth freedoms) to transport passengers and cargo from one foreign country to another by routing through the home country.

Service within a country was to be reserved for a carrier of that country. These internal or cabotage rights, as they were known from international maritime tradition, were of considerable importance in countries of great area such as the United States.[2] At Chicago, the United States, not unexpectedly, was in favor of retaining cabotage rights and for a multilateral acceptance of the first five freedoms. The Chicago Conference brought no such multilateral agreement but rather demonstrated the great disparity of views among the participants. A disparity of particular importance was the desire of the United States for "open skies" (free competition in world aviation markets) and the United Kingdom's wish for international regulation of the skies.

The differences between the United States and the United Kingdom were formally resolved at a meeting in Bermuda in 1946 where an agreement was signed (subsequently known as Bermuda I) that set the pattern of bilateral international aviation agreements for three decades after World War II. Bermuda I required that rates be set under procedures established and administered by the International Air Transport Association (IATA), an international association of airlines that had existed prior to World War II but was reestablished after the war in a new and expanded form.[3] Under Bermuda I, IATA fare setting mechanisms were given exemption from the U.S. antitrust laws by the CAB. Since Bermuda I was subsequently used as a template for other bilateral international agreements, the fare-setting mechanisms of IATA soon gained widespread use in international airline markets.

With fares largely controlled by the IATA system, international competition came to focus on service, as had been the case in the United States under CAB fare regulation.[4] To contain service competition, IATA set standards, and often surcharges, for such items as excess baggage, food services, in-flight movies, drinks, and the use of headphones. Price competition came almost solely from non-IATA airlines and charter (nonscheduled) services outside the IATA system. Indeed, during much of the postwar period, liberalization of charter rules was a chief U.S. tool for introducing some competition in international aviation.[5]

During the Bermuda I years, whatever the agreement's merits or demerits, international aviation grew at spectacular rates. Scheduled international traffic, measured by revenue passenger miles, doubled in volume every five years from 1950 through 1970.[6] The decade of the 1970s, though, brought a decline in this growth rate.

The Bermuda I period was marked not only by growth but also by dramatic change, both politically and technologically for international aviation. Membership in the International Civil Aviation Organization (ICAO) grew rapidly from 54 in 1950 to 118 by 1980.[7] The greatest numbers of new members (countries) have been in Africa (31), the Middle East (9), and the Far East (11) as many countries shed their colonial past or found increasing affluence. For these emerging countries, the operation of a national airline became important not only for passenger services but also as a means of carrying the flag to distant places.[8]

Improved technology, particularly advances in aircraft, navigation, and landing systems also spurred growth in international aviation. The need for refueling stops which had typified long-distance flights even after World War II were largely removed with the advent of jet aircraft. Bermuda I had specified international routes and rights on the basis of propellor technology and many landing rights became less valuable as carriers opted for more direct jet routes. The introduction of wide-bodied jets in the late 1960s and early 1970s was also an important change but, unfortunately for the airlines, coincided with slower growth in the demand for international air travel. Airlines had projected otherwise and therefore struggled with excess capacity, especially when faced with the higher costs from the OPEC oil crisis of 1973. Ostensibly to save fuel, capacity control agreements (in parallel with similar concessions granted within the United States) were established in early 1974 on North Atlantic routes between Britain and the United States.[9] The CAB rejected a British request for a continuation of these capacity agreements in 1976. The British, believing that the Bermuda I agreement was then heavily in favor of the United States, gave notice to terminate the agreement on June 22, 1976.

Subsequent negotiations between the United States and the United Kingdom led to a second Bermuda agreement (Bermuda II) which was signed on June 23, 1977.[10] This agreement was termed by some critics as "perhaps the greatest abdication [ever] of U.S. interests in international aviation."[11] Ironically, its signing also coincided with a new drive by the United States for greater competition in commercial aviation, both domestic and international.

The New "Open Skies" Policy

The Bermuda II agreement increased the number of U.S. gateways for air service to Britain from 6 to 14 but restricted entry at those gateways.[12] Only two gateways, New York and Los Angeles, were to be allowed service by two carriers of both countries. All other gateways were restricted to single-carrier service from each country, with some routes being initially restricted to service by only one U.S. carrier or one from the U.K. with competition from the other nation to be introduced at a later date. A more stringent capacity control clause was also incorporated into Bermuda II; approval was required by both governments prior to capacity additions rather than after.[13] Additionally fifth freedom rights were substantially reduced (i.e., the rights for U.S. carriers to fly from U.K. airports to points beyond in other countries).

CAB Chairman Alfred Kahn saw Bermuda II as contradicting the principles of market competition then being pursued by the CAB.[14] In particular, Kahn was concerned that Bermuda II did not include any liberalization of charter rules that would have continued the opportunity for U.S. charter carriers to compete and to provide a vital stimulus for low-cost service. Indeed, by November 1977, the CAB under Kahn's leadership had already reached an agreement with Belgium that differed substantially from Bermuda II.[15] Instead of the many restrictive provisions of Bermuda II, the Belgium-U.S. agreement contained few restrictions and was in line with Chairman Kahn's six stated objectives for international aviation:

1. Elimination of anticompetitive restrictions on charters and supplemental carriers.

2. Expanded opportunities for new low-priced scheduled services.

3. Maximum access to markets by expansion, and not contraction, of nonstop U.S. gateways.

4. Adequate multiple-carrier designations.

5. Avoidance of capacity or frequency restrictions.

6. Maximum flexibility for air carriers to operate to points beyond, or on the way to, the country of the bilateral partner.

The liberal bilateral agreement with Belgium, agreed to only a few months after adoption of Bermuda II, as well as subsequent development of liberal bilaterals with other countries, so contrasted with the terms of Bermuda II that many felt legislation was required to ensure that U.S. bilateral negotiators would have a clear set of guidelines under which to work. This guidance came in the form of the International Air Transportation Competition Act of 1979 (IATCA) which became law on February 15, 1980.[16] Embedded in this legislation were goals very much like those stated by Kahn. International aviation was to be encouraged by lowering fares, by eliminating operational and marketing restrictions, by liberalizing charter rules and operations, and by allowing the maximum degree of multiple and permissive international authority for U.S. air carriers so that they would be able to respond quickly to shifts in market demand. The objectives also included: better integration of domestic and international air transportation, increased numbers of nonstop U.S. gateway cities, and opportunities for carriers of foreign countries to increase their access to U.S. points in exchange for benefits of similar magnitude for U.S. carriers or the traveling public (with permanent linkage between rights granted and rights given away).[17]

All these moves toward more liberal bilateral agreements echoed earlier U.S. policies aimed at enhancing competition in international aviation. Like those earlier "open skies" policies, however, implementation of the new "open skies" policy was difficult.[18] To start, the United States still needed to have the agreement of a bilateral partner for implementation. In most countries only one airline existed, and it was usually government owned or an airline in which the government had a considerable financial stake (so that few countries were likely to welcome unconstrained entry of

U.S. airline companies on their routes to and from the United States). The international scene also had no structure of antitrust law, whereas the domestic U.S. deregulation movement could rely, at least to some extent, on antitrust laws to ensure an orderly transition to a free market.

IATCA also produced a problem for the CAB by specifying multiple objectives. To ensure that consumer interests would be well attended and that airline companies would simultaneously receive healthy profits was obviously a difficult task. Furthermore those negotiating bilateral agreements on behalf of the United States had only a limited set of tools and incentives for persuading other countries to adopt policies compatible with U.S. goals.

Liberal Bilaterals: Definitions and Trade-offs

To enhance competition within a market, more airlines are obviously better than fewer. From a traveler's viewpoint, more airlines also provide more opportunities for convenient connections to international flights. Yet, for quite obvious reasons, multiple airline designations on international routes have generally been of little interest to foreign countries with only one airline.

Opening additional U.S. gateways, by contrast, is very desirable to foreign carriers as it gives them direct access to more of the U.S. market and means that fewer passengers have to travel part of the way on a U.S. domestic carrier. From the U.S. standpoint, additional gateways: (1) create the possibility of competition between gateways, an important aspect if multiple-carrier routes from a particular gateway are not permitted, (2) improve access for U.S. residents to foreign destinations via shorter flights and fewer stops en route, and (3) stimulate foreign travel to the United States (because of improved service and reduced costs).

The U.S. pursuit of more liberal bilaterals also usually incorporated some promotion of fifth freedom rights. Extending fifth freedom rights increases, of course, the possibility of more carriers competing on a route (although only with the agreement of yet another bilateral partner). In any negotiation fifth freedom rights may not be equally desired by both parties. For example, the United States, because of its large geographical size and relatively few close neighbors, may not present the same fifth freedom opportunities as, for example, a small European or Asian country.

Indeed, in one important aspect U.S. aviation policy has never been liberal or even negotiable. The maintenance of cabotage rights, which reserved domestic traffic to U.S. carriers, was embedded in various U.S.

transportation statutes; even a foreign ownership position in an airline with U.S. cabotage privileges has been restricted.[19] Other countries, particularly small ones, have claimed that these cabotage rights give U.S. carriers as unreasonable advantage in bilateral traffic because of the large U.S. market area from which to funnel traffic toward U.S. international airlines.

Still another conventional goal in liberal bilaterals, achieving nondiscriminatory practices in marketing and operations, can often be difficult to achieve or even define in practice. What may appear as a discriminatory practice from one nation's viewpoint may be seen as having an economic basis in equity, or even in efficiency, by another nation. Endless haggling about the application of such terms as "discriminatory" or "anticompetitive" has thus long plagued international aviation negotiations.

Of course no procompetitive considerations will have much meaning if airline prices are agreed on between competing airlines, as in the IATA traffic conference mechanisms. Similarly, to make the market work, competing carriers should be free to determine their own capacity levels. Indeed, this had been a U.S. negotiating objective since the 1944 Chicago convention. Most intra-European bilaterals, by contrast, removed virtually all competitive elements by having not only tight bilateral control of price and capacity but some type of revenue pooling as well.[20]

Few countries in the western world in fact have maintained a strong procompetitive stance on international aviation throughout the post-World War II period. France, Italy, Norway, Sweden, Denmark, Japan, and Australia have all been powerful voices in favor of more rather than less international regulation. Only Iceland and Luxembourg sanctioned much scheduled competition to the IATA airlines on the North Atlantic. However, from the late 1960s on, an association of airlines in South East Asia, numbering some fourteen by 1980, competed directly with the airlines of IATA. The United States therefore had some allies in principle.

Progress in aviation technology, coupled with the very size of the United States, has brought most of the major population centers of the world within the range of direct flights from U.S. gateways. These centers are composed of some whose governments favor liberalization, some fervently opposed, some where adjacent countries fear a traffic diversion should their agreements be insufficiently competitive, and some that are relatively undeveloped with thin markets.[21] In facing this patchwork, the U.S. negotiator cannot hope for quick conversion to liberal philosophies of most U.S. bilateral partners.[22]

Nevertheless, between July 1977 and August 1981, the United States concluded new bilateral agreements with 25 countries (in addition to extending existing Bermuda I type agreements). The most liberal of these agreements were with Belgium, Finland, Israel, Jordan, Jamaica, Singapore, Korea, and Thailand. These liberal bilaterals included such features as:

1. *Mutual disapproval of pricing*. Both partners must disapprove of a tariff for its rejection.
2. *Capacity discretion*. No restrictions on schedule or aircraft type or size.
3. *Route freedoms*. Granting full fifth freedom rights to the bilateral partners.
4. *Charter freedoms*. Each country determines its own charter rules for operations originating within its own country.

Relatively little acceptance of the liberal philosophy has occurred in Africa, South America, and Eastern Europe. Although the number of liberal bilaterals is small in relation to the number of international aviation markets, the United States has achieved liberal agreements with three (if the United Kingdom is included) of its top five European markets and with three of its top four Asian markets. U.S. liberal influence in Asia may be somewhat overstated though, as the fourth market is Japan, by far the largest market in the Far East. On the other hand, any assessment of the impact of liberal bilaterals purely by the number of agreements ignores the competitive stimulus felt by competing markets through the fear of traffic diversion.

U.S. International Aviation Performance

Market Shares

Nations take an immense pride in being a world leader of a visible industry. For Britain, for example, in the days of its Empire, one presumed measure of its "superiority" was its dominance of world maritime shipping. For the United States, a world leader in a different age, pursuit of a leadership position in aviation may be equally natural. At any rate a steady postwar loss of U.S. market share as a percentage of world international scheduled traffic, as shown in table 9.1, has been viewed by some U.S. policymakers as unsatisfactory. This loss may have been largely due, though, to the United States being the pioneer nation in international aviation on many of the continents of the world. At the end of World War II the United States dominated the airline routes of the Pacific, the Atlantic and South America and had made significant inroads into Asia and Africa. U.S. airlines were providing service in many countries that were without their

Table 9.1 Market share of revenue passenger miles, in total international scheduled traffic, 1950–1980 (selected countries as percent of world total, excluding USSR)

	1950	1955	1960	1965	1970	1975	1980
World War II non-Axis powers							
Belgium	2.4[a]	1.4	2.7	2.1	1.5	1.4	1.1
France	11.4[a]	8.6[a]	7.3	8.4	6.9	6.6	5.7
Netherlands	7.8	7.8	6.6	4.2	3.6	3.9	3.2
Switzerland	1.5	2.7	2.8	3.1	2.8	2.9	2.2
United Kingdom	11.7[b]	14.5	15.8	13.6	10.6	10.7	11.8
United States	43.8	38.1	33.4	34.4	24.2	16.6	18.1
World War II Axis Powers							
Germany	—	0.4	3.0	4.3	4.5	4.6	4.1
Italy	0.6	1.6	2.9	4.3	4.4	3.3	2.5
Japan	—	0.6	1.2	2.4	4.1	4.6	4.9
Rest of world							
By difference	20.8	24.3	24.3	23.2	37.4	45.4	46.4

Source: *ICAO Digest of Statistics* (1950–1975) and *Civil Aviation Statistics of the World* (1980).
a. Includes some domestic traffic.
b. BEA and BOAC only.

own airlines. Much of this traffic was not based on U.S. gateways and was fifth freedom in nature. As countries became more developed economically, or shed their colonial ties, a new national airline became a common way of showing their flags around the world, with a concomitant diversion of traffic away from prior carriers (including those of the United States).

The United States was not alone in seeing its world market share diminish. As table 9.1 demonstrates, most of the major non-Axis aviation powers of World War II experienced similar declines. Obviously revival of the World War II Axis powers has contributed to the decline of the market shares of the other developed nations. However, with the exception of Japan, this market share growth trend has reversed, and even for Japan, market share growth had all but ceased by the late 1970s.

The group entitled "rest of the world" displays a dramatic growth in market share after 1965. This period coincided with the creation of a large number of new independent nations in the former colonial territories. Similarly, increasing affluence in some third-world countries (e.g., the Arab oil states) made the establishment of a national airline a virtual necessity for economic and political reasons. Finally, the advent of the jet brought some small, but affluent, non-European countries such as Austra-

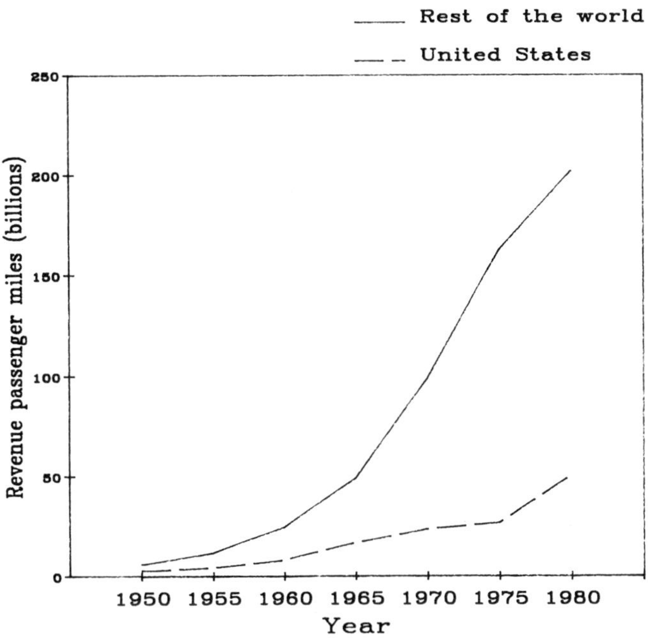

Figure 9.1 Growth in international scheduled aviation, 1950–1980.

lia and New Zealand into more convenient and direct contact with other developed countries.

As illustrated in figure 9.1, loss of U.S. market share does not necessarily mean an absolute decline in traffic (because of offsetting overall growth in the international aviation market). Participation in international aviation has not, however, followed a simple smooth pattern. The United States experienced accelerating growth through the mid-1960s, only slightly lagging the world pattern. During the late 1960s and early 1970s, however, U.S. market growth rates were considerably lower than the rest of the world. But then a period of U.S. growth resurgence followed, coinciding with the procompetitive policies of the late 1970s.

While world market share patterns give a measure of the changing forces in international aviation, the market shares of routes based in a country are often a matter for special review by policymakers. Specifically, bilateral market shares that become very one-sided can be expected to increase pressure for action from the nation with the smaller share.

Measured in shares of total passengers (arrivals and departures), the U.S. market share of traffic between the U.S. and other countries (both scheduled and nonscheduled) hovered close to 50 percent for the 1975 to 1981 period, with a slight fall in 1980 and 1981. This was roughly the same market share that the United States had in the 1960s. That share had been much higher, though, in the 1950s; in 1955, for example, the level was 68.6 percent. Indeed, only two areas showed significant market share growth for U.S. carriers between 1975 and 1981 in U.S.-based traffic: the Middle East (from 25.4 to 34.9 percent) and the Caribbean (from 63.9 to 69.9 percent). Increased U.S. economic activity in the Middle East and a possible propensity for travelers to seek the security of U.S. carriers in this troubled region may explain some of these market share gains. The Caribbean is largely a tourist market where many of the charter passengers originate in the United States.

Significantly, U.S. citizens, like those of other nations, show some predilection to travel on their own carriers. U.S. citizens form a consistently higher share of U.S. carrier traffic than they do for foreign carriers. Some of the decline in U.S. market share, even for U.S. origin or destination traffic, is thus attributable to travel by foreign citizens growing more quickly than that of U.S. citizens. In 1979 for the first time U.S. citizens were outnumbered by foreign citizens on flights arriving in the United States.[23] Chief among many causes for the relative decrease of U.S. citizens' travel in world markets is probably the increasing affluence of other parts of the world.

Table 9.2 examines this picture by market region with the areas of the world ranked roughly by the relative decline of U.S. citizens as a percentage of the market (regions with the greatest relative loss of U.S. citizens are

Table 9.2 Change in U.S. citizen importance to airlines in markets with the United States

Approximate rank by greatest decrease in U.S. citizens in market	Percent change in U.S. citizen proportion of carrier traffic, 1975–1981		1981 level of U.S. citizen proportion	
	U.S. carriers	Foreign carriers	U.S. carriers	Foreign carriers
Africa	−54	−33	43	32
South America	−47	−33	24	22
Europe	−39	−34	49	39
Middle East	−17	−25	58	47
Central America	−18	−17	50	43
Caribbean	−9	−26	68	42
Far East	−19	0	30	20
Oceania	−10	+10	47	32

Source: INS arrivals data.

ranked highest). To illustrate, U.S. citizen participation in Africa–U.S. markets declined 54 percent on U.S. carriers and 33 percent on foreign carriers. These declines were associated with an absolute U.S. citizen participation rate of 43 percent on U.S. carriers and 32 percent on foreign carriers. A propensity to fly the carrier of citizenship suggests that U.S. carriers will find it extremely difficult to increase their market shares while U.S. citizen participation percentages are falling; to do so, U.S. carriers must achieve an increased share of the non-U.S. citizen market.

By the early 1980s U.S. citizens formed a minority of the travelers in the biggest noncontiguous (i.e. Canada and Mexico excluded) U.S.-based international markets. The ability of U.S. carriers to maintain a total share of these markets of around 50 percent (in terms of passenger numbers) was remarkable in light of these trends. U.S. carriers apparently have successfully appealed to the travelers of other nationalities in greater numbers than in the past, either because of price and service flexibility or U.S. government efforts to open up competition.

Suggestively, as shown in table 9.3, the growth experiences of liberal U.S. bilateral markets have generally been better than those in markets with restrictive agreements (e.g., of the Bermuda I type). In the cases of

Table 9.3 A comparison of growth rates of U.S. liberal bilateral markets with restrictive markets, 1975–1981

	1976/75	1977/76	1978/77	1979/78	1980/79	1981/80
Europe						
Three liberal bilaterals—Belgium, Netherlands, West Germany	13.7	4.0	9.4	18.6[a]	11.0	1.3
Three restricted bilaterals—France, Spain, Italy	4.7	5.0	9.4	6.8	−4.3	−1.9
Moderately liberal bilateral—United Kingdom	20.2	80.5	24.1	4.4	9.7	4.6
Far East						
Two liberal bilaterals—Korea and Singapore	8.7	0.5	3.5	65.2[a]	50.9	4.5
Restrictive bilateral—Japan	4.0	1.9	6.7	19.9	4.3	5.5

Source: INS data; includes arrivals, departures, scheduled, and charter.
Note: Growth rate in percent increase of total arrivals and departures (scheduled and charter) over previous year between the United States and the designated countries.
a. Liberal bilaterals put in force.

Table 9.4 U.S. market share in liberal bilateral markets, 1975–1981 (percent of total passengers)

	Prior to liberal bilaterals				After liberal bilaterals		
	1975	1976	1977	1978	1979	1980	1981
Europe							
Belgium	29.4	30.8	22.1	21.2	36.5	44.5	39.1
Netherlands	14.2	8.6	8.6	11.6	23.4	12.3	7.3
West Germany	43.2	50.5	49.1	44.4	45.3	50.6	46.4
United Kingdom	57.8	56.9	55.5	53.4	52.6	47.8	50.0
Far East							
Singapore	99.6	99.5	97.5	96.5	21.5	22.6	18.0
Korea	18.7	21.1	11.8	6.5	13.2	18.5	20.7

Source: INS data; includes arrivals, departures, scheduled, and charter.

Europe and the Far East the liberal bilateral markets have experienced a considerably higher growth rate than the restrictive markets. However, the market with Japan, subject to a restrictive bilateral, experienced higher growth rates for a few years than did the liberal European markets.[24] This probably had little to do with international aviation policy but was more a reflection of the rising level of economic interaction between Japan and the United States.

As shown in table 9.4, U.S. carriers have also held their market shares in most liberal bilateral markets. For example, the liberal agreements with Belgium and West Germany seem to have helped the U.S. carriers; by contrast, most other markets continued to demonstrate the overall trend away from U.S. carriers. The Singapore market is, incidentally, a special case in that liberalization meant an end to a U.S. monopoly in that market.

The Impact of New Gateways

As the U.S. population shifted to the south and west in the postwar years, more and more international travelers had to be routed through the established gateways of the older population centers to reach international destinations. By definition, opening up new international gateways changed this and meant that the old gateways as a group lost market share. Few of the old gateways, though, experienced an absolute decline in international activity. As shown in table 9.5, only Anchorage, Detroit, and Washington/Baltimore of the fourteen gateways included in the Bermuda II agreement experienced an absolute decline in passenger volumes over the 1976 to 1981 period. The largest of the traditional gateways—New York, Miami, Chicago, Los Angeles, and Boston—grew absolutely over those same

Table 9.5 Market share of international arrivals and departures at U.S. gateways designated in Bermuda II, 1976 vs. 1981 (scheduled plus charter)

	Total passengers		Percent growth	Percent market share	
	1976	1981	1976–81	1976	1981
Gaining market share					
Atlanta	163,417	957,799	586	0.6	2.3
Dallas	404,891	924,003	128	1.5	2.3
Houston	622,544	1,361,402	119	2.3	3.3
Los Angeles	2,114,498	4,096,137	94	7.8	10.0
Miami	3,510,967	7,609,314	117	13.0	18.7
San Francisco	432,567	1,277,387	196	1.6	3.1
Losing market share					
Anchorage	416,185	352,167	−15	1.5	0.9
Boston	1,021,280	1,310,498	28	3.8	3.2
Chicago	1,357,807	1,503,344	11	5.0	3.7
Detroit	208,677	86,069	−58	0.8	0.2
New York	9,834,696	12,492,964	28	36.5	30.9
Philadelphia	302,347	307,208	2	1.1	0.8
Seattle	476,093	686,523	44	1.8	1.7
Washington/ Baltimore	666,449	596,019	−11	2.5	1.5
Others	5,419,799	7,127,927	32	20.1	17.5

Source: INS data; includes arrivals, departures, scheduled, and charter.

years. Indeed, Miami and Los Angeles even increased their shares of the U.S. market.

The spectacular growth of Miami is worthy of special note. This airport gained 18.7 percent of the U.S. international travel market in 1981 by providing not only a gateway to and from U.S. domestic points but also a base for U.S. carriers or for sixth freedom operations between Europe and Central or South America.

Opening new gateways, it is sometimes argued, is against U.S. self-interest because it represents an automatic loss for the U.S. domestic airline system as a whole. When a traveler uses a new gateway, business is lost to the domestic system because the traveler would have flown to an old gateway first on a domestic carrier. Through the old gateway the flight segmentation (and U.S. share of the flight) would typically be (1) a domestic leg on a domestic carrier and (2) an international leg (which in the U.S. case would be flown approximately 50 percent of the time on a U.S. carrier). Through a new gateway U.S. carriers would be expected to have only about 50 percent of the entire traffic; thus by the traveler going through the new gateway, U.S. carriers (as a system) lose a market approximately equal to 50 percent of the eliminated domestic leg.

This argument, however, overlooks several considerations. To start, insistence on the use of the domestic system as part of an international journey discriminates against those who do not live near existing gateways. Would proponents of this argument suggest, for example, that New Yorkers be forced to fly via Atlanta to London? Yet this is what, in reverse, was effectively the situation before Atlanta became an international gateway. The argument against opening up new gateways thus aligns itself against the idea of service to the traveling public. The argument also assumes that travelers from the new gateway also live in that gateway city. They may of course live in another city and still require some use of the domestic airline system to reach the new gateway. The market "loss" as measured by 50 percent of the former domestic leg is therefore overstated and represents an upper bound estimate.

A full analysis of the actual loss to the domestic system of opening up new international gateways would be quite complex. Account would have to be taken of a host of difficult to assess factors: for example, the full origin and destination patterns of travelers and the usage of the domestic airline system under the old and new gateway arrangements. Furthermore proper assessment of the impact of a new gateway on the market for international travel would involve assessing the likelihood that reduced costs, time savings, gateway competitive effects, and new services and fares would stimulate some additional traffic.[25]

To illustrate, table 9.6 shows the time savings of a direct flight from several U.S. gateways opened in the early 1980s against the previous best routing through New York to London or to Brussels. For each new

Table 9.6 Direct flight service time gains from new gateways to London and Brussels over previous routing via New York, 1982

U.S. city	To	Time reduction of schedule
Atlanta	Brussels	4 hr 18 min
	London	2 hr 49 min
Chicago[a]	Brussels	6 hr 50 min
Detroit[a]	Brussels	5 hr 0 min
Houston[b]	London	3 hr 25 min
Minneapolis[b]	London	4 hr 50 min
New Orleans[b]	London	4 hr 14 min

Source: *Official Airline Guide*.
a. Chicago and Detroit previously had direct service to London.
b. Houston, Minneapolis, and New Orleans did not have direct service to Brussels in 1982.

gateway an area of influence extends to the point where a traveler becomes indifferent to using a new or old gateway. Thus the service benefits extend to not only the inhabitants of the new gateway cities but also for considerable distances beyond, depending on the domestic services available and distances separating competing gateways.

International Fares

International aviation has been subject to a patchwork of pricing similar in some ways to the world patchwork of different aviation development philosophies. Standard fares in areas around the world are routinely reported by the International Civil Aviation Organization (ICAO). These ICAO fares can be compared to the CAB's standard fares, as produced by the U.S. Domestic Passenger Fare Investigation (DPFI) formula for the years 1976 and 1977 and the Standard Industry Fare Level (SIFL) thereafter. The CAB's standard fare represents an average of U.S. domestic carrier operations (e.g., as contrasted with an average of "efficient" carriers only) and is probably reasonably representative of international operations as well since the technologies of domestic and international aviation are much the same.

Table 9.7 shows how world fare levels have progressed in relation to the DPFI and SIFL standard fares for the United States. The markets in the table are grouped by distance. A ratio of, for example, 2.03 in the case of local Europe for 1976 implies that fares in that area were over twice the U.S. standard domestic fare level at that time. As the percentage change calculated for 1976 to 1980 shows (in the far right column of table 9.7), a large number of the international markets experienced a drop in markups over DPFI/SIFL during those years. All of the markets (with the exception of the local Middle East) that experienced markup reductions of more than 10 percent are markets directly influenced by U.S. bilateral agreements. In contrast, markets that are either intra-Europe or between Europe and someplace other than the United States have moved least, and indeed, markups in these cases have remained more or less constant. Furthermore areas subject to the least U.S. influence, such as intra-Europe and Africa, have consistently had the highest markups.

Substantial reductions in markups have also been achieved in the longer-distance markets. This finding is consistent with the commonsense view that diversion may be more likely in longer-distance markets, but it may also have been significantly affected by new liberal bilaterals between the United States and several Pacific Rim countries that experimented

Table 9.7 Normal economy passenger fares as a ratio of DPFI and SIFL rates for similar distances, 1976–1980

	1976	1977	1978	1979	1980	Percent change 1976–1980
Route group of 100–2,000 km[a]						
Between Canada/U.S./Mexico	1.13	1.06	1.01	0.87	0.87	23
Between North and Central American/ Caribbean			1.29	1.11	1.10	
Local South America	1.19	1.16	1.24	1.08	1.18	−1
Between and within Central America and Caribbean			1.54	1.30	1.26	
Local Middle East	1.76	1.77	1.81	1.44	1.49	−15
Local African	1.77	1.79	1.88	1.70	1.82	3
Local Europe	2.03	2.03	2.31	2.17	2.10	3
Route group of 3,000–4,000 km						
Between North/Central and South America	1.52	1.51	1.50	1.26	1.25	−18
Local Asia/Pacific	1.65	1.73	1.82	1.50	1.51	−9
Between Europe and Middle East	2.23	2.21	2.43	2.05	2.09	−6
Between Europe/Middle East and Africa	2.16	2.19	2.34	2.06	2.16	0
Route group of 7,000–10,000 km						
North Atlantic	1.49	1.56	1.53	1.28	1.21	−19
North and Mid-Pacific	1.61	1.32	1.54	1.20	1.06	−34
South Pacific	1.72	1.73	1.68	1.29	1.13	−34
South Atlantic	1.64	1.78	1.85	1.65	1.67	2
Mid-Atlantic	1.81	1.66	1.81	1.66	1.73	−4
Europe/Middle East/Africa to Asia/Pacific			1.91	1.64	1.68	

a. Group defined by ICAO "Survey of International Air Transport Fares and Rates," Circular 161-AT/59, 1981, pp. 2, 3.

Table 9.8 First-class fares as ratio of U.S. SIFL, 1978–1982

From	To	1978	1979	1980	1981	1982
New York	Brussels	2.53	2.37	2.22	2.18	2.63
	London	2.56	2.50	2.59	3.00	3.63
	Paris	2.55	2.56	2.60	2.86	2.80
	Rome	2.56	2.51	2.48	2.98	3.06
Chicago	Brussels				2.22	2.50
	London	2.66	2.53	2.60	2.94	3.64
	Paris	2.63	2.58	2.61	2.85	2.79
	Rome	2.63	2.51		3.02	
Los Angeles	Brussels			1.32		
	London	2.51	2.24	2.28	2.50	3.14
	Paris	2.49	2.28	2.29	2.47	2.43
	Rome	2.50	2.26	2.22	2.57	2.77
Miami	Brussels				1.16	
	London	2.12	2.15	2.26	2.68	2.80
	Paris		2.22	2.30	2.60	2.39
	Rome					

Sources: OAG and CAB.
Note: Absence of figures indicates no service as of March 1 of year.

with innovative pricing schemes in long-haul South Pacific and Far East markets.

Markups apparently also were reduced in many instances during 1979 only to rise again in 1980. This reversal may be due to a lag in adjusting fares to the very considerable fuel cost rises that occurred in mid to late 1979.

Examination of international first-class fares in relation to SIFL (as shown in table 9.8 for four major U.S. gateways to four European cities) displays a somewhat different picture to that of the standard fares. Two of the European cities, Brussels and London, operated under liberal bilaterals in the late 1970s, while the second two, Paris and Rome, operated under restrictive policies. Not surprisingly, under IATA pricing there was considerable uniformity of fares to the different European gateways in 1978. But liberal bilaterals evidently did not necessarily bring down first-class fare levels. Indeed, in the case of London, freedom for carriers to set first-class fares apparently resulted in higher markups. First-class service, however, did improve on many routes after deregulation as first class increasingly incorporated sleeper seats and other refinements. Furthermore, a new business class often emerged equal in quality to earlier first-class service and typically priced only a bit above standard economy fares.

The same effect, an increase in the fare range as a consequence of

Table 9.9 Economy fares in several international markets, 1978 and 1982

		1978		1982	
From	To	Economy fare (U.S. $)	Economy as ratio of SIFL	Economy fare range (U.S. $)	Economy/SIFL range
New York	Brussels	325	1.20	538–258	1.10–0.53
	London	313	1.22	526–261	1.13–0.56
	Paris	325	1.21	612–561	1.25–1.14
	Rome	414	1.33	581	1.03
Chicago	Brussels	402	1.33	642	1.18
	London	390	1.35	710–691	1.35–1.32
	Paris	402	1.33	735–648	1.34–1.18
	Rome	483	1.40		
Los Angeles	Brussels	498	1.24		
	London	486	1.25	1109–306	1.58–0.49
	Paris	498	1.24	899–775	1.23–1.06
	Rome	589	1.32	771	0.95
Miami	Brussels	377	1.14		
	London	365	1.14	555–177	0.96–0.31
	Paris	377	1.22	750–604	1.25–1.01
	Rome	464	1.25		

Sources: OAG and CAB.
Note: All fares as of March 1. All missing entries indicate no direct route on date.

liberalization, is evident in an examination of these same markets' economy or lowest fare levels in table 9.9. The 1978 fares and markups show little or no variation as these were set by agreement. But by 1982 the range of standard markups and fares had become substantial, including some fares well below the 1978 economy fare. Several fares unquestionably fell considerably in real terms, particularly in U.S.-based markets, and some even fell in nominal terms.

The Impact on the U.S. Airlines

One obvious way for airlines to adjust to generally lower fares or markups is to increase load factors. The average load factor increase for U.S. international carriers following the implementation of liberal bilaterals in 1978 was about 6 percentage points. In particularly competitive areas the increase was even more pronounced, as in the North Atlantic where load factors increased steadily from a 1976 level of 57.6 percent to 67.7 percent in 1981.

Under policies adopted by the CAB in the late 1970s, airlines willing to offer innovative services and rates generally have been selected to represent the United States on new international routes. These airlines have often been low-cost, former charter operators or the more efficient of the domestic scheduled carriers. Financial data for specific markets is difficult to obtain. However, the CAB does publish some international financial statistics on a regional basis.[26] Table 9.10 shows the ratio of out-of-pocket costs in relation to total transport revenues for several U.S. carriers' international operations in the Atlantic, Latin American, and Pacific regions. Obviously few would want to continue the Braniff experience reported in the table. In sharp contrast, Northwest in the Atlantic and Continental in the Pacific display an encouraging trend. The major established U.S. international carriers, Pan Am and TWA, apparently improved their operating ratios in the Atlantic in the long run, but not immediately after the advent of the procompetitive strategies. This improvement is all the more remarkable given the large fuel price rises of 1979 and the accompanying downturn in the economy of the developed world.

Conclusion

Somewhat surprisingly, U.S. carriers have held their market share against foreign competition in U.S.-based markets despite a declining proportion of U.S. passengers carried on these routes. This relative decline of U.S. citizen participation in international travel implies that U.S. carriers will find it increasingly difficult to maintain their traditional market shares, regardless of the international aviation policy adopted by the United States.

Since liberalization of U.S. international aviation policies in the late 1970s accompanying domestic deregulation, international fares in U.S.-based markets have been reduced in real terms. In some cases fares have even declined in nominal terms. Furthermore service, measured in terms of variety and convenience (e.g., number of flights and gateways), has improved. On the other hand, load factors have increased so that last minute scheduling and crowding may be worse than before. Some U.S. gateways have also experienced a reduction in traffic during the period of the "new open skies" policy, but the effects have been slight, mainly because of the overall boost in total traffic volumes over the liberalization period.

The financial performance of the major established U.S. international carriers seems to have improved marginally as a result of the liberalization policies. Indeed, neither TWA nor Pan Am actually experienced a decline in traffic after new international route awards were made to other U.S. carriers. International airlines have also achieved improvements in load

Table 9.10 U.S. carrier international operating: ratios out-of-pocket costs as a percent of total revenues, 1976–1983

	1976	1977	1978	1979	1980	1981	1982	1983
Atlantic region								
Air Florida					68.2	75.5	66.6	103.2[a]
American							100.9	76.5
Braniff			79.2	109.5	118.4	112.6	88.3	—
Capitol								97.6
Delta			81.3	79.3	87.0	86.3	77.1	73.2
Flying Tiger/Metro							96.3	97.6
National			74.6	93.2				
Northwest				135.0	117.9	102.0	92.4	88.5
Pan Am	83.9	79.9	80.2	81.8	89.6	94.2	87.9	76.3
People Express								87.3
TWA	77.1	77.4	77.5	82.8	83.7	80.6	75.5	70.2
Western					297.8	158.9		
World							104.0	71.4
Latin America								
Air Florida					45.3	43.9	41.4	76.7[a]
American			83.4	84.9	88.7	89.4	86.4	87.7
Braniff			74.2	85.0	91.7	96.9	85.9	—
Capitol								86.5
Continental				229.1	180.0	137.7	99.2	89.7
Delta			90.8	111.7	98.8	88.1	90.2	75.2
Eastern			82.4	89.7	93.5	98.5	89.1	95.1
National				176.2				
Pan Am	87.0	77.7	73.0	77.4	81.3	81.1	81.5	87.1
Western					99.9	92.0	89.7	94.1
Pacific region								
Braniff				160.6	138.6			
Continental			99.5	120.9	109.7	100.4	94.4	73.6
Northwest			80.4	87.5	97.7	91.1	88.1	86.5
Pan Am	83.7	76.8	71.3	80.1	92.4	96.6	96.2	81.8
United								122.5

Source: *CAB Air Carrier Financial Statistics.*
Note: Out-of-pocket operating costs are defined to include flying operations, maintenance, passenger service, aircraft and traffic servicing, promotion and sales.
a. Air Florida ceased operating during 1983.

factors, some pruning and rationalization of routes, and at least a slight improvement in aircraft utilization since liberalization. And with the opening of new gateways both airlines and travelers alike are faced with less interlining to move passengers and baggage from origin to destination.

North American experience with airline deregulation has not been lost on European travelers. Proponents of airline deregulation in Europe have long held that the Treaty of Rome, the foundation agreement of the European Community, provided for the establishment of a common transport policy. This, they argued, meant that the airline industry should be governed by the antitrust rules that governed other European industries. These arguments were strengthened in some quarters by the many studies of North American deregulation that had been undertaken by European governing bodies, industry associations, and others, despite strong disagreement with the idea of deregulation by some of these. On April 30, 1986, the French government's practice of regulating French air fares was ruled to be in violation of the Treaty of Rome by the European Court of Justice. This landmark decision did not, however, provide clear guidelines for antitrust control of the European airline industry, though officials of the European Economic Commission felt that the ruling would accelerate the process for applying antitrust rules to European aviation. Some in Britain, and the Netherlands in particular, had long been pushing for the establishment of new routes and lower air fares, and this position was supported by officials of the European Commission and the European Consumers Union. The direction of change is clear, though the rate of change and final outcome are hard to predict.

The most striking consequence of U.S. efforts to extend the competitiveness unleashed by domestic deregulation into international aviation, however, is that international markets with a "U.S. connection" experienced substantial reductions in fare markups in the late 1970s and early 1980s while such experiences were relatively rare elsewhere. This happened, moreover, despite those U.S.-connected markets always experiencing relatively low markups by international standards. In short, U.S. international travelers have always received *relatively* good value from the airlines, and the "new open skies" policy associated with domestic deregulation has apparently provided even better values.

II

THE ECONOMICS OF COMPETITION IN INTERCITY PASSENGER TRAVEL

10

The Other Modes: Rail, Bus, and Auto

with José A. Gómez-Ibáñez and Marni Clippinger

Airline deregulation clearly has put increasing pressure on the other modes to adhere to competitive principles—to lower costs, to bring charges (tariffs, user fees, or rents) into better alignment with costs, and so forth. Specifically, since airline deregulation the other modes are subject to fewer regulatory restrictions, receive less in public subsidies, and are involved in fewer cross-subsidy schemes where profits on one kind of service make up for losses on another. Thus intercity buses have been largely deregulated, much like the airlines. Rail passenger service, after being recapitalized and reorganized under government aegis in the 1970s, has been subjected to increasing congressional pressure to adhere to "commercial principles." Autos using the public highways are less and less protected from the vagaries and dynamics of the energy market and increasingly asked to pay the "full cost" (whatever that might be) of their highway use, including allowances for such externalities as congestion, noise, and air pollution.

This trend toward an increasingly competitive intercity passenger travel market is not due, of course, to airline deregulation alone. Rather, it is largely attributable to the same basic political forces that created airline deregulation in the first place. Nevertheless, airline deregulation did heighten and hasten these tendencies in the other modes.

This chapter presents a brief summary of the characteristics and histories of the nonairline intercity modes—passenger rail, intercity bus, and auto—followed by a description of the roles played by each in the market for intercity travel. Particular emphasis is placed on how these roles have changed since airline deregulation and its attendant events. In a broad sense this chapter is concerned with more than the impact of airline deregulation on these other modes; it addresses the changes encompassed by a general movement in public policy toward fewer regulatory restrictions, reduced public subsidies, and minimum cost operating practices.

Intercity Rail Passenger Service

Early Origins

In the second half of the twentieth century, rail became the smallest of the intercity passenger modes, accounting for 1 percent or less of all intercity passenger miles of travel. As recently as the turn of the century, however, rail accounted for almost all intercity travel, and railroad regulation served as a model for later government restrictions on intercity bus and air carriers.

Before railroads, long-distance passenger travel was extremely slow and costly, particularly away from coastal areas, rivers, or canals where boats or ships could be used.[1] The earliest railroads were developed by entrepreneurs in Baltimore, Charleston, and Philadelphia who were worried that their cities' ports were losing inland trade to New York and other cities served by canals. Unable to build canals of their own because of mountainous terrain, they experimented with primitive horse and steam drawn railway lines to connect their cities with navigable inland rivers.

By 1850 railroad technology had improved to the point where its superiority over canals was widely recognized. These technological improvements brought continual reductions in railroad construction costs and operating costs as well as increases in operating speeds. Travel by stagecoach or packet boat typically averaged less than 5 miles per hour, including stops for meals.[2] As early as the late 1850s, by contrast, a rail passenger could purchase a through ticket from eastern cities to the midwest and complete the journey at an average speed of around 25 miles per hour, including time for meals and changing trains.[3] Speeds increased even more as railroads began to use faster equipment, operate through trains, and add dining cars and sleepers. By the close of the nineteenth century most railroads offered crack "limited" stop trains between major cities, often equipped with all Pullman luxury cars. By 1902 the two most famous limiteds, New York Central's Twentieth Century Limited and Pennsylvania Railroad's Broadway Limited, both offered an unprecedented 20-hour service between New York and Chicago, for an overall average speed (including several intermediate stops) of around 45 miles per hour.[4]

Not only did average speeds increase, but fares declined as well. Fares varied widely in the turnpike and canal eras, but 5 cents per passenger mile was typical on the faster packet boats.[5] Early railroad fares averaged around 3 cents per passenger mile, but by the turn of the century declined to an average of around 2 to 2.5 cents per mile for standard day coach service, with a 1 cent surcharge for Pullman or other luxury accommodations.[6]

By the early 1900s railroads had become the dominant mode for all but the very shortest local trips, and improved performance and lower costs stimulated a tremendous increase in the volume of intercity passenger travel. Not only did commercial and business travel in the interior of the nation increase, but the railroads developed vacation travel. Resorts ranging from Bar Harbor to the Grand Canyon and Yellowstone National Parks all flourished under railroad service.

Increasing Government Regulation: 1887–1920

Local, state, and federal governments were not heavily involved in the development of the early railroads, in part because they had owned or sponsored many canals and turnpikes that had been bankrupted by rail competition and were wary of repeating the experience. Even though state and local governments often bought stock in railroad companies, few were outright government owned. Between 1850 and 1870 the federal government did, though, offer alternate sections of land along the right-of-way as an incentive for some western railroads to be built.

By the 1870s the nation's honeymoon with the railroads began to sour. Ignited by over capacity, rate wars broke out among carriers competing for freight traffic in the Chicago–Atlantic, Chicago–Pacific, and southern routes. These rate wars ultimately resulted in monopolistic rate agreements between carriers, which were soon augmented by traffic and revenue pools, as well as price discrimination against less competitive routes.

It was not until the late 1880s, however, that the federal government took an active stand on railroad regulation. In 1887, a year after a Supreme Court decision held that state control over interstate commerce or traffic was unconstitutional, Congress passed the Act to Regulate Commerce, more frequently known as the Interstate Commerce Act. The Interstate Commerce Commission (ICC) was created to oversee regulation of common carriers involved in interstate or foreign commerce. The act required that rates be set at reasonable and just levels, and prohibited discriminatory pricing practices and the pooling of money and traffic between carriers.

Ten years after its founding the ICC's hands were tied by a Supreme Court ruling that the commission had no power to enforce a rate, although it was authorized to request that a rate be lowered. In response, Congress passed the Hepburn Act in 1906 and gave the ICC legal power to set rate ceilings and to issue regulations aimed at further eliminating discriminatory pricing and various other ostensibly antisocial practices of the railroad companies. The commission's authority over rates was subsequently strengthened by passage of other laws, including the Mann-Elkins Act in 1910.

Meanwhile, in 1906 and 1907 to be precise, a strong wave of antirailroad feeling swept the country, and more than half the state legislatures passed laws limiting railroad passenger fares for any class of intrastate service to no more than 2 or 2.5 cents per passenger mile, a substantial reduction over the ICC's customary maximum of 3 cents per mile.[7] In a few states the railroads successfully challenged these laws on the grounds that they amounted to confiscation of property, but in many states the new laws were successfully enforced.

The railroads were nationalized during World War I, and six months after the federal takeover the director-general of railroads, in tacit recognition that past fares were uncompensatory, raised basic passenger fares to 3 cents per mile.[8] Furthermore, when Congress turned back the railroads to private stockholders after the war it instructed the ICC, in the Transportation Act of 1920, that its job was not only to prevent discriminatory rates but also to ensure "a fair rate of return on a fair value of railroad property." Soon after the railroads were returned to private control, the ICC ordered a general rate increase including a 20 percent increase in passenger fares to 3.6 cents per mile.[9]

Fighting off the Competition: 1920–1945

In 1920, the same year that Congress broadened the ICC's responsibilities, intercity rail ridership reached its peak of 47 billion passenger miles. Rail travel dropped off during the recession of 1921–1922 and recovered to 38 billion passenger miles in 1923, but then fell slowly but steadily until the great depression of the 1930s, when it dropped precipitously. Many contemporaries blamed the infant bus industry for the railroads' passenger losses, but the spread of the automobile was also a key factor since the railroads' losses were far greater than the growth in bus traffic.[10]

The railroad industry responded to the loss in passenger traffic with improved service and equipment. The most notable innovation was the introduction in the 1930s of streamlined equipment, a misnomer since the advantages stemmed more from lightweight construction than reduced air resistance. The lighter cars had lower capital costs per seat, used less energy, and permitted higher-speed operations.[11] The 1930s also saw the introduction of mechanical air conditioning on many of the deluxe trains as well as more widespread provision of private rooms in sleeping cars. Streamlining and other improvements seemed to increase ridership, but it was costly to replace existing equipment, much of which was not fully depreciated; by the end of the 1930s lightweight equipment accounted for only 15 percent of all train miles, mainly on the luxury trains.[12]

Rail passenger travel did increase slowly in the 1930s, but by 1941, just before the war, it was still slightly below 1929 levels and only 62 percent of the 1920 peak. Nevertheless, the recovery of the 1930s and the boom in the wartime years led some railroad executives to hope for a resurgence of traffic after the war.

Accelerating Abandonment: 1945–1970

Rather than a resurgence, rail passenger traffic declined rapidly after 1945, as peacetime prosperity brought a surge in automobile ownership and highway construction. Since streamlining had "saved" traffic in the 1930s, the railroads again experimented with new equipment in the 1940s and 1950s. Some of the new designs, such as "super lightweight" cars and trains with a low center of gravity, were failures while others, most notably dome and bilevel cars, proved both popular and cost-effective, although not enough to stem the decline in rail passenger traffic.[13]

Passenger service became a large financial drain on the railroads, and shippers began to complain that the ICC was forcing them to subsidize passenger traffic through high freight rates. The extent of the passenger losses was controversial, however, because of uncertainty about how to allocate costs between freight and passenger service.[14] Whatever the cost estimates used, passenger earnings were far lower after World War II than they were before, as shown in table 10.1 (third and fourth rows from the bottom). By the 1950s rail passenger deficits were enough to offset 30 to 40 percent of the railroad industry's freight operating profits, and thus were a key cause of the railroads' overall financial weakness. For many of the eastern roads which were more heavily involved in passenger service, the passenger losses were an enormous strain.

Most railroads saw no recourse but to cut back passenger service during the 1950s, but state regulatory commissions often denied their abandonment petitions in response to local political pressures to retain service. Nevertheless, because of rapidly deteriorating railroad finances, Congress enacted several regulatory relief measures in the Transportation Act of 1958, including power for the ICC to overrule state requirements to retain intrastate passenger service where it would be a burden to interstate operations. Although service abandonments accelerated after 1958, the ICC still ordered the retention of highly unprofitable trains when political influences were strong enough. Toward the end of the 1960s the ICC became even more reluctant to approve abandonment as it sought to retain a minimum route network for the nationalized rail passenger system that Congress was then debating.[15]

Table 10.1 Selected railroad passenger operating results, 1923–1967

	1923 (decline begins)	1929	1933	1936	1941	1944 (war peak)	1955	1967
Passenger miles (in billions)								
Intercity	31.6	24.2	12.0	19.8	25.3	90.2	23.7	10.9
Coach	19.5	11.3	6.9	12.5	16.1	63.3	17.3	9.3
Parlor or sleeping car	12.1	12.8	5.1	7.3	9.2	26.9	6.4	1.6
Commutation	6.4	6.9	4.3	4.0	4.1	5.3	4.8	4.3
Total	38.0	31.1	16.3	23.8	29.4	95.5	28.5	15.2
Passenger service revenues (in $ millions)[a]	1,452	1,232	490		751	2,248	1,267	878
Passenger operating profit (or loss) after deducting (in $ millions)								
Solely related costs[b]	na	na	na	51	74	1,036	−85	−138
Solely related and apportioned costs[c]	266	128	−111	−233	−226	234	−637	−485
Rail share of intercity travel								
By common carriers	na	77.1	68.4	67.6	64.6	75.8	36.5	11.7
By all modes	na	17.1	9.5	10.2	9.8	34.9	4.0	1.4

Sources: Data from Interstate Commerce Commission documents as reported by the American Association of Railroads, Economics and Finance Department, *Statistics of Passenger Service*, Washington, 1968; James C. Nelson, *Railroads and Public Policy* (Washington: Brookings Institution, 1959), pp. 18, 295, 474, 475; and Lewis C. Sorrell and Harry A. Wheeler, *Passenger Transport in the United States, 1920–1950* (Chicago: Railway Business Association, 1943).

a. Includes revenues from mail, express, and other head end service as well as from passengers.

b. The solely related profit or loss is calculated by deducting only those costs that can be directly identified with passenger rail services.

c. Data before 1936 excludes the costs of tax accruals and net rents.

Amtrak and the Future

In 1970 Congress created the National Rail Passenger Corporation, a quasi-governmental but for-profit corporation better known as Amtrak, to take over the operation of the nation's rail passenger service. Amtrak supporters hoped that the corporation would only need a one-time infusion of federal aid and that by modernizing equipment, consolidating and coordinating routes, and replacing tired and discouraged railroad management, Amtrak would soon be self-supporting. The authorizing legislation provided for $40 million in grants and $100 million in loan guarantees from the federal government and $197 million in contributions from the railroads.

Railroads were not compelled to join Amtrak, but carriers who chose not to do so were required to maintain their existing levels of passenger service until 1975. The carriers who joined were required to "buy out" their losses from passenger operations by making a contribution (based on their 1969 passenger losses) in cash, equipment, or future service. Amtrak had the option of operating trains themselves or contracting with the railroads to do so.

Amtrak began operations in May 1971, and during its first decade it replaced or rebuilt the aging rolling stock that it had inherited from the private railroads. The federal government, under a separate appropriation, bought the rail passenger right-of-way in the northeast corridor (Boston to Washington) for Amtrak and authorized spending to refurbish and upgrade the track, signals, and power distribution system. Over the period from 1972 to 1981 Amtrak managed to increase rail passenger ridership by 55 percent, from 3.0 to 4.7 billion passenger miles per year, with much of the gain coming in the energy crises of 1973–74 and 1979.

These gains were not enough, however, to achieve profitability for Amtrak. Only six months after it began operations in 1971, the corporation had to return to Congress for more aid to cover heavy operating deficits. By 1981 the operating deficit paid by the federal government had grown to $777 million per year. Passenger revenues covered only 38 percent of operating costs, and the federal operating subsidy amounted to 16 cents per passenger mile or $38 per passenger trip. Congress, recognizing defeat, in 1978 changed the original "for-profit" statutory description to read "operated and managed as a for-profit corporation."[16]

Since Amtrak has never broken even, let alone made a profit, the fundamental determinant of its service levels has been the annual appropriation of federal operating and capital assistance. The executive branch, led by the U.S. Department of Transportation and the Office of Management and Budget, has repeatedly tried to reduce the federal subsidy by pressing Amtrak into dropping unprofitable routes and improving productivity. In the first years of the Reagan administration, for example, the Office of Management and Budget proposed to cut Amtrak's operating aid by 35 percent initially and eventually to phase out aid altogether. Congress, on the other hand, has typically been more generous to Amtrak, especially because the corporation has argued that any substantial cut in federal aid would mean the loss of trains in many congressional districts.

By the mid 1980s the public policy debate on rail passenger service focused on two important sets of issues. The first and most obvious was whether direct aid to railroad passenger service should be reduced or eliminated and, as a corollary, how much of the intercity rail system could be self-supporting. A particularly interesting question, especially in light of the airline deregulation experience, was how much of the rail passenger network might be self-supporting if all excess costs were "wrung" from the system. In general, the rationale for continuing federal subsidies to rail seemed weak, since it was hard to believe that a mode capturing less than 1 percent of all intercity passenger miles was contributing significantly to energy conservation, congestion reduction, or any other public policy goals.[17] The increased availability of low air fares after airline deregulation also did not help Amtrak's case.

A second emerging issue was whether more modern technology, in the form of high-speed trains, could help save the U.S. rail passenger business. Both the Japanese Shinkansen or bullet train (opened in 1964) and the French Train de Grand Vitesse or TGV (opened in 1981) operated at maximum speeds of 140 to 170 mph compared to 80 mph for conventional rail equipment.[18] Although the capital and operating costs of these trains were high, they had also attracted heavy ridership. In early 1981 a group of private entrepreneurs proposed building a bullet train between Los Angeles and San Diego with private capital, and in the next few years local governments and entrepreneurs were studying or proposing similar trains in half a dozen other intercity corridors, including Los Angeles–Las Vegas, Chicago–Milwaukee, Cleveland–Cincinnati, and Houston–Dallas.[19]

A first step in evaluating these issues—self-supporting sustainability and the potential of new rail technologies—resides of course in costs. Two types of intercity rail service would seem relevant for these cost comparisons: conventional service operated at top speeds of 80 mph or so, similar to that currently provided by Amtrak, and service with 140 mph top speeds like that offered on the high-speed rail lines of Japanese and French railways. Furthermore some indication would be desirable of what rail costs might be if rail operations were fully freed from government influences and otherwise permitted to rationalize their operations, including elimination of any excess costs. Of course a full analysis would also require an incorporation of demand as well as cost considerations and a comparison of these over all modes; this is done in the next chapter.

On the basis of cost considerations alone, however, rail is not very competitive with the other modes under 1980 operating conditions (as shown in appendix A). Basically a conventional train's full costs at moderate market densities (250,000 passengers per year or about 700 passengers per day) are always higher than those for bus or auto and below air only on very short hauls of less than 75 or 100 miles. If time is assumed to have a value of $10 per hour, then the greater speed of the airplane makes rail travel more costly even on very short trips. Rationalization of rail operations would improve rail's relative cost performance only slightly. Similarly high-speed rail becomes cost competitive with air only at very high volumes (10 million passengers per year) and would always appear more expensive than bus or auto.

In general, rail remains somewhat competitive with the other modes in the United States only because of generous government subsidies. These permit Amtrak to charge fares of less than 10 cents per passenger mile even if costs are rarely less than 15 cents per passenger mile. Abolition of these subsidies, even if accompanied by rationalization and investment in high-speed capabilities, would at most leave rail with a cost advantage in only a few selected niches in short-haul, high-density markets (as more fully explained in appendix A).

The Intercity Bus Industry

Early Growth, Regulation, and Consolidation: 1913–1945

The first reported regular intercity scheduled bus service in the United States began in 1913, transporting miners between Hibbing and Alice, Minnesota, using a seven-passenger Hupmobile.[20] As might be imagined, early bus trips were arduous excursions. Roads were generally unpaved, vehicle breakdowns were common, and arrival times were unpredictable at best. Despite these problems the industry grew by leaps and bounds. By 1926 no less than 4,040 intercity bus companies, many quite small, operated within the United States.

The rapid growth of the industry attracted the attention of state governments. Pennsylvania was the first state to regulate passenger bus operations in 1914, and the other states soon followed. By 1930 all states except Delaware had enacted some form of regulation of the intercity bus industry.

The earliest state regulations focused primarily on issues of passenger safety and highway maintenance, but beginning in the mid-1920s state regulators increasingly became concerned about the financial stability of carriers. This new emphasis was motivated in part by the financial failure of a large Indiana bus company, as well as the prevailing view among state regulators that the industry was a capital-intensive public utility similar to the rail industry. Financial capability became a high priority in evaluating carriers' applications for certification. The larger the carrier, it was reasoned, the lower the fixed costs per trip and the fare levels that could be offered. In keeping with these beliefs, mergers and consolidations between carriers were viewed favorably, even encouraged.

Bankruptcies, mergers, consolidations, and acquisitions reduced the number of carriers in the industry during the mid-1920s, starting a trend that has characterized the bus industry almost ever since. While the number of bus miles traveled increased 28 percent between 1926 and 1930, the number of companies in operation decreased 13 percent. Industry consolidation continued into the mid-1970s. Subsequently, though, some reversal was evident: between 1975 and 1980 the number of carriers rose from 950 to 1,330, though much of the increase was in the form of carriers whose primary business was charter rather than regular route service.

Increased demand for long-distance passenger service, combined with the positive attitude of state regulatory commissions toward mergers, set the stage for the emergence of national bus systems. In December 1926 a \$10 million holding company, The Motor Transit Corporation, was organized by Eric Wickman (the man who had started the very first bus company in Hibbing, Minnesota). Wickman's Motor Transit Corporation was restructured as the Greyhound Corporation on February 5, 1930.

Wickman's holding company grew rapidly, acquiring many small local and regional carriers holding intrastate rights as well as all major competing interstate transcontinental carriers. By 1930 Greyhound carriers operated major routes over most of the United States. Greyhound's success in becoming the dominant national motorbus operator was largely made possible by the regulatory policies of the states that restricted competition and encouraged mergers. In 1980 Greyhound still dominated the industry, accounting for 43 percent of industry revenue, trailed distantly by Continental Trailways which collected only 17 percent and Carolina Coach, the third largest firm, with only 2 percent.

Before 1925 carriers were protected from competition on both interstate and intrastate routes by state regulations. In 1925, however, the U.S. Supreme Court ruled that state commissions had no regulatory authority over motor carriers operating interstate routes, except in matters of safety and highway protection. This decision opened interstate markets to new entrants and encouraged carriers to devise ingenious routes to cross state lines to avoid the jurisdiction of state regulators. Certificated bus carriers suddenly were confronted with competition on what previously had been monopoly routes. These developments encouraged the Interstate Commerce Commission, the state regulatory commissions, certificated bus operators, and railroad companies to lobby Congress to enact some form of federal regulation of the interstate bus industry.

The result was passage of the Motor Carrier Act of 1935; this act established the ICC as regulator of interstate bus fares, safety, routes, entry, exit, mergers or transfers of operating rights, service adequacy, and financial fitness. Like other federal regulatory activities established during the 1930s, the ICC was mandated to promote the bus industry while protecting the public interest. As in other industries, these goals frequently came into conflict!

Unlike the state regulatory commissions, the ICC did not automatically assume that "natural monopoly" characterized the industry. Rather, the ICC acted to increase competition for incumbent carriers in some cases and to limit competition in others. In efforts to increase competition, the commission certificated new interstate bus operators and many railroad motor bus subsidiaries. A most notable consequence was the formation of the National Trailways System in 1936. National Trailways was started by three railroad-owned bus companies—Missouri Pacific Trailways, Burlington Trailways, and Santa Fe Trailways—as an association formed to provide nationwide through service in competition with Greyhound. As other bus companies joined, National Trailways evolved into the Continental Trailways System.

Increasing Competition and Regulatory Problems: 1945–1982

Like the railroads, buses enjoyed a sharp increase in patronage during World War II with traffic increasing from approximately 10 billion passenger miles in 1940 to 27 billion in 1945. Unlike the railroads, however, buses maintained traffic at near wartime levels well into the 1950s.

Although bus ridership remained relatively steady in absolute terms, the bus share of the intercity travel market (as measured by revenue passenger miles) fell steadily from nearly 10 percent at the end of the war to approximately 2.5 percent in 1960 and then more or less stabilized at that level.

Continuing improvements in the highway system during the 1950s and 1960s undoubtedly improved bus service, but during that same period improvements in auto and air service coupled with rising household incomes also worked against the industry. By the 1970s the bus was used largely for short-distance intercity trips (200 miles or less) and by retirees, students, and other persons who were too young or old to drive or who could not afford an automobile.[21] The bus filled a vital role for autoless groups, however, especially in small towns that were not served by either rail or air service. In 1980 scheduled air service was available in approximately 650 U.S. communities, and Amtrak served 550 communities; in contrast, intercity bus service was available in about 14,000 places.[22]

During this same period the profitability of regularly scheduled bus service declined, inducing several adaptations by bus management. Beginning in the 1950s, bus operators began to diversify their services to emphasize more charter operations and to carry packages on regular bus runs. For example, though regularly scheduled passenger service accounted for 92 percent of all operating revenue in 1950, by 1980 it accounted for only 68 percent, with the remaining share almost equally divided between charter and package express services.[23] By 1981 charter service accounted for half of the revenue passenger miles in intercity bus service. Bus operators also adjusted by selectively pruning scheduled services, especially to small towns. The number of vehicle miles of service and the number of passengers carried remained roughly constant in the 1970s, but the number of places receiving regularly scheduled intercity bus service declined by nearly 15 percent.[24]

These adjustments in scheduled passenger service brought operators into increasing conflict with some state regulatory authorities who, much as they had with the railroads in earlier decades, sought to retain extensive service and low intrastate fares. The ICC did not have the authority to override state regulations on intrastate service, even for interstate carriers, and thus some bus companies complained that they were being forced to cross subsidize small town intrastate service with profits from interstate or charter operations.[25] A handful of states began programs of direct subsidy to private bus operators, but most of the funds were used to support commuter rather than intercity routes.[26]

During the 1970s the bus industry also faced new competitive threats to its profitable scheduled services between large- and medium-sized cities from Amtrak and the airlines. Amtrak priced its rail fares just at or below bus fares and, particularly in the Northeast Corridor, bus operators were forced to reduce fares to avoid losing traffic to their new and heavily subsidized competitor. Furthermore, with the onset of airline deregulation in 1978, People Express and a few of the other new entrant airlines began to offer fares at or below the bus tariffs in some selected markets.[27]

All these factors combined to reduce bus profitability substantially and increased pressure for regulatory reform. Industry operating ratios (operating costs divided by revenues), which had averaged 85 to 88 percent since World War II, increased to around 95 percent in the late 1970s. Greyhound began lobbying for complete deregulation to allow the industry to adjust to changing economic conditions while the rest of the industry, fearful that Greyhound would benefit the most from complete freedom, generally supported more limited forms of regulatory relief. The ICC liberalized entry regulations in 1977 and 1978, and in 1980 Congress amended the Motor Carrier Act to require faster decisions and simplified application procedures for new operating authorities. Two states, Florida and Arizona, also completely deregulated their intrastate bus services in 1980 and 1982, respectively.

The 1982 Federal Reforms

Significant regulatory relief was not forthcoming, however, until the passage by Congress of the Bus Regulatory Reform Act of 1982. This law did not completely deregulate the bus industry, but it loosened regulatory controls significantly. Entry was liberalized by granting authority to any "fit, willing, and able" carrier unless a protestant could show that the new authority was contrary to the public interest. After a three-year transition period the ICC would be allowed to suspend or investigate only those rates that were predatory or discriminatory. The key and most controversial feature of the act, however, was the provision that the ICC could overrule stage regulatory authorities on intrastate rate and exit issues if the state rulings caused undue burdens on interstate commerce.[28]

The Bus Regulatory Reform Act raised some of the same concerns apparent in airline deregulation, most notably the threat to small community service and possible dominance by large existing companies, especially Greyhound. A detailed study of service to more than 3,900 communities in 12 states in the 1975 to 1984 period has revealed that although there were service losses following passage of the act, the rate of service loss was not dramatically different than that observed prior to passage.[29] Total service, as measured by weekly bus departures, declined at an average annual rate of 4.8 percent between 1975 and 1982. Service continued to decline with drops of 16.0 percent and 4.0 percent, respectively, in the first two years following passage of the act. The drop in the number of communities receiving bus service was somewhat sharper. Between 1975 and 1982 the number of communities receiving service declined at an average annual rate of 3.3 percent, whereas in the first two years following the act, the annual declines were 9.2 percent and 11.6 percent, respectively. In addition to these service changes many cases came before the ICC requesting rate increases of 25 to 40 percent in intrastate fares to bring them into parity with interstate fares.[30]

Some changes in small town service were probably inevitable absent direct government subsidies, since the history of the railroads suggests that the bus industry could not cross subsidize small town losses with charter or package profits indefinitely. One can argue, moreover, that rationalization will eventually strengthen and extend bus service to other small communities by reducing the drain caused by supporting extremely unprofitable service. Nevertheless, the service reductions and fare increases have stimulated discussion of federal or state direct subsidy programs modeled on either the 10-year "essential service" guarantees in the Airline Deregulation Act of 1978 or the less specific and more open-ended commitment to Amtrak.[31]

The implications of lessened regulation for competition within the bus industry are even less clear than those for small town service. The major fear has been that Greyhound, and to a lesser extent Trailways, could use size and national route networks to drive most smaller competitors out of the market. But Greyhound, in a striking parallel to the large airlines' experience, faced a critical disadvantage after deregulation in that its wages and costs were 10 to 20 percent higher than those of Trailways' affiliates and 20 to 30 percent above the average of the smallest carriers.[32] Greyhound moved to reduce labor costs directly by successfully weathering a strike in 1983 and Trailways has attempted to reduce its costs by shifting selected routes from the high-cost National Trailways System to lower-cost Trailways affiliates.[33] The small, low-cost, and independent carriers have also applied for expanded route authority, and just as with the airlines, their expanded services are likely to keep substantial competitive pressures on the old guard bus companies for some time to come. Indeed, in 1985 Greyhound began to franchise other carriers to operate as part of its intercity bus network.[34] Greyhound offered training, maintenance, insurance, and finance, while the franchisees operated using the Greyhound name, logo, color scheme, and, more important, terminals. Such an arrangement obviously provided Greyhound another mechanism with which to counter the competitive threat of the low-cost carriers and strikingly parallels the development of ever-closer working affiliations between trunks and commuters in the deregulated airline industry.

Overall, since regulatory reform the bus industry, like the airline industry before it, has sought to keep its costs as low as possible. Indeed, the techniques used to lower costs—work rule changes, franchising, withdrawal from high-cost services, and so on—are much the same in the bus industry as in airlines. Obviously bus managements believe that their future, including definition of the markets they serve, will depend on minimizing their costs for the services they render.

Actually (as shown in appendix A) bus costs in 1980 were very low under a wide array of market circumstances, even without further rationalization. Rail, as already noted, can compete only because of subsidization. Indeed, bus costs are very close to those of the ubiquitous and highly economical private auto, with the advantage depending on how many people are in the travel party and whether an auto is owned for other purposes than intercity travel. Airline transportation costs are much higher than for bus, but if the time savings from going by air are valued at $10 per hour, then air travel is cheaper for trips of more than 100 miles or so. Accordingly, although further cost economies would probably help the bus industry, they are not likely to enhance greatly the overall bus market. However, cost control and minimization could be crucial in determining which bus operators survive and which do not.

The Automobile and the Highway

Early Development: 1910–1940

In the first few decades of the twentieth century the automobile made a remarkable transition from a curiosity for the very rich to an accepted necessity of everday American life. Commerical auto production in the United States began in earnest shortly after 1900, and the number of passenger automobiles in use jumped from eight thousand to almost half a million in the first decade of the century. The next two decades were the periods of most explosive growth, however, with eight million passenger cars registered in 1920 and an astonishing 27 million registered by 1930.[35] As early as 1927 more than half (55.7 percent) of all U.S. families owned at least one automobile and 10 percent owned two or more.[36] By 1929 there was one automobile for every five persons in the United States. The explosive growth in automobile ownership of the 1920s did not reoccur, however, until the postwar prosperity of the 1950s and early 1960s, when the percentage of households owning a car jumped from 59 percent in 1950 to 84 percent in 1980 by which time there was one car for every two persons.

The growth in auto ownership was due in large part to technological improvements in the design of the vehicle and the manufacturing process. Between 1900 and the early 1920s metal alloys were developed to increase the horsepower-to-weight ratio of the engine, the electric starter motor replaced the hand crank, steel was used for stronger frames and body panels, gasoline additives were discovered to improve performance, and the closed body replaced the touring body to make the car a lockable and all-weather vehicle.[37] At the same time Henry Ford used mass production techniques and the moving assembly line to reduce the cost of producing an automobile while also increasing its quality and reliability. In the first few years of the century a modest car cost $1,000 to $1,500 and in 1908 the first Model T's were sold for $850 each. By 1916 mass production techniques had reduced the retail price of a Model T to only $360.[38]

The rapid growth in automobile registrations led to strong pressures for highway improvements which, when successful, encouraged further auto ownership and use. At the turn of the century the United States already had a system of 3 million miles of roads connecting nearly every place in the country, so the issue was not adding road route mileage as much as rebuilding the existing mileage to meet the needs of the automobile. The principle improvement during this period was to provide a durable, hard, all-weather surface. Between 1904 and 1930 the proportion of road mileage with some kind of improved surface (including gravel or dirt with drainage) grew from 7.1 to 23 percent while the paved proportion increased from 0.1 to 18.1 percent.[39] These highway improvements were extremely costly, but the financing problems were largely solved during the 1920s when most states adopted, with automobile owners' encouragement, registration fees and gasoline taxes to pay for road improvements. In 1921 these highway-user fees financed only about one quarter of all road improvements while property taxes or general revenues accounted for the rest; by 1929, however, the ratio had completely reversed, with user tax receipts covering the bulk of road improvements.[40]

The Great Depression slowed but did not stop the growth in auto ownership and use. Annual new car sales dropped by 75 percent from 1929 to 1932, and they did not recover to their 1929 levels until after World War II. Many people responded to the Depression by holding on to their old cars longer, however, and thus registrations dropped by only 10 percent in the depth of the Depression and soon recovered and continued to grow. The Depression also had little effect on the rate of highway improvement, since federal relief agencies took up the slack from hard pressed state and local governments by using road construction as a way of alleviating unemployment.[41]

The effect of this growth in automobile ownership and highway improvements was an extraordinary increase in the volume of automobile travel, partly at the expense of the railroads but mostly through an increase in the number and length of trips that American families made. According to one set of statistics, total intercity travel by all modes (but excluding commuting) grew from 42 billion passenger miles in 1916 to 198 billion in 1929, with the automobile accounting for all the growth and its share increasing from less than 20 percent to over three quarters of the market in 1929.[42] By 1940 intercity travel had increased to 330 billion passenger miles, and auto's share had reached 89 percent.[43]

Experiments in Highway Design and Finance: 1940–1956

Most of the major technical features of the automobile had been developed by the end of the 1920s. The major breakthrough of the 1930s was, by contrast, in the design of the roadway. Although paved surfaces and drainage were a major improvement over rutted dirt roads, they were not enough to take advantage of the full potential of high-speed automobile travel. Most intercity highways passed through the centers of the cities and towns along the route, mixing long distance with local traffic. There was little or no control of highway access by abutting land owners and no grade-separated intersections, so motorists had to slow or stop frequently to avoid traffic entering, leaving, or crossing the highway. A national route of trunk highways designed with limited access and full-grade separation was clearly needed.

There were some models for such an expressway system, particularly in Europe where the Italians had built an autostrada in the 1920s and the Germans had built autobahns in the 1930s. In the United States the metropolitan parkways built in New York in the 1920s and 1930s had limited access and grade separation, although they were not intercity highways nor designed for very high-speed travel.

The first U.S. models for such a system were Connecticut's Merritt Parkway, which opened in 1937, and the Pennsylvania Turnpike, which opened in 1940. Although the Pennsylvania Turnpike was the second, it was perhaps the most important because it was substantially longer and opened to trunk as well as auto traffic. Both of these highways were financed through tolls, ostensibly because of the great expense of expressway construction and the perceived inequity of using state gasoline taxes for roads that would be heavily traveled by out-of-state motorists.[44]

Further expressway construction was halted during World War II, but the Connecticut and Pennsylvania experiences demonstrated the merits of high-performance highways. Traffic on these facilities greatly exceeded projections, and the Pennsylvania bonds were retired earlier than scheduled. Time savings of 30 to 40 percent or more over parallel routes were common, accident rates dropped by 70 percent or more, and the savings in gasoline consumption and maintenance from eliminating stops and gear changes often more than offset the cost of the tolls, especially for trucks.[45]

In 1941 President Roosevelt appointed an Interregional Highway Committee to recommend postwar federal highway policy. Motivated by both the need for improved highways demonstrated during the war and the expectation of unemployment problems during demobilization, the committee in 1944 proposed construction of a 32,000 mile national express highway system.[46] Congress responded by authorizing "a national system of Interstate Highways, not exceeding 40,000 miles" in the Federal-Aid Highway Act of 1944, but it authorized such low expenditure levels for the total highway program that all the funds were absorbed in rehabilitating the primary and secondary systems with little left for the new interstate system.

Faced with inadequate federal funding, several eastern and a few midwestern states began to imitate Pennsylvania and Connecticut by constructing a network of toll roads that eventually exceeded 3,000 miles. Thus by 1956 one could drive from New York to Chicago on a continuous 840-mile express highway system passing through six states.[47] During this period California also began to construct a statewide freeway system financed by gasoline taxes rather than tolls, apparently at least in part because out-of-state travelers were of less concern in that large state.[48] The eastern toll roads and the California freeways provided a valuable laboratory in express highway design, leading to such improvements as wider medians with plantings or barriers, longer merging lanes for exits and entrances, and shorter straight sections to prevent highway hypnosis.

Constructing the Interstate System: 1956–1970

Responding to the obvious need and the example of the eastern toll roads, the federal government in 1956 finally assumed the primary responsibility for building a national express highway system, restating the commitment of the 1944 act to a system of 41,000 miles (later increased to 42,500 miles). The Interstate and Defense Highway System, as it was named in the 1956 legislation, was to be toll free, but 2,300 miles of the existing eastern toll road network were incorporated in the system (even though federal aid could not be used for improvements on the toll segments).

A key element of the 1956 act was that funding for the system was secured by earmarking increased federal highway-user taxes for highway construction. Toll financing had been advocated by those concerned with the size of the federal budget and the desire to get politics out of road building, but a national toll road system was ultimately abandoned because of doubts that toll financing could support some of the rural and lightly traveled links in the proposed system.[49] Instead, the 1956 act raised federal gasoline taxes and excise taxes on motor vehicles and parts and dedicated them to a special Highway Trust Fund that would expire upon the completion of the system. Under the Interstate program the federal government paid 90 percent of all construction instead of a previous maximum of only 50 percent, but only road segments on the federally designated route system were eligible for aid and the plans had to meet strict Interstate design standards.[50]

Construction of the Interstate System proceeded remarkably rapidly, especially during the 1960s. As early as 1970, 74 percent of the system (31,543 miles) was already open to traffic, 22 percent was under construction, and only 4 percent was not yet started. By 1980 the system was almost complete with 95 percent of the mileage open, 4 percent under construction, and 1 percent not yet started. Most of the uncompleted mileage was in urban areas, where opposition to home taking and neighborhood disruption slowed highway construction; a few unfinished segments were also in particularly scenic and unspoiled rural areas. The cost to complete the system escalated from the original $27 billion estimate in 1956 to $104 billion in 1977, due largely to inflation but also to added mileage, design changes, and other factors.[51]

Postwar highway construction, coupled with population growth and rising real incomes that made automobiles and new suburban housing more affordable, induced a dramatic surge in automobile travel. Between 1946 and 1970 intercity auto travel increased threefold from 324 billion passenger miles (approximately the level previously achieved in 1941) to one trillion passenger miles. The automobile's share of the intercity travel market rose steadily from 87 or 88 percent in the early 1950s to reach a peak of 90 percent in the early 1960s; by 1970, however, it had declined to 86 percent apparently because of airline cost reductions and speed improvements that occurred with the introduction of jet aircraft.[52]

Disenchantment and Regulation: 1970–1980

During the 1960s many social and environmental costs of increased automobile use became painfully apparent. By the end of that decade several government programs and regulations had been initiated to ameliorate these problems.[53] The 1962 Federal Highway Aid Act mandated relocation assistance and compensation for persons and businesses displaced by federally aided highway construction and required, as a precondition of federal aid, that every metropolitan area prepare a comprehensive transportation and land use plan that considered mass transit as well as highway alternatives. These provisions were substantially strengthened under the National Environmental Policy Act of 1969 which required a federally approved environmental impact statement for federally funded projects in both urban and rural areas. In 1970 federal legislation also gave states the option of redepolying the highway funds allocated for controversial Interstate highway segments to mass transit alternatives as long as the U.S. Secretary of Transportation certified that the omitted segments were not essential to the completion of the Interstate System. These laws contributed to a slowdown in highway construction in the 1970s by making it substantially easier for local citizen groups and governments to stop highways that they thought were unnecessary or disruptive.

Automobile safety also became a focus of government activity in the mid to late 1960s. Although the accident rate steadily declined per mile traveled, thanks in part to the new highways, the increase in auto traffic offset these improvements and total traffic fatalities increased from around 32,000 per year in the late 1940s to 55,000 per year in the late 1960s. The National Highway Traffic Safety Administration (NHTSA) was established in 1965 with the authority to set safety standards for new cars and to order manufacturers to recall and correct defects.

At about the same time the air pollution problems caused by automotive emissions of hydrocarbons, carbon monoxide, and nitrogen oxides became more noticeable, especially in large metropolitan areas with high concentrations of automobiles. California began setting standards for automobile pollutants in 1963 to alleviate the smog problems caused by the combination of high auto use and unfavorable topography in the Los Angeles air basin. Spurred on by the California example, Congress required that all cars meet the early California standards starting in model year 1968. The Clean Air Act of 1970, a watershed in pollution regulation, required an additional 90 percent rollback in the hydrocarbon, carbon monoxide, and nitrogen oxide emissions rates of new automobiles by the 1975 model year. Although high costs and technological uncertainties forced several extensions of the deadlines for these emissions standards and the relaxation of the nitrogen oxide target to a 75 percent rollback, the emissions standards set in the 1970 act were largely achieved by model year 1982.[54]

Energy conservation was added to the list of automotive problems after the oil price increases that followed the Arab oil embargo in 1973 and the Iranian revolution in 1979. In 1975 Congress passed a law requiring that average new car fuel efficiency be improved in stages from 18 miles per gallon in model year 1978 to 27.5 miles per gallon in 1985. The 1985 target amounted to a nearly 50 percent reduction compared to the 14.2 miles per gallon average for new cars sold in 1973 and 1974. Nevertheless, U.S. automakers were in compliance with the schedule until the 1984 model year, when weakness in gasoline prices induced a consumer shift away from small and more fuel-efficient vehicles. The standard was reduced to 26 miles per gallon in 1986 for the 1986 to 1988 period.

Auto ownership and use continued to grow despite the social and environmental regulations of the late 1960s and 1970s. Auto travel grew at an average annual rate of 2.3 percent per year in the 1970s which, though lower than the 4.5 percent average annual increase in the 1950s and 1960s, was still impressive. However, the automobile's share of the intercity market drifted down slightly from around 86 percent in 1970 to around 83 percent in 1980.

This continued growth in automobile use appears to be due to an ability to improve automobile air pollution, safety, and fuel economy without greatly affecting auto user costs. Despite the substantial increases in energy prices and the stringent pollution and safety standards applied to motor vehicles in the 1970s, the inflation-adjusted cost of owning and operating an automobile increased by only 12 percent for a standard size car and around 20 percent for a compact or subcompact.[55]

Auto costs in 1980 thus remained quite competitive with other modes (as shown in appendix A). How competitive mainly depended on whether the car was owned for other purposes anyway (e.g., commuting), on how many people were in the travel party, and whether time was of value. Basically, even if the auto were assigned the full costs of all its environmental and other consequences, it would be difficult to find a cheaper mode for a family trip of four to five people traveling 500 miles or less. On the other hand, a single business traveler, placing even a relatively nominal $10 per hour value on his time, would rarely find the auto cost competitive.

Conclusion

In the past 75 years a veritable revolution has occurred in intercity passenger travel within the United States. At the turn of the century the passenger train was effectively the only high-speed mode suitable for long-distance travel. All that quickly changed with the coming of the internal combustion engine and a national network of paved intercity highways. From a standing start of essentially no intercity passenger mileage at the turn of the century, the automobile came to account for over 80 percent of such mileage by the 1950s. The only "counter force" to this steady progression and growth in intercity automobile passenger mileage has been the development of domestic airlines, particularly after the development of jet aircraft and, more recently, lower fares stimulated by airline deregulation.

The demise of passenger railroads is of course a virtual mirror image of the automobile's progression. However, that demise was also abetted by the rise of other public modes, initially the bus and then the airplane. Indeed, the airplane by most measures has been the dominant mode of intercity public passenger transportation in the United States throughout most of the second half of the twentieth century, a position that has strengthened with the passage of time.

Deregulation would appear to have enhanced the airlines' relative market strength, but a full evaluation of that possibility depends on demand and cost considerations and their interaction with each other. Furthermore other changes in public policy, particularly deregulation of buses and growing insistence that users of every mode pay a "reasonable approximation" of their full costs, could modify the ultimate distribution of market shares among the different intercity modes. An analysis of these more comprehensive issues is undertaken in the next chapter.

11

Toward an Equilibrium in Intercity Travel Choices

by José A. Gómez-Ibáñez and Don H. Pickrell

Intercity passenger travel patterns are determined by the interaction of transportation costs and passenger demand. In this chapter, cost and demand characteristics are combined to analyze the likely effects on intercity travel of continued deregulation and other changes in government policy. Policies examined include projecting likely eventual effects of deregulation in the bus industry, extending procompetitive cost-rationalizing policies to the rail mode, and eliminating government subsidy to all modes. In addition the possible effects on intercity travel of demographic trends, such as increasing incomes and smaller household sizes, are considered. Finally, special attention is devoted to the prospects for intercity rail of offering high-speed services similar to those found in Japan and Europe and to the problems that might be created by increasing congestion and access problems at airports. Overall, the goal is to determine how deregulation and other public policy changes might affect long-standing trends in intercity travel, particularly relative market or modal shares. Simulation models are used to compare the results achieved under different public policy and demographic scenarios, embodying different assumptions about costs and market demand characteristics.

Assumptions

Costs

Three alternative estimates of the costs and related service characteristics of the modes are examined: (1) a base estimate of user-paid costs, (2) full costs, and (3) potential deregulated or rationalized costs. These cost concepts are described in detail in appendix A (where specific cost estimates for the various modes are also given).

User-paid costs represent the status quo as of 1980 and are typical of operations in 1980 for all the modes. They are the direct charges paid by the traveler and exclude any subsidies that are borne by the *general* taxpayer.[1] The user-paid cost estimates also assume that only airlines are deregulated and that other modes operate without the benefit of any increased efficiencies that might accompany regulatory reform. The airline costs used are those typical of a low-cost, new entrant air carrier characterized by relatively low overhead expenses, intensively utilized equipment, and low unit labor costs.

The *full-cost* estimates differ from user-paid costs by including the costs of any subsidies paid from general government funds. For example, estimates of the actual costs of publicly provided highway, airport, and airway systems are used instead of the fuel taxes and other fees paid by users to help finance these facilities. All capital and operating expenses are included.

The *potential deregulated cost* estimates are based on full costs but also assume that the bus and rail modes are freed from government regulation. At the risk of substantial oversimplification, the estimates of *potential deregulated costs* assume that deregulation would allow intercity bus operators to achieve the same kinds of improvements in vehicle utilization and unit labor costs that some of the deregulated airlines have achieved. Although rail passenger service is no longer heavily regulated, the estimates of potential deregulated costs also assume that policies to promote competition in other intercity modes might provoke similar improvements in productivity and costs in railroad service.

Demand Characteristics

The purpose for which a trip is made, the distance traveled, the income levels of travelers, and the size of the traveling party all affect travelers' responses to the costs and service characteristics offered by different travel modes (see appendix B for data and documentation). For example, as shown in table 11.1, on all types of routes business travelers are far more

Table 11.1 Relationship of trip purpose to travel mode shares for selected route types, 1977

			Percent of trips made			
Route type	Median trip length (miles)[a]	Trip purpose	Auto	Air	Bus	Rail
Origin and destination cities with populations exceeding one million	485	Business	26.6	66.1	1.5	4.9
		Other[b]	65.1	25.4	5.4	3.9
Routes connecting nonmetropolitan areas and cities with populations exceeding one million	335	Business	46.1	48.3	1.9	3.5
		Other[b]	73.4	19.3	4.8	2.1
Origin and destination cities with populations under one million	360	Business	83.0	14.3	1.1	0.4
		Other[b]	87.2	6.9	4.7	0.9
Origin and destination points outside metropolitan areas	345	Business	88.4	7.9	1.3	0.2
		Other[b]	94.2	3.1	1.7	0.3

Source: Tabulated from individual trip records of the 1977 National Travel Survey (sample size = 52,086).
a. Estimated from trip distances reported by travelers.
b. Social, entertainment, and recreation.

likely to use air than nonbusiness travelers, since air offers large travel time savings (over surface modes) that are important to travelers who value their time highly. Air's share of both business and nonbusiness travelers also increases the longer the route and the larger the cities that the route connects. Longer distances increase the time advantage air has over surface modes. Routes connecting larger cities also can support a greater frequency of air and other common carrier departures; with greater frequencies a traveler is more likely to find a common carrier departure that closely fits the desired travel schedule and thus makes the carrier competitive with the instantly available (but slower) automobile. The time savings achievable by air would therefore be greatest for the relatively longer and better served trips between big cities (first row in table 11.1) and least for trips originating and terminating outside metropolitan areas (last row of table 11.1).

Travelers' valuations of time savings also appear to increase roughly in proportion to their income, as suggested by the data in table 11.2. The activities that are sacrificed or disrupted by traveling apparently have higher forgone monetary values for travelers with higher incomes, thus inducing relatively more use of air, particularly for business travel.

Individuals traveling alone also much more commonly utilize common carrier service than do groups. In fact, as shown in table 11.3, the total share of travel by common carrier modes falls sharply with increasing group size, and the mix of air, rail, and bus travel seems to change as well. For both business and other trips the fraction of individuals traveling via the three common carrier modes is well over twice that among pairs of travelers, and approximately six to eight times as large as that among large

Table 11.2 Relationship of traveler's income to travel mode shares for different trip purposes, 1977

Travel purpose	Household income level of traveler	Percent of trips made			
		Auto	Air	Bus	Rail
Business	$0–15,000	85.6	11.4	2.6	0.4
	15,000–25,000	72.9	25.3	1.1	0.7
	25,000–50,000	58.5	38.0	1.1	2.4
	over 50,000	44.4	52.8	0.1	2.7
Other (social, entertainment, recreation)	$0–15,000	86.7	4.9	7.3	1.1
	15,000–25,000	91.0	6.7	1.7	0.6
	25,000–50,000	87.9	10.6	0.6	0.9
	over 50,000	81.6	16.9	0.4	1.1

Source: Tabulated from individual trip records of the 1977 National Transportation Survey (sample size = 89,074).

Table 11.3 Relationship of travel party size to travel mode shares for different trip purposes, 1977

		Percent of trips made			
Travel purpose	Travel party size	Auto	Air	Bus	Rail
Business	One	61.2	35.6	1.7	1.5
	Two	84.2	13.4	1.7	0.7
	Three or more	93.5	3.8	0.5	2.2
Other (social, entertainment, recreation)	One	75.2	17.7	5.5	1.6
	Two	90.7	7.5	1.2	0.6
	Three or more	95.1	3.6	0.4	0.9

Source: Tabulated from individual trip records of the 1977 National Travel Survey (sample size = 89,074).

travel parties. Conversely, the fraction of trips made by private automobile increases with the size of the traveling party. Within the range of the comfortable seating capacity of a single vehicle, the cost of traveling by automobile varies only slightly with travel party size so that the per-person cost falls directly with the size of the group. By contrast, the cost of common carrier travel is usually the group size multiplied by the appropriate fare, the only major exception being occasional discounts for immediate family members, such as young children or spouses, traveling together.

The impact of these various demand characteristics has been quantified in a modal share demand model, as described in appendix B. In the policy simulations reported later in this chapter, this model is used to estimate the share of trips in an intercity market garnered by air, bus, rail, and private auto in response to the different cost and service characteristics of the modes. This modal share demand model, it should be noted, does not predict the total volume of travel but rather how a fixed volume is allocated among the different modes in the market.[2] As a consequence only the effects of policy changes and demographic factors on shifting modal shares are examined with this model.[3]

Typical Markets

In the cost-demand simulations reported later in this chapter, each market is viewed as a pair of cities (or metropolitan areas) connected by an expressway and, initially, by a minimum of three daily direct, nonstop departures on each of the bus, rail, and air modes. The distances between the cities range from 200 to 1,000 miles, and the volumes of intercity travel range from 500,000 to 50 million person trips per year in each direction.[4]

The assumption that each city-pair is served by at least three direct, nonstop departures may bias the results slightly against rail and, to a much lesser extent, buses. Where several major cities are located close together, as in the northeastern United States, a single train route may serve several major city-pairs along a corridor simultaneously. Such proximity is particularly advantageous for rail service because the average cost of carrying a railroad passenger falls rapidly with increasing passenger volume while the average rail line-haul speed is not greatly affected by making a few intermediate stops. Buses sometimes serve intermediate points too, but the practice is usually confined to routes serving very small towns since the relatively small passenger-carrying capacity of a bus means that economies of traffic density are exhausted at low passenger volumes. Intermediate stops are less attractive for airlines, particularly where they involve flights of under 200 miles, because there are limited economies from higher volumes and intermediate stops greatly reduce airline speeds and increase operating costs.

To offset this potential bias against rail, some of the simulations assume that the actual volume of rail traffic on the route is four times higher than the volume that could be supported by the particular city-pair being considered. A few simulations also raise air fares to reflect high accessibility costs and congestion at some major airports; in effect these simulations assume that the average distance to the rail or bus terminal is shorter than to the airport.

The Average Traveler

As noted, the share of the market carried by each mode is a function of the income, trip purpose, travel group size, and other characteristics of the travelers as well as the costs and quality of the services offered. Table 11.4 compares the average characteristics of the travelers assumed in the simulations with the actual characteristics of the average intercity traveler in 1977. Most simulations assume the characteristics of the hypothetical average traveler in the year 1980 (column 2 of table 11.4), with the same ratio of business to nonbusiness trips and the same average party size as in 1977 but a slightly higher average household income (to reflect increases experienced in the intervening years).

A few simulations assume possible characteristics of travelers in the mid-1990s (far right column of table 11.4), including higher average real incomes and a smaller average size of the travel party. In these extrapolations real household incomes are assumed to increase by 2.0 percent per year, about the median of available projections.[5] The size of the average travel party is assumed to decline proportionately with the projected decline in size of households.[6]

Table 11.4 Hypothetical 1980 and 1995 average traveler's characteristics compared to actual 1977 characteristics

	Actual average traveler	Hypothetical average traveler[a]	
	1977[b]	1980[c]	1995
Percent of travel for business purposes	21.4	21.4	21.4
Percent of travel for nonbusiness purposes	78.6	78.6	78.6
Mean income	$20,261	$21,320	$29,665
Mean party size (persons)	2.35	2.37	1.99

a. Assumed by authors. The simulations incorporated 18 different hypothetical travelers for three different income levels ($10,000, $20,000, and $40,000), three different party sizes (1, 2, and 4 persons), and two trip purposes (business and nonbusiness). The reported results are the weighted averages.
b. Actual 1977 traveler's characteristics are from tabulations by Alan Grayson and the authors from unpublished data for the full sample of the National Travel Survey.
c. Characteristics of the hypothetical 1980 travelers are identical to those of the actual 1977 travelers with one major and one minor exception. The major exception is that average traveler income was deliberately increased in proportion to the growth in family incomes between 1977 and 1980. The minor exception is that average party size is assumed to be 1 percent larger (2.37 vs. 2.35 persons). This exception is simply due to the difficulty of deriving weights for the 18 hypothetical travelers that will reproduce 1977 conditions exactly.

Test against 1977 Travel Patterns

To test the plausibility of these assumptions, simulated 1980 modal shares were compared with the actual 1977 modal shares in several travel markets, as shown in table 11.5. The simulated 1980 shares assume user-paid costs and average traveler characteristics for that year, whereas the actual 1977 shares are computed from sample data collected in the 1977 National Travel Survey. Since the National Travel Survey does not estimate the total travel volumes for individual city-pairs, the effects of travel volumes had to be approximated by varying the populations of the cities involved. The simulated shares between a city-pair with 500,000 trips per year are compared with actual shares for trips between cities with populations of 500,000 to 1 million persons, for example, whereas simulated shares between a city-pair with 1 million trips per year are compared with actual shares for trips between cities with populations of 1 to 3 million persons.[7] Since no city-pairs are exactly 200, 500, or 1,000 miles apart, the simulated shares are compared to two actual shares: one for city-pairs slightly closer than the simulated distance and a second for city-pairs slightly more distant.

The results of the simulation are reasonably similar to the actual data. The simulated shares of the largest modes—automobile and air—are usually well within the appropriate ranges of actual shares. The simulated

Table 11.5 Comparison of simulated 1980 with actual 1977 modal shares

City-pair distance and annual passenger volume	Source[a]	Percent carried			
		Auto	Bus	Rail	Air
200 miles[b]					
500,000 passengers	1980 simulated	78.6	1.6	5.2	14.6
	1977 actual	86.0–89.2	4.8–5.1	0–0.8	4.2–7.6
1 million passengers	1980 simulated	76.0	2.6	0.4	19.5
	1977 actual	72.6–76.1	2.4–4.3	0–10.1	14.3–19.3
5 million passengers	1980 simulated	60.7	6.8	4.5	28.0
	1977 actual	47.3–73.8	8.0–13.1	5.5–6.1	7.5–38.0
500 miles[b]					
500,000 passengers	1980 simulated	68.6	0.9	10.4	20.1
	1977 actual	56.6	7.5–8.5	0–2.8	28.3–30.2
1 million passengers	1980 simulated	56.7	0.8	5.9	36.8
	1977 actual	30.0–59.0	0–2.8	0–0.8	35.9–66.0
5 million passengers	1980 simulated	38.5	2.1	3.3	56.2
	1977 actual	9.3–56.5	0.6–6.1	0.6–1.4	36.1–88.2
1,000 miles[b]					
500,000 passengers	1980 simulated	49.7	0.3	12.5	37.5
	1977 actual	32.8–56.6	1.6–8.5	2.8–4.9	30.2–60.7
1 million passengers	1980 simulated	32.9	0.1	2.7	64.3
	1977 actual	21.0–30.0	1.1–2.8	0.8–1.5	56.0–76.5
5 million passengers	1980 simulated	16.4	0.1	2.7	80.8
	1977 actual	5.0–9.3	0.6–0.8	0.4–0.6	88.2–93.7

a. Actual 1977 statistics are tabulations for specific trip length and route density categories prepared by Alan Grayson and the authors using the full sample (89,074 trip records) of the 1977 National Travel Survey. The "1980 simulated" numbers are those produced by the simulations, assuming the 1980 hypothetical average traveler from table 11.4.
b. Simulated 200-mile trips are compared to actual trips of 150 to 200 and 200 to 300 miles, while simulated 500-mile trips are compared to actual trips of 400 to 500 and 500 to 1,000 miles; and simulated 1,000-mile trips are compared to actual trips for 500 to 1,000 and over 1,000 miles (domestic trips only).

air share in short-distance, low-density markets is slightly high, perhaps because commuter carriers had had only limited impact on most markets by the time of the 1977–1978 travel survey.[8] Rail's share is almost always overpredicted, probably because the simulations assume that a minimum of three daily trains are available when in reality many city-pairs have far less rail service. Bus shares are often slightly underpredicted, probably also because the simulations exaggerate the quality of rail service (the bus' principal competitor).

The Effects of Rationalized Public Policies

Table 11.6 compares the simulated effects of continuing present public policies with the possible impacts of eliminating government subsidies and extending deregulation or similar procompetitive policies to the bus and rail modes. In all cases the simulations assume the 1980 hypothesized traveler characteristics.

Eliminating Subsidies

The major impact of reducing subsidies is to all but eliminate the share of intercity passenger trips carried by rail. In 1980 government subsidies represented over 60 percent of full costs for rail but a far smaller percentage for every other mode. The principal recipients of rail's share are auto and bus in short-haul travel markets and auto and air in long-haul markets.[9]

The elimination of government subsidies might be a major boon for the bus industry, as the bus industry has long maintained. In short-haul markets, for example, the simulated bus shares increase by as much as 50 percent, although the actual effects would be somewhat lower since, as noted earlier, the base simulations exaggerate rail's share of the market.

Extending Deregulation

If, in addition to eliminating subsidies, buses are fully deregulated and similar procompetitive policies are extended to rail service (e.g., resulting in about a 20 percent overall reduction of bus and rail costs), bus shares could increase by a further 20 to 40 percent in most short-haul markets while rail shares might regain a small fraction of traffic otherwise lost because of elimination of subsidies. Both bus and rail gain largely at the expense of the automobile rather than the airplane, although the percentage decline in auto use is still quite small since bus and rail capture a very small share of the total intercity passenger market.

Table 11.6 The effects of alternative public policies on modal shares, assuming 1980 traveler's characteristics

City-pair distances and annual passenger volume		Percent carried			
		Auto	Bus	Rail	Air
200 miles					
500,000 passengers	Continue present	78.6	1.6	5.2	14.6
	Eliminate subsidy	82.7	1.8	0.1	15.4
	Extend deregulation	82.2	2.3	0.1	15.4
1 million passengers	Continue present	74.2	2.0	4.3	19.5
	Eliminate subsidy	76.6	2.1	0.3	21.0
	Extend deregulation	76.0	2.6	0.4	20.9
5 million passengers	Continue present	60.7	6.8	4.5	28.0
	Eliminate subsidy	62.6	7.1	0.9	29.4
	Extend deregulation	61.0	8.6	1.3	29.2
10 million passengers	Continue present	51.2	9.3	13.9	25.5
	Eliminate subsidy	56.9	10.2	0	32.9
	Extend deregulation	55.1	12.3	0	32.5
500 miles					
500,000 passengers	Continue present	68.6	0.9	10.4	20.1
	Eliminate subsidy	76.5	1.2	0	22.3
	Extend deregulation	75.9	1.8	0	22.3
1 million passengers	Continue present	56.7	0.8	5.9	36.6
	Eliminate subsidy	58.4	0.9	0.0	40.7
	Extend deregulation	57.9	1.4	0.1	40.6
5 million passengers	Continue present	38.5	2.1	3.3	56.2
	Eliminate subsidy	37.8	2.1	0.3	59.8
	Extend deregulation	36.7	3.1	1.0	59.1
1,000 miles					
500,000 passengers	Continue present	49.7	0.3	12.5	37.5
	Eliminate subsidy	49.1	0.7	0	40.2
	Extend deregulation	58.6	1.3	0	40.1
1 million passengers	Continue present	32.9	0.1	2.7	64.3
	Eliminate subsidy	31.6	0.1	2.7	64.3
	Extend deregulation	31.5	0.2	0	68.3
5 million passengers	Continue present	16.4	0.1	0.7	82.7
	Eliminate subsidy	14.5	0.1	0	85.4
	Extend deregulation	14.5	0.2	0	85.4

The Effects of Demographic Changes

Demographic changes have substantial potential for altering future modal shares, and particularly for inducing a major shift from auto to air travel. Table 11.7 illustrates the effects of assuming that the average traveler has the 1995 profile shown in the far right column of table 11.4; as compared with 1980 intercity travelers, the 1995 travelers are assumed to have 34 percent higher average household incomes and a 16 percent smaller average travel party size. The simulations do assume, however, a continuation of 1980 government subsidies and regulation.

Higher traveler incomes increase air's share by a surprising 20 to 40 percent in most markets, largely because air offers a faster albeit more costly service that appeals to high-income groups. Most of air's gains come at the expense of the private automobile and, to a far lesser extent, bus. Rail also gains slightly in a few short-haul markets where, under the assumptions of the simulations, rail offers relatively high-quality service, but it loses market share in most longer-haul markets.

Smaller party size also decreases the automobile's share of the market. With smaller party sizes, however, air is not the only winning mode: bus and rail market shares also increase in every market.

In combination, changes in income and size of travel party produce a bigger shift from auto to air than either change singly. Auto still remains the dominant mode for short-distance markets, particularly if the volume of travel is also modest. Nevertheless, air's market share increases by around 50 percent in many markets, a gain large enough to replace the auto as the largest mode in several intermediate distance and medium volume markets. Rail and bus shares also increase slightly in a few short-distance markets. But at intermediate and long distances the effects of income growth swamp those of declining party size, and the shares of both rail and bus decline.

A shortcoming of these simulations is that they may exaggerate the shift from auto to air by not incorporating the full effects of higher incomes on auto ownership and use. For households with incomes below around $40,000 per year (in 1980 dollars), the number of automobiles owned increases substantially as income rises; above $40,000 per year, additional income produces a much smaller increase in auto ownership.[10] In the demand model, income affects only the value placed on travel time savings; separate variables for income's effect on auto ownership are not included.[11]

Even allowing for this possible bias the simulations strongly suggest that future demographic trends will have a greater influence on modal shares than public policy. Although future trends in household and travel party size are uncertain, any reduction in size will help air at the expense of auto. Continued growth in household incomes, which seems likely, may cause an even more pronounced shift in the same direction.

The Prospects for Rail Passenger Service

International Comparisons of Rail Competitiveness

Foreign experience with rail passenger services contrasts sharply with that in the United States. Foreign passenger trains, and particularly high-speed trains, enjoy relatively high ridership levels.[12] For example, the Japanese National Railway's (JNR) share of total passenger traffic (including both conventional and high-speed services) was 51 percent in 1960 and 25 percent in 1980 (the decline being largely due to increasing auto ownership and use, particularly in rural areas).[13] JNR's share of the total market is obviously substantially higher than the few percentage points captured by Amtrak in the United States; and in corridors served by the high-speed Shinkansen or bullet train JNR is thought to capture a significantly larger share than the national average.[14] Indeed, the bullet train alone carries about 125 million riders per year, down from a peak of 157 million riders in the early 1970s but still several times greater than the volume carried by Amtrak on all its routes.[15]

Several factors may account for the high ridership on Japanese and French high-speed trains. In the first place, not only are the terminal cities usually extremely large, but the trains often serve several major intermediate cities as well to increase passenger volumes further and reduce the average cost per passenger. Such corridor service appears to play a major role in the success of the Japanese bullet train, for example. The initial line of the bullet train connects Tokyo and Osaka (a distance of 322 miles) but also serves such large intermediate cities as Yokohama, Nagoya, and Kyoto. Since train deceleration, passenger loading, and acceleration at an intermediate stop delay the bullet train by only about four minutes, the quality of service is not greatly degraded by making a few such stops.

Rail patronage in Japan and Europe may also be enhanced because their rail stations are more accessible. Many foreign cities have higher population densities than U.S. cities, so that more people live or work within a given radius of the central station.[16] Foreign cities sometimes also have relatively attractive mass transit systems, the use of which reduces problems of parking and traffic congestion for intercity travelers wanting access to a centrally located rail station.

Table 11.7 The effects of changing demographics on modal shares, assuming 1980 public policies

City-pair distance and annual passenger volume	Income and travel party size	Percent carried			
		Auto	Bus	Rail	Air
200 miles					
500,000 passengers	1980 base case	78.6	1.6	5.2	14.6
	1995 income	71.4	1.4	5.8	21.4
	1995 party size	74.1	2.1	5.8	18.0
	1995 income and size	67.7	1.7	6.4	24.3
1 million passengers	1980 base case	74.2	2.0	4.3	19.5
	1995 income	67.1	1.5	4.6	26.8
	1995 party size	70.7	2.3	4.9	22.0
	1995 income and size	62.1	1.8	5.0	31.1
5 million passengers	1980 base case	60.7	6.8	4.5	28.0
	1995 income	53.5	4.7	4.5	37.2
	1995 party size	55.7	7.8	4.8	31.7
	1995 income and size	47.0	5.3	4.6	43.0
10 million passengers	1980 base case	51.2	9.3	13.9	25.5
	1995 income	43.6	6.4	16.2	33.7
	1995 party size	46.9	10.3	14.1	28.7
	1995 income and size	37.9	7.8	16.2	38.1
500 miles					
500,000 passengers	1980 base case	68.6	0.9	10.4	20.1
	1995 income	58.5	0.5	12.4	28.4
	1995 party size	64.0	1.2	12.4	22.3
	1995 income and size	52.0	0.7	13.9	33.3
1 million passengers	1980 base case	56.7	0.8	5.9	36.6
	1995 income	44.1	0.4	5.2	50.4
	1995 party size	49.3	1.1	6.6	43.1
	1995 income and size	34.3	0.5	5.0	60.3
5 million passengers	1980 base case	38.5	2.1	3.3	56.1
	1995 income	22.2	0.7	1.9	75.3
	1995 party size	31.4	2.6	3.7	62.3
	1995 income and size	16.5	0.8	1.9	80.8
1,000 miles					
500,000 passengers	1980 base case	49.7	0.3	12.5	37.5
	1995 income	38.7	0.1	10.6	50.6
	1995 party size	40.5	0.5	14.6	44.4
	1995 income and size	28.1	0.1	10.4	61.4

Table 11.7 (continued)

City-pair distance and annual passenger volume	Income and travel party size	Percent carried			
		Auto	Bus	Rail	Air
1 million passengers	1980 base case	32.9	0.1	2.7	64.3
	1995 income	18.9	0.0	1.0	80.1
	1995 party size	23.8	0.1	3.1	73.0
	1995 income and size	12.2	0.0	1.0	86.7
5 million passengers	1980 base case	16.4	0.1	0.8	82.7
	1995 income	5.5	0.0	0.2	94.2
	1995 party size	10.6	0.1	0.8	88.4
	1995 income and size	3.5	0.0	0.2	96.2

Rail ridership may also have been historically higher in Japan and Europe because real per capita incomes are lower and travel party sizes smaller. Although the gap between Japanese and U.S. income levels has narrowed rapidly in the past two decades, mean per capita incomes were still roughly 20 percent lower in Japan in the early 1980s.[17] Also, compared to the United States, the average household is smaller in Europe and larger in Japan.[18]

Perhaps the key factor contributing to rail's popularity in Europe and Japan, however, is the relatively high cost and inconvenience of competing modes, particularly the airplane and the automobile. As noted in chapter 9, European short-haul air fares are about twice as high as comparable U.S. air fares, in part because the Europeans protect their airlines from intramodal competition. These high air fares also serve to protect rail from intermodal competition from air. Although Japanese internal air fares are not quite as high as those in Europe, they appear to be significantly higher than the deregulated fares assumed in the policy simulations of table 11.6.[19] Japanese airports are also often located far from the city center, which increases access costs considerably and particularly affects short-distance air travel.[20] In France not only have air fares been high, but the government has suppressed bus competition with rail by prohibiting intercity bus operations on expressways.[21]

Automobile use may also be discouraged in Japan and Europe by a combination of higher fuel prices and less extensive intercity highways, as shown in table 11.8. Regular gasoline costs more than twice as much in Europe and Japan as in the United States in 1980, due to heavy taxes

Table 11.8 Comparative highway and railway statistics for the United States, Japan, France, West Germany, and Great Britain, 1980

	United States	Japan	France	West Germany	United Kingdom
Highway systems					
Gasoline price ($/gallon regular)[a]	$1.19	$2.72	$2.97	$2.46	$2.60
Expressway, national, and other main roads:[b]					
kilometers (000)	846.6	42.8	33.0	40.0	14.9
km per square km of land	0.09	0.11	0.06	0.16	0.06
km per 1,000 persons	3.81	0.36	0.61	0.64	0.07
km per motor vehicle	5.49	1.13	1.51	1.60	0.88
Autos per capita[a]	0.54	0.20	0.36	0.38	0.28
National railway systems[c]					
Total cost ($ billion)	$1.1[d]	$17.5	$10.4	$16.1	$6.4
Freight and passenger revenue ($ billion)	$0.4[d]	$11.8	$7.3	$9.3	$5.4
Deficit or government subsidy ($ billion)	$0.7[d]	$5.7	$3.0	$6.8	$1.0
Passenger revenue as a percentage of total freight and passenger revenue	100.0[d]	83.0	53.0	43.0	52.0

a. U.S. Bureau of the Census, *Statistical Abstract of the United States, 1982–1983* (Washington: Government Printing Office, 1982), p. 621.
b. International Road Federation, *World Road Statistics*, 1976–1980 (Switzerland, Geneva and Washington: International Road Federation, 1981).
c. U.S. statistics are for Amtrak only, and foreign statistics for national railways; see International Railway Union, *International Railway Statistics, Statistics of Individual Railways, 1980* (Paris: International Railway Federation, 1981).
d. Statistics for Amtrak only.

designed to discourage petroleum consumption. Comparisons of the highway systems are difficult because the standards for classifying roads vary among countries and the greater geographic size of the United States requires a larger minimum road network to connect major cities. Nevertheless, in 1980 the United States had far more miles of highways classified as expressways or national routes than did France, West Germany, Britain, or Japan. Although the number of miles of main road per square mile of land area is roughly similar in the United States and Europe, the United States has approximately five times as many miles of main road per capita or per motor vehicle.

Rail passenger service is heavily subsidized in both Europe and Japan, although probably no more so in relative terms than in the United States. The extent of foreign rail passenger subsidies is difficult to determine because separate costs of passenger and freight services are seldom re-

Table 11.9 The effects on modal choice of Japanese or European conditions in a 200-mile travel corridor with 10 million passengers per year

Assumptions	Public policy	Percent carried			
		Auto	Bus	Rail	Air
A. Original assumptions (1980 base case)	Continue present	51.2	9.3	13.9	25.5
	Eliminate subsidy	56.9	10.2	0.0	32.9
	Extend deregulation	55.1	12.3	0.0	32.5
B. Above plus rail twice normal ridership	Continue present	50.7	9.2	14.5	25.5
	Eliminate subsidy	56.7	10.2	0.1	32.9
	Extend deregulation	55.6	12.4	0.1	32.0
C. Above plus rail four times normal ridership	Continue present	50.6	9.2	14.7	25.4
	Eliminate subsidy	56.8	10.2	0.1	32.8
	Extend deregulation	55.6	12.4	0.1	21.9
D. Above plus auto and air twice as costly	Continue present	49.6	7.5	24.8	18.1
	Eliminate subsidy	65.8	9.8	0.2	24.3
	Extend deregulation	63.6	12.9	0.2	23.3
E. Above plus air access penalty	Continue present	51.3	9.3	28.1	11.3
	Eliminate subsidy	70.8	12.1	0.3	16.8
	Extend deregulation	67.6	16.1	0.3	16.0
F. Above plus auto speed avg 40 mph	Continue present	40.1	11.6	36.1	12.2
	Eliminate subsidy	63.1	16.1	0.3	16.8
	Extend deregulation	58.9	22.2	0.3	18.6
G. Above plus incomes 20% lower	Continue present	49.6	14.8	27.3	8.4
	Eliminate subsidy	67.9	19.1	0.3	12.7
	Extend deregulation	63.4	24.8	0.3	11.5
H. Above plus smaller travel party size	Continue present	54.1	12.5	26.7	6.7
	Eliminate subsidy	72.3	16.2	0.2	11.3
	Extend deregulation	67.9	21.1	0.2	10.8

ported. As shown in table 11.8, however, government subsidies or deficits amounted to between 15 and 40 percent of the combined costs of the freight and passenger operations of European and Japanese national railways. Subsidies on some of the high-speed services, though, are far lower than these averages; the Japanese report a profit on their original Shinkansen line between Tokyo and Osaka, for example, and the French claim to be covering operating expenses (but not capital) on their Paris–Lyon TGV line. Nevertheless, the most recent or planned extensions of the Japanese Shinkansen and the French TGV are not expected to cover even operating costs.[22]

Simulating Foreign Conditions

A simulation of the effects Japanese and European conditions might have on U.S. rail ridership is shown in table 11.9. To simulate a corridor with several major intermediate cities, ridership is assumed to be two to four times higher than the rail ridership between the two principal cities at each end. The disadvantages of remote airports are simulated by increasing the price of air travel by the cost of a 20-mile round trip by auto to and from the airport.[23] To approximate the higher costs of foreign auto and air services, the out-of-pocket costs and fares of automobile and air are doubled, and the average intercity auto speed is reduced to 40 miles per hour. Foreign demographics are simulated by reducing average traveler incomes by 20 percent (approximately the 1980 differential between U.S. and Japanese households) and by reducing average party sizes by the same amount (approximately the U.S.-European differential). These assumptions are applied to a 200-mile corridor with 10 million passengers per year traveling between the principal city-pair, conditions that should be quite favorable to rail. Several alternative public policies are also considered, including the continuation of rail subsidies at 1980 U.S. levels, as well as the elimination of subsidy and the extension of procompetitive policies.

If continuation of rail subsidies, presence of major intermediate cities, better accessibility, and more costly auto and air service are all assumed in combination, rail's share of high-density, short-haul markets increases to 36 percent, approximately the levels seemingly experienced in Europe and Japan. Rail's share is increased significantly, however, by only two key factors: continued rail subsidies and higher costs for air and auto travel. No matter what other favorable assumptions are made, rail captures less than 1 percent of the market if subsidies are discontinued and never drops below 14 percent if subsidies are maintained. Rail's share increases appreciably above the 14 percent level only if higher auto and air costs are assumed in combination with rail subsidies.

Intermediate cities and alternative income and party sizes have a relatively small effect on rail's share. A doubling or quadrupling of rail passenger volumes, such as might conceivably occur in a dense corridor with several intermediate cities, adds less than 1 percentage point to rail's market share. Lower income levels reduce, rather than increase, rail's share and do so by as much as 8 percentage points, although the effect of lower incomes on rail may be exaggerated because of the failure of the demand model to account for the full effects of income on auto ownership. Smaller party sizes have relatively little effect as well, modifying rail's market share by, at most, a percentage point or two.

Implications for the United States

These simulations suggest a very pessimistic future for rail passenger service in the United States. Although some short-distance corridors, principally in the northeast, have high travel volumes and intermediate cities that favor rail, these circumstances alone will not be enough to ensure rail a significant share of the market. Apparently rail will capture a significant share of the market only if the United States is willing both to continue rail subsidies and substantially increase the cost of air and automobile travel.[24]

It is at least conceivable that rising energy prices might eventually push the costs of auto and air above those of rail, but it must be remembered that rail costs are affected by energy prices as well. High-speed rail, moreover, is substantially more energy intensive than slower conventional rail (although even high-speed rail is probably less energy intensive than auto or air in high-density markets). The experience of the 1970s also suggests that rising energy prices can be absorbed or deflected in a variety of ways where there are strong underlying advantages to doing so. The fuel efficiency of new U.S. cars increased by roughly 40 percent over the decade, so that the total costs of owning and operating an automobile were barely affected by a doubling in the real price of petroleum.[25] New aircraft models show similar, though less dramatic, improvements in fuel efficiency which promise to dampen significantly the effects of any fuel price increases on airline costs.[26] The success of these conservation efforts in transportation and in other sectors of the economy has also served to reduce demand for energy and thereby weakened pressures for further energy price increases. In short, even if real energy prices were to resume rising at the same rate as in the 1970s, a seemingly improbable event, they are unlikely to alter the economics of intercity modes enough to modify market shares to any great extent.

Airport Congestion

Growth in air travel, as encouraged by deregulation, rising incomes, and changing demographics, might ultimately be limited or dampened if the nation's airports became seriously congested. Airport congestion is normally divided into two components: the land side and the air side. Land-side congestion includes delays on the highways approaching the airport, parking shortages, and other access problems, while air-side congestion involves delays in takeoffs and landings due to congestion on the ramps, runways, or in the immediately surrounding airspace. Nationwide air-side delays have increased since 1978 at a faster rate than the growth in air travel, although the increase in both traffic and delays has been concentrated at only a few of the largest hub airports.[27] There are no systematic data on land-side congestion at the nation's airports, but many travelers have the impression that land-side delays have also increased since deregulation.

Any major increase in airport congestion would probably reduce air's share of the intercity travel market. A comparison of rows D and E in table 11.9, for example, shows the effects of serious airport congestion; in row E a penalty was imposed on air travelers equivalent to an additional 10 mile drive to and from the airports at either end of the trip compared to access to and from the terminals of other modes. For a 200-mile trip, such a severe airport congestion penalty reduces the air share by about one-third (row E compared with D). Air's share would be less strongly affected on longer trips, in which terminal congestion makes up a smaller portion of total travel time and cost, or for smaller increases in airport congestion.

The big uncertainty, however, is whether airport congestion will continue to increase as traffic grows or whether present trends in delays will moderate or even reverse themselves. Airport congestion can be reduced in many ways that, applied in some combination, might permit air travel to grow without any or much increase in airport delays. Historical precedent supports optimism in such matters, moreover, given the favorable experience in solving a similar or even more dramatic increase in airport delays during the early 1960s when the introduction of jets stimulated air travel. By the middle of the 1960s the increase in aircraft-holding delays, especially in the northeast, led federal and state governments to consider a variety of radical solutions such as construction of a fourth New York City airport, high-speed trains in the Washington–New York–Boston corridor, and even vertical takeoff and landing aircraft from downtown airports.[28] Within a few years, however, airport delays abated as a variety of less dramatic developments increased effective airport capacity.

Much of the congestion relief of the late 1960s and early 1970s can be attributed to technological developments, particularly in air traffic control and aircraft design. Improvements in air traffic control systems allowed planes to land and take off at closer intervals, and the introduction of wide-bodied jets in the 1970s meant that a single wide body might replace two or even three smaller aircraft.[29] Similar technological improvements and trends may offer relief in the future.[30]

Changes in airline schedules and routings offer other opportunities for congestion relief. At many airports both land- and air-side congestion is confined to a few hours each day, so that flights in off-peak hours can accommodate traffic growth without increasing congestion. Many metropolitan areas also have relatively uncongested satellite airports that can easily accommodate additional traffic. At major hubs where connecting traffic is a source of congestion, airlines can overfly the hub with direct flights or establish other hubs at less congested airports (as discussed in chapter 5). These scheduling and route changes may inconvenience some travelers by reducing available connections or requiring off-peak travel or the use of less centrally located airports. But avoiding land- and air-side delays is a convenience to travelers too, and results in cost savings to airlines from improved crew and equipment utilization. Since deregulation, these cost savings can be, and increasingly are, reflected in lower fares for less convenient schedules and routings. Fare discounts of 50 percent or more are common on off-peak flights to extremely congested New York airports, for example, or for flights to a satellite airport such as Dulles (in Washington), Newark, Midway (in Chicago), or Ontario, California (in lieu of Los Angeles).[31]

Other possibilities for congestion relief involve better management of the existing capacity of airfields, airways, and access roads at airports. For example, landing fees are often determined largely by the need to meet airport operating costs and perhaps finance a small fraction of the local share of airport expansion costs. These charges usually fail to reflect the full costs of building airport capacity or the costs that a landing imposes on others in the form of delays, noise, or safety hazards. Low landing fees, in turn, reduce the incentives for airlines to substitute large aircraft for small or to reschedule and reroute flights and even, in some cases, permit small private general aviation planes to delay large commercial airliners by landing during congested hours. More sensible landing fees, better aligned to marginal costs of using airspace and terminal areas, would reduce congestion by reallocating the available capacity to those who value its use most, while inducing others to shift their travel or operations to less heavily utilized hours or airports.[32]

A final, but perhaps less promising, possibility to relieve congestion is to increase the capacity of the airport by building additional runways, terminals, access roads, and other facilities. Since 1970 the federal government has led a major effort to expand the nation's commercial airport system through the Airport and Airways Trust Fund. The fund is intended to finance the expansion of airports and the modernization of the nationwide air traffic control system and is supported by special taxes on domestic passenger tickets, international departures, air cargo shipments, and a variety of other aviation-related activities. Although the fund underwrote about $6 billion in investment during the 1970s ($3.5 billion of which was in federal grants and the balance in local match), it has not been enough to prevent increased congestion at large hubs. This discouraging performance is partly due to airport capacity being expensive to build and often engendering opposition from surrounding communities, but also partly to a disproportionate share of the funds being allocated to small airports, where congestion has never been a serious problem.[33] With some reallocation of investment from small to large airports, capacity improvements could undoubtedly reduce congestion, but perhaps at greater cost than through technological improvements, route and schedule changes, and better management practices.

Conclusions

Future changes—in public policy, personal incomes, or demography—are unlikely to alter the fundamental patterns of intercity passenger travel in the United States: autos will continue to dominate at short distances and air will dominate long-distance markets; bus and rail will serve minor and specialized niches, primarily in short-haul markets.[34] The two major modes, auto and air, have such strong and obvious advantages in their respective markets that together they will continue to account for the vast majority of U.S. intercity travel.

Elimination of government subsidies and regulations would have little effect on auto and air but could have a major impact on the particular or specialized roles played by rail and bus. For example, the elimination of subsidies (expecially for rail) coupled with deregulation of buses might nearly double the bus market share, principally at the expense of rail but partly at the expense of the private automobile. Similarly procompetitive policies that reduced rail costs would increase rail's market share slightly, but not by nearly enough to offset loss of government subsidies. Indeed, the elimination of government subsidies could essentially eliminate rail in all but a few extremely dense, short-distance markets.

Demographic changes should have a moderate effect on auto and air market shares. If the average size of the intercity travel party declines, the auto could lose a few percentage points to the air mode as well as a fraction of a point or two to bus and rail. Increasing incomes could bring an even more pronounced shift from auto to air, since higher incomes increase the ability and willingness to pay for high-speed air travel.

A revival of rail passenger travel in the United States also seems improbable even if high-speed rail service of the type found in Japan and Europe were introduced. Rail's large market share in Japan and Europe appears primarily attributable to government policies that subsidize rail while raising auto and air costs to nearly double U.S. levels. Since the United States is unlikely to follow the European and Japanese lead with respect to increasing the relative costs of the auto and air modes, rail is likely to remain a minor mode.

Air travel, whose growth generally seems ensured under U.S. conditions, might be inhibited, even capped in a few locations, by a worsening of congestion in and around airports. Several rather simple scheduling and pricing solutions are available for these congestion problems, however, and a deregulated industry should have the flexibility to pursue these successfully. Furthermore a better matching of expenditures from available public airport and airway trust funds with identified bottlenecks would largely eliminate any congestion constraint on air travel growth. Thus, regardless of public policies, the purpose for which travel is undertaken, or the level of air and other common carrier service provided, a shift to air travel will probably occur to some extent in almost all major intercity travel markets, primarily as a result of the increased values attached to faster travel as personal incomes continue to rise.

In short, the outlook would appear to be one in which airlines will continue to expand in *relative* market terms while most of the other modes stagnate or decline. Most of the airline expansion will be at the expense of the automobile, although probably not greatly reducing the absolute level of intercity auto travel. Buses and trains will continue to occupy limited and specialized market niches; these niches will be slightly declining or stagnant in total scope largely due to economic and demographic changes that are quite independent of deregulation or any other probable changes in public policy.

12

Market Structure, Public Policy, and the Future of Intercity Passenger Transportation

By the mid-1980s the intercity passenger transportation market in the United States had become essentially free of economic regulation. Although unleashing the modes from the constraints of regulation did not, and as shown in the last chapter apparently will not, dramatically change modal shares, deregulation obviously has had some impact on the industry. If nothing else, the industry's scale, structure, and practices have been inalterably changed.

Certainly since deregulation, many of the public carriers' costs have been lowered. Capital as well as labor are more efficiently deployed and effectively used. More rational and less costly route networks have been developed. The deregulated airline and bus industries have also better tailored their offerings to market needs, most dramatically in the case of small community service where both substantial expansions and contractions of service have occurred. Furthermore the deregulated airlines, and to a lesser extent bus companies, have also experimented with entirely new service concepts, ranging from stripping away so-called extras such as baggage handling and meals to offering enhanced "business class" or "super first-class" services.

The public modes' new marketing freedoms have also been used to experiment with fare differentials and promotional fares. These have been aimed not only at diverting traffic from other modes (mainly the automobile) but also at stimulating entirely new traffic. Much of the early surge in airline traffic under the administrative deregulation of 1976 to 1978 was apparently new. Subsequently the new entrepreneurial airlines have seemingly continued to develop new markets for air travel, while diverting traffic from older airlines and from the other modes as well. Similarly the bus industry has experienced a surge of new charter operators, offering low fares and new service combinations, in response to removal of regulatory restrictions.

Under deregulation cost reductions should also be more quickly passed on to travelers as fare reductions, thus advancing the development of entirely new markets. As a consequence, even if technological change and productivity improvement were not enhanced by deregulation (which, as shown in chapter 6, they probably were), the total market for intercity passenger travel should expand somewhat faster with deregulation. By contrast, under regulation technological change and attendant cost reductions tended to be captured as factor rents, particularly in higher union wages.

Ultimately too deregulation should encourage a subtle but important change in the recruitment of management. The requisite mix of managerial skills has changed with deregulation, shifting from law and politics to marketing and cost control. With deregulation the public modes should also provide more opportunities for managers with an entrepreneurial bent, strengthening the prospects for innovation and further market development.

In sum, deregulation should induce more intercity travel by lowering average costs and fares. A slightly higher percentage of that travel may also go by public rather than private modes, all else equal. Of course not all else will be equal. Specifically, as shown in chapter 11, demographic and income trends should reinforce deregulation's tendency toward a larger public market share. For example, an expected decline in family size will make the private auto relatively less attractive as an intercity travel mode. Similarly higher personal incomes should favor the airlines because higher-income households place a higher valuation on their time and therefore find air travel, which normally saves time, increasingly preferable to surface travel. Of course, a larger percentage of travel by public modes may not result in less total private automobile travel in absolute terms if the total market for intercity travel expands sufficiently, as indeed it probably will.

Potential Pitfalls of Deregulation

Three potential pitfalls have been widely cited that could undermine the efficiency and consumer benefits of deregulation in the long run. The first is that deregulation might lead to the creation of a concentrated, almost monopolistic, industry structure that denies consumers the benefits of deregulation and competitive markets. Second, deregulation could create so much financial instability that capital becomes less available to the industry, preventing prompt realization of the technological gains available and thereby offsetting cost efficiencies or similar benefits created by deregulation. Third, without the political and social control of regulation, intolerable inequities or social losses might be created, the most common concerns being that too little service will be provided to outlying or rural areas of the country, or that inequitable fare structures will be created (e.g., as exemplified by having to pay more for a relatively short trip than for a much longer trip).

Industry Structure

It has been widely argued both prior to and after the fact that deregulation could result in a highly concentrated industry structure that would eliminate competition and eventually might make reregulation necessary.[1] Some suggestions have even been made as to how this more concentrated structure might evolve. Under deregulation, it has been said, too much competition would be created, destroying industry earnings and capital and eventually resulting in survival of only a few of the strongest firms.

Market structures, to be sure, have not remained static in most industries after deregulation.[2] Deregulation of U.S. transportation, in rail and trucking as well as airlines, hastened an already existing trend toward end-to-end mergers because of the marketing advantages in providing single-carrier service. A freight carrier's salesmen, for example, have always found it advantageous to approach shippers with an offer of one carrier assuming sole responsibility and thereby providing service guarantees that were not otherwise available.[3] Similarly an airline traveler usually found it easier to establish tight connections with less opportunity for lost baggage and other such difficulties, by traveling on the same carrier when a change of plane was required rather than transferring from one carrier to another.

In general, some service advantage has always inhered to transportation companies having as comprehensive and ubiquitous a network as possible. Prior to deregulation, however, the ability to develop such comprehensive networks was usually thwarted by regulators wishing to distribute routes so as to achieve "balanced" competition or wishing to maintain some sort of rough equity or size parity in the industry.[4]

After deregulation, the advantages of end-to-end expansion or mergers often became even more pronounced. For example, rate making is usually simpler and more flexible if one carrier serves both the origin and destination—and simplicity and flexibility became highly prized qualities as transportation markets became more competitive. Deregulation has also been accompanied in the United States by elimination of many antitrust exemptions and other collaborative arrangements that permitted the different carriers to establish, under regulatory "oversight," joint rates, rate divisions, and so forth. Thus "end-to-end" cooperative arrangements by two carriers to gain some of the advantages of single carrier service are no longer as immune to antitrust considerations. Of perhaps equal importance, such close cooperation was easier to negotiate when regulatory authorities restricted competition. A strong argument can also be made that end-to-end mergers, unlike parallel mergers, sometimes increase rather than reduce competition, and increased competition usually has become a major public policy goal after deregulation.

It is therefore not too surprising that several mergers have occurred in the U.S. airline industry since deregulation. Many of these were end-to-end in character, particularly just after deregulation, and seemed primarily motivated by considerations of route extension. However, a second wave of postderegulation mergers, starting in 1985, seemed as much oriented to market control and scale economies as to route expansion (see the discussion of route strategies in chapter 5). Indeed, this second wave of mergers in the mid-1980s revived and intensified concerns about the possibility of the airline industry becoming a tight and uncompetitive oligopoly.

Despite these many mergers, however, a few systems have not come to dominate the industry. To the contrary, the number of jet carriers in the industry was up from less than 20 prior to deregulation to over 50 by 1984; furthermore the largest carriers (the trunk airlines) as a group lost 11 percentage points of market share to other types of airlines between 1976 and 1982 under deregulation. In those years over 200 new airlines were created, though less than half have probably survived as independent entities. Subsequently, as the economy recovered between 1982 and 1984, the trunks as a group apparently continued to lose some market share to the new entrant jets and commuters. However, after 1984, reflecting the second postderegulation wave of merger activity in the industry, market concentration may have increased by some measures; for example, in 1984 the largest six carriers had about 65 percent of the domestic market but by 1986 were approaching 75 to 80 percent (assuming all proposed mergers were consummated).

Shifts in market shares and industry structure have largely been a reflection of the extent to which firms in the industry have implemented successful cost control, route, and pricing policies (as discussed in chapters 4 through 7). In airlines, as in most industries, firms basically have a choice of establishing themselves either by providing a "better" product or by having lower costs than their competitors. Such differentiation or superiority, in turn, permits a firm to settle itself either in a particular market niche or across the whole relevant market, depending on the circumstances and the firm's strategic positioning.[5]

Before deregulation the U.S. domestic airline industry had three reasonably well established and defined overall cost leaders: Delta, Northwest, and National. None of these cost leaders, however, could assert itself industrywide (although Delta came reasonably close) because the CAB placed definite limits on the scope of individual airline activities by controlling route awards. As a consequence all three of these cost leaders had to focus their activities to some considerable extent prior to deregulation: Delta on the southeastern United States and southern transcontinental routes; Northwest on transpacific service and the upper midwest; National on southern transcontinental and longer-haul eastern seaboard to Florida service (mainly originating from New York south). Their activities were also limited by their inability and lack of incentives under regulation to translate their lower costs into lower fares.

Prior to deregulation there were also three carriers (American, United, and TWA) that, with varying degrees of success, differentiated themselves by their service qualities and competed on an industrywide basis. All three carriers had good route coverage across much of the nation and were generally perceived to have as good or better cabin service and amenities than most of their competitors.

Several U.S. airlines pursued focused strategies prior to deregulation, often because the regulatory authorities did not permit any other choice. For example, Pan American was exclusively in international service, and to a considerable extent Braniff, Northwest, and TWA, though they each had some domestic routes, concentrated on developing their international routes. The local service airlines (LSAs) each served a particular region of the country under what amounted to a CAB-sanctioned monopoly of medium- and short-haul service in their region. Very short-haul and low-density routes shunned by the LSAs were the province of so-called commuter airlines and were largely unregulated even before deregulation. Most of the successful commuters pursued very focused strategies (reliable, timely hub to small community service in a particular geographic area). Finally, in a few of the larger states (e.g., California, Texas, and Florida) a few intrastate carriers with low costs and low fares (e.g., Pacific Southwest and Southwest Airlines) were well established prior to deregulation.

A rough schematic representation of the strategic positioning of U.S. commercial airlines under regulation is shown in figure 12.1. Market focus decreases with movement upward on the vertical axis while cost leadership or advantage increases with movement to the right on the horizontal axis.[6] Thus cost leadership combined with a very specific market focus would put an airline (e.g., Southwest Airlines) in the lower right corner, while industrywide coverage and unique but costly service characteristics would place a carrier (e.g., United Airlines) in the upper left quadrant.

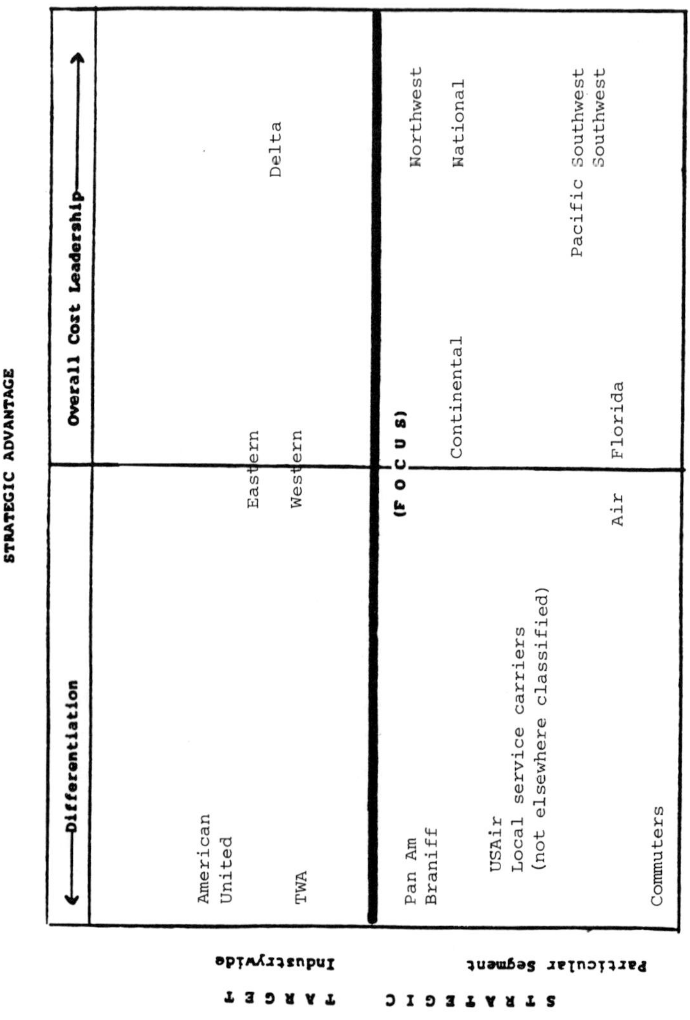

Figure 12.1 Market structure of U.S. commercial aviation industry prior to deregulation.

A key consideration in determining the long-run impact of deregulation on market structure is evaluating how deregulation may have changed the strategic positioning of different firms in the industry. To start, deregulation changed the cast of players quite considerably. In particular, new entrant jets, enlarged commuter airlines, and deregulated bus lines filled market voids that existed prior to deregulation. For the most part, relatively focused strategies were pursued by the new airline entrepreneurs (see chapter 4), including not only some entirely new jet-equipped airlines (e.g., People Express, New York Air, and Midway) but greatly expanded activities by some commuter airlines (e.g., Empire, Britt, and Air Wisconsin).

After deregulation Northwest and Delta could still be characterized as cost leaders, but they now had opportunities to expand their activities industrywide. (National had "disappeared" as a separate entity because of its merger with Pan Am.) Delta clearly seized on this opportunity (see chapter 5) with systematic moves to extend the scale of its domestic network. Pursuit of this strategy eventually led Delta, in 1986, to acquire Western Airlines. Northwest, by contrast, initially did not expand much domestically but continued to focus on its international markets, which it enlarged (see chapters 5 and 9); in 1986, however, Northwest also expanded its domestic preserve substantially, albeit not through internal expansion but by acquiring Republic Airlines.

A strategy of differentiation, mainly through an emphasis on service quality, was still pursued by American and United Airlines, the previous leaders in this activity, but with an increasing emphasis on lowering costs and meeting the fares of new low-cost competitors (see chapters 5 and 6). Both American and United developed additional hubs to bring their systems to near-national coverage. These expansions, coupled with their dominant positions in computer reservation systems, may have permitted American, and perhaps United as well, at least to consider whether a further competitive advantage could be gained by withdrawing from interline arrangements with other carriers and "going it alone." TWA, the other prederegulation pursuer of a broadly diffused service differentiation strategy, retrenched and focused on one or two selected hubs within the United States and on its North Atlantic trade; even its acquisition in 1986 of Ozark Airlines could be considered an extension of this strategy since a major impact was to consolidate further TWA's already dominant position at the St. Louis hub.

Most of those pursuing a focused strategy before deregulation have generally pursued a somewhat more diffuse strategy afterward. Indeed,

Braniff so hastily expanded that it brought itself into bankruptcy. Pan Am abandoned its exclusive emphasis on international travel by acquiring National in an attempt to build a system balanced between domestic and international travel while, hopefully, providing complementary traffic feeds between the two activities. When these hopes foundered, Pan Am sold its Pacific division to United, thereby permitting United to realize its long-standing ambition to expand aggressively in the Pacific Rim. Local service (or national) carriers, and their kinsmen the major intrastate carriers (e.g., Southwest and PSA), have with few exceptions pursued a policy of extending outward from their original regional bases. At the extreme Republic Airlines through a series of mergers (North Central, Southern, and Hughes Air West) created a nationwide network, albeit of relatively short hauls; when Republic was acquired by Northwest, these short hauls complemented and fed Northwest's relatively long hauls, domestic and international. Finally, although most of the commuter airlines remained at their basic business of connecting small outlying communities with major hub airports on very short hauls, a few reached out to higher-volume and longer-haul routes. The larger commuters also forged close ties with one (or in a few cases several) major jet airlines via marketing alliances or, in a few cases, outright merger as the major jet carriers intensified their battle for feed traffic.

A crude synopsis of the U.S. commercial airline industry's strategic positioning six or seven years after deregulation (e.g., in 1984 or early 1985) is shown in figure 12.2. A somewhat disturbing aspect is the number of companies seemingly stuck in the strategic middle—and therefore potential candidates for exit with neither a well-defined market niche nor a cost or service advantage. Indeed, three of these middlers (Western, Eastern, and Republic) had either merged or agreed to proposed mergers by 1986.

Perhaps this tendency toward middling strategies was an inevitable consequence of bestowing economic freedom on managements that had grown up in a cocoon of regulation. Whatever the explanation, such early prederegulation "middlers" as Eastern Airlines and Western Airlines were quickly joined after deregulation by Braniff, Pan American, and Republic, with apparently less than favorable consequences for their viability. Indeed, by way of further documenting the potential dilemma of being a strategic middler, many observers would argue that People Express drifted toward such a positioning in 1985 and 1986, thus setting the stage for its exit from the industry via merger with Texas Air in late 1986.

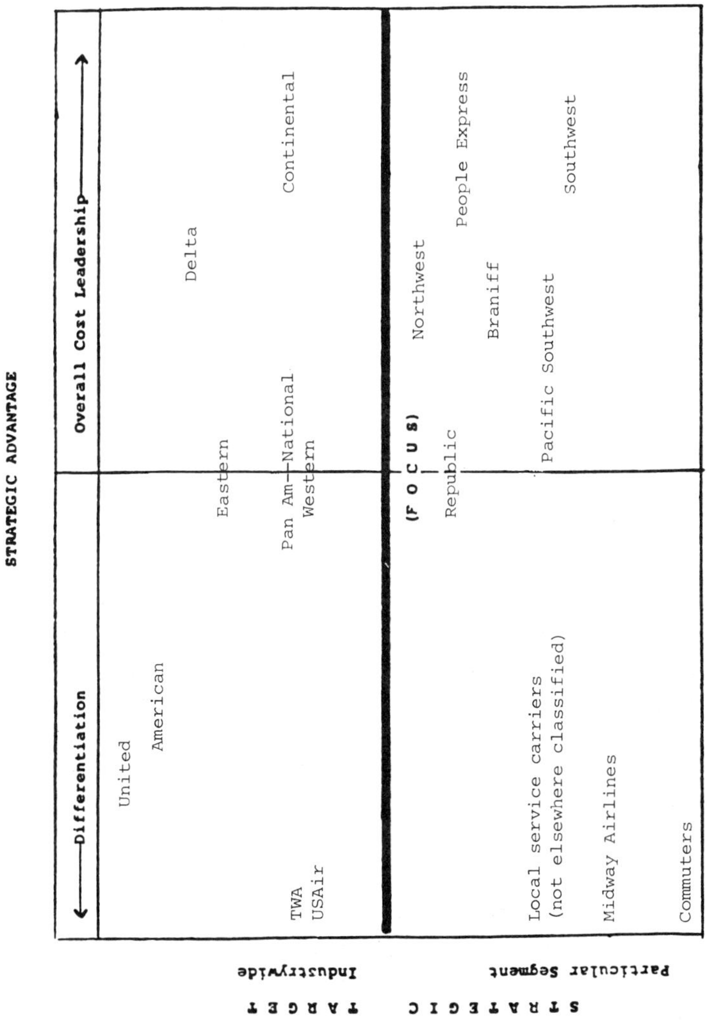

Figure 12.2 Market structure of U.S. commercial aviation industry after deregulation, in the mid-1980s.

Inclusion of the other public modes, as shown in figure 12.3, does little to alter this picture, which is not unexpected given the other modes' relatively modest market roles. Amtrak would seem to be a middler, although an increased emphasis on cost control in the mid-1980s created by congressional deficit concerns may alter the situation. The Greyhound and Trailways bus companies operate large comprehensive networks but at low costs compared to most airlines and Amtrak, placing them in the northeast quadrant. The independent bus lines in most instances seem to provide very low-cost service in particular local market segments; this positions them in the southwest quadrant much like most low-cost new entrant airlines.

Even though much of the strategic repositioning triggered by deregulation may be ill-advised or misdirected, reflecting the competitive market inexperience of recently deregulated firms, the net outcome nevertheless seems to be an industry structure not unlike that to be found in most industries operating in market economies: a few very big firms (achieving dominance either through being the lowest-cost producer or through product differentiation) surrounded by several smaller competitors operating in more narrowly defined market niches, but also well poised to expand if their bigger brethren become inattentive. This "fringe" includes not only the smaller airlines but the other modes as well; not only can the buses provide competition in certain short-haul niches, but even Amtrak can be a presence in certain high density short-haul markets, such as that between New York and Washington (where even in 1985 rail accounted for about 30 percent of travel by public carriers). Furthermore the early experience with deregulation saw some reduction in market concentration and enhancement of competition, rather than the contrary. Nevertheless, the increase in the number of strategic middlers has meant that several firms have disappeared as independent entities, and a few more may yet follow. Obviously this could eventually create a more oligopolistic industry structure (paralleling the experience of many other industries as they matured). Whether such a development will require special public policy responses (e.g., vigorous antitrust enforcement and expansion of airway and airport capacities to permit easy entry) remains an interesting and open question. Certainly an increasingly oligopolistic structure poses the issue and enhances the probabilities that such policy responses will be needed.

Financial Instability

The financial instability argument is based on assumptions and forecasts quite the opposite of those leading to an excessively concentrated and

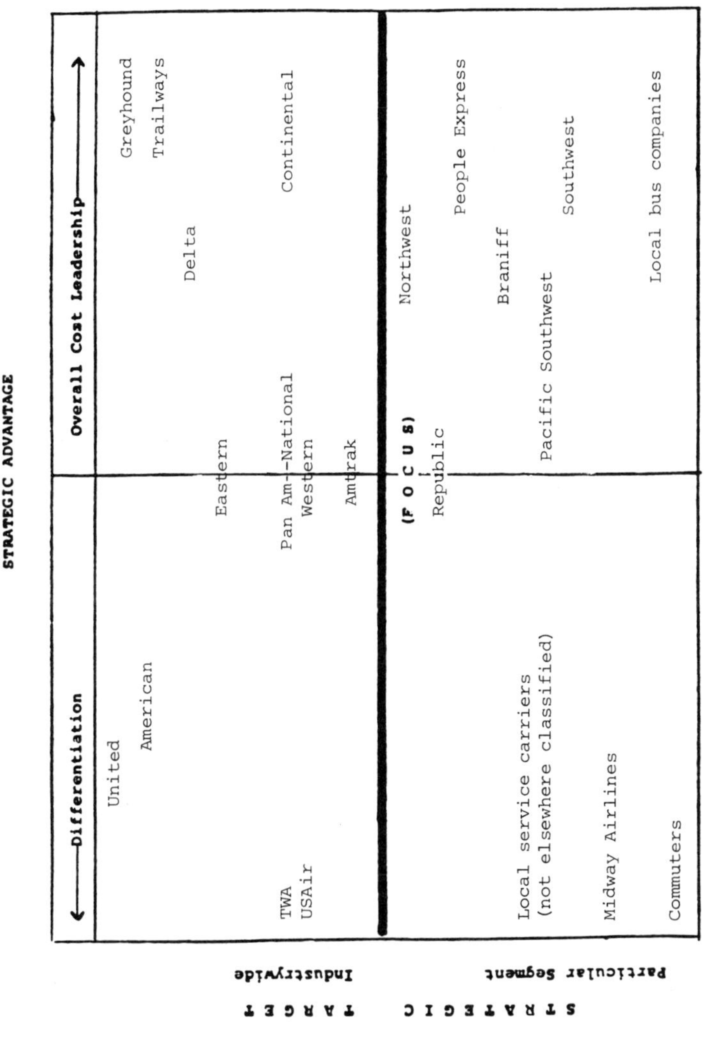

Figure 12.3 Market structure of U.S. intercity passenger transportation industry, in mid-1980s.

oligopolistic industry. Rather, deregulation is seen as creating too much competition. Earnings would therefore be so insufficient and cyclically unstable that needed new capital equipment could not be financed. Financial difficulties, in turn, could lead to reduced productivity, costs higher than they otherwise should be, slower growth of markets, and so on. The industry in the long run would thus be less well positioned to serve consumers than if deregulation had never occurred.

A major difficulty with these arguments is establishing cause and effect. Are fare wars a result of deregulation or a "hangover" from the previous excesses of regulation itself? As repeatedly noted, the perverse incentives created by regulation led to airlines investing in too many wide-bodied aircraft which, in turn, led to fare wars in transcontinental and other long-haul markets when regulation was relaxed. Or, how much of any postderegulation profit decline was due to deregulation, to factor price increases, or simply to recession? The evidence in chapter 3 would suggest that all three were clearly at work in the early 1980s, shortly after airline deregulation occurred, and that the recession and fuel price increases accounted for the bulk of any such effects.

The airlines have also long been an industry characterized by a good deal of cyclical instability. Financial market perception of these cyclical or nondiversifiable risks can be measured by so-called "betas" reflecting the relative volatility of airline equity prices compared with those of the stock market in general. As reported in chapter 3, betas for most airlines (especially when corrected for additional debt) were actually lower in 1984 than they were in the early 1970s when CAB regulation was still in force, suggesting that deregulation has not enhanced the perceived financial risk of airline equities.

Destructive competition, if it exists, may also simply represent a transition problem. For instance, if and as excess supplies of particular aircraft are eliminated (by retirement, obsolescence, or whatever), then any resultant tendency toward fare wars should also be diminished. Similarly much of what might appear to be destructive competition may simply be a churning of market strategies and structures (as outlined earlier and discussed in greater detail in chapters 4, 5, 7, and 8), created by the unleashing of various entrepreneurial possibilities that were suppressed under regulation; these, in turn, might be expected to dampen themselves as time elapses and a greater awareness develops as to what can and cannot be done in various markets. In general, managements may simply have much to learn in shifting from the political and legal game emphasized under regulation to the competitive give and take of a free market.

The evidence is also mixed on the extent to which airline deregulation may have affected the financial or debt capacity of the airlines. Several airframe contracts or options consummated in the 1970s were canceled during the early 1980s. The question arises, though, of whether this was attributable to the business cycle downturns of the early 1980s or to deregulation, particularly since there have been several large aircraft orders placed subsequently (in 1984, 1985, and 1986). Furthermore factor prices, particularly fuel prices, had an impact. A major reason for ordering new airplanes in the late 1970s was to save on fuel as the new planes consumed less fuel per seat mile than the older aircraft they replaced. The declines in energy prices that occurred in the early 1980s therefore lowered the expected return on investments made in newer and more fuel efficient aircraft.

Any argument that deregulation greatly limited the financial capacity of the airlines is also not easily reconciled with the remarkable number of new airline equity and debt issues made during the early 1980s (as reported in detail in chapter 3). These issues occurred moreover at a time when airline earnings were hurt by recession, higher energy prices, high interest rates, and all the other complexities and difficulties besides deregulation that the industry endured during the early 1980s. Indeed, so substantial and prevalent were new financial issues by the airlines during the early 1980s, even as many of the airlines' fortunes otherwise foundered, that one industry observer (anonymously) suggested that "even though the airlines might not be able to sell tickets, they were certainly able to sell brightly colored green-and-white pieces of paper."

It should also never be forgotten that many airlines have long had rather highly leveraged balance sheets, prior to deregulation as well as after. All else equal, such leverage tends to reduce debt capacity available for further investment and to heighten the risk of bankruptcy. As Braniff, Air Florida, Continental, and several smaller airlines have demonstrated, bankruptcy *is* a real possibility for an airline since deregulation, whereas under regulation bankruptcies were assiduously avoided through CAB-arranged mergers, almost regardless of cost or other considerations. Thus the character of airline financing has surely been modified to at least some extent by deregulation: leases and equipment trusts tied to particular pieces of equipment will be the virtually universal rule in the industry, whereas prior to deregulation that rule was *almost*, but not quite, universal. In essence, those few cases in which airlines could obtain money on their general credit, never all that prevalent, will become even less prevalent under deregulation. This does not mean, though, that the industry will necessarily lack for capital. Indeed, in the early years of deregulation, the industry has shown a remarkable ability to find new sources of financing. However, these financings may be subject in the absence of regulation to greater scrutiny and more careful evaluation prior to the fact. For example, it might be harder in a deregulated environment to finance a surplus of wide-bodied jets than it was in the late 1960s and early 1970s under regulation. Of course that may not be a totally adverse development, especially when viewed from a national rather than a strictly industry perspective. In short, little in the record suggests that deregulation will make financing of needed equipment additions or replacements impossible, or even all that difficult, though deregulation might make pursuit of haphazard and ill-conceived expansion plans rather more difficult than previously.

Social Inequities

A major contention in prederegulation debates, for both freight and passenger transportation, was that deregulation would result in a serious diminution or even elimination of service to many small towns in the United States. Transportation links to small communities are of course part of the long-standing federalist agenda of knitting the country more closely together. Reflecting this concern, Congress over the years has repeatedly provided substantial subsidies to ensure various small town services: in airlines it meant creating and subsidizing so-called local service carriers; in telecommunications it meant extending the rural electrification administration beyond its original mandate of providing rural electrical service to that of providing telephone service; in postal operations it meant subsidizing post offices in remote small town locations.

Regulatory actions also reflected these same concerns. Thus the Civil Aeronautics Board (CAB) attempted to establish cross subsidization wherein higher returns were earned in long-haul, high-density markets in order to keep fares below cost on short hauls to smaller communities. A somewhat similar pattern of cross subsidization (from freight to passenger service) was also discernible in railroading, at least until the creation of Amtrak. Finally, in bus operations, some state regulators pursued policies of cross-subsidizing small town service with earnings on charter operations or on longer and denser scheduled interstate hauls.

Significantly there is no evidence that deregulation per se has caused much loss of small town service in either the airline industry or the bus industry. In the airline case commuter airlines, operating small propeller-driven aircraft well suited to the short-haul, low-density markets that are characteristic of small community service, filled the void when the jet carriers moved their aircraft to longer-haul and higher-density markets. The commuters in fact almost tripled their share of the domestic airline market after deregulation so that no systemwide loss of air service to small communities has resulted. Moreover, although some subsidies were still required to maintain this local air service, the amount of subsidy was substantially less than had regulation remained in effect.[7]

The case of bus service to small communities is somewhat different. First, the average size of community served by buses is much smaller than that served by aircraft. Although fewer than 600 communities in the United States had regularly scheduled air service, well over 10,000 communities received scheduled bus service in the early 1980s. Second, bus service was (quite unlike commuter airline service) on a declining trend for at least seven years prior to bus regulatory reform. Following passage of the Bus Regulatory Reform Act of 1982, bus departures declined abruptly. Once, though, the "pent-up" demand to withdraw from scheduled service was satisfied (about six months to one year after passage of the act), the decline in departures proceeded at about the same annual rate as had been the case between 1975 and 1982. The number of communities receiving service also continued to decline following deregulation, but at a somewhat higher rate. Significantly, however, from a public policy standpoint these service terminations did not fall disproportionately on the poor or aged; if anything, the communities terminated were somewhat richer (as measured by average median income) and had a lower percentage of their population over age 65 than those communities continuing to receive service.[8] Indeed, the median income in communities losing all bus service was about 6 percent higher than in those communities retaining service, and the fraction age 65 and older was about 7 percent lower in communities losing all service. Not surprisingly, the bus companies apparently did not cut service as much, if at all, to communities with high concentrations of their most frequent riders!

Overall, the evidence suggests that bus deregulation, after a brief initial adjustment period, did little more than simply allow trends to continue that were already well under way. Moreover Florida, a state that had deregulation at the state level in 1980 and thus has had more time to adjust to a deregulated environment than the other states, experienced increases in small town service between 1983 and 1984. Thus, in the bus case as in the airline case, the preponderance of the evidence suggests that deregulation did not cause or greatly aggravate service losses to small communities.

The dimensions or qualities of small town service have changed, though, because of deregulation, particularly for the airlines. Specifically, the commuter airlines provide more service frequencies and more convenient schedules than their predecessors but render these services in smaller, less comfortable planes. Since the commuter airlines seem to garner as much or more traffic than their jet predecessors in most instances where they have replaced small town jet service, the commuters have apparently established an appropriate trade-off between service frequency and size and comfort of aircraft. Furthermore the "comfort gap" between the commuter replacement aircraft and the jets formerly assigned to local service could be largely closed as new and more comfortable aircraft specifically designed for commuter service become available; the lack of such aircraft, incidentally, is also partly a residue of regulation, since under regulation very little incentive existed for aircraft manufacturers to do the necessary research and development to provide these alternative small aircraft.

There is no formally established classification of bus operations that is as clearly definable and observable as that of commuter airlines. In large measure this simply reflects the greater fragmentation and ease of entry into the bus industry that is inherent in its simple technology and relatively low capital costs; as minimal as terminal and aircraft investment costs might be for commuter airlines, they are even less for a small bus operation. Bus operations may be even more divisible than commuter airline operations and certainly require a lesser level of specialized labor skills. Furthermore, once school bus, sightseeing, local airport limousine, and other such services are taken into account, a larger base almost surely existed prior to deregulation in the bus than the airline industry on which to build new local small town services. In the bus industry, in fact, the main problem, especially from the standpoint of the larger companies in the industry, may not be so much finding smaller carriers willing to replace them when they withdraw from local small town service but rather keeping these lower-cost replacements from encroaching on larger markets that the established older carriers wish to preserve. Just as in the case of the airlines, this competitive threat by the smaller bus carriers has been based to a considerable extend on lower labor and other operating costs so that they can achieve successful entry on the basis of cost-justified lower fares.

Finally, and most significant from the standpoint of public policy, the cost to society of maintaining services to local communities has almost surely been reduced by deregulation.[9] Not only have government subsidies declined, but indirect or cross subsidies have been eliminated by the market pressures created through deregulation. Cross subsidy is of course virtually impossible in a deregulated world characterized by easy entry and exit, especially one in which specialization in a particular niche of the market seems to be an emerging trend. Indeed, this specialization has even gone a step further in small town airline service, in that those local commuter airlines continuing to receive some subsidy tend to be in a special niche within the commuter airline industry itself; apparently applying for and collecting subsidies requires rather different skills (legal and public relations) than those needed to succeed in the unsubsidized portion of the industry.

The experience with small town intercity passenger travel under deregulation raises interesting and broader issues of public policy. Specifically, the emergence of new specialized carriers efficiently serving this niche in the market, and even inducing expanded supplies of equipment better suited to such service, poses the question of whether the ability of the market to provide such service has not been long overlooked in political and public policy deliberations. A certain large-scale myopia may have been at work historically: the initial application of any new technology may have a tendency toward serving the largest, most obvious markets first, resulting in a premature conclusion that these technologies could not be adapted to serve smaller and less dense markets. Or, from a somewhat different perspective, the federalist concern with "knitting the country together" may have generated an impatience that led to premature development of subsidies and other specialized schemes to ensure service to small communities, service that might have been provided only slightly less quickly (and probably less expensively) if left entirely to the market.

The other major social equity issue is that associated with fares. This issue emerged after deregulation and was not widely anticipated prior to the fact—somewhat surprisingly since fare equity issues are rooted in many of the same "federalist" concerns that motivated anxieties about small town service. Indeed, the allegation of inequity in some people paying more for short hauls than others pay for long hauls is hardly a new policy concern in American transportation. Clauses concerned with such matters were actually incorporated into the Interstate Commerce Act of 1887. In essence, both the new fare equity issues uncovered by deregulation and the older concerns embodied in the original regulatory acts represent a long-standing American political interest in achieving as much "horizontal equity" as possible: that is, a belief that people in different parts of the country should pay roughly the same for what appears, at last superficially, to be the same service.

Unfortunately different services are not usually so directly comparable as initial observation might suggest. Specifically, mileage is hardly the only determinant of cost in transportation operations. First, and most obviously, there are almost invariably some terminal costs involved with almost any transportation operation; in the case of airlines, in fact, if one includes the cost of achieving and coming down from cruising altitude as a form of terminal costs, then terminal costs can be a major proportion, particularly on relatively short hauls. For buses and rail, terminal costs will normally be a lesser percentage of total costs but still significant. The volume or density of demand in a particular market can also have an impact on the utilization and the unit cost of service, and therefore on fares.

The legacy of regulation has also imposed prior conditions that required different fare adaptations in different markets. An important characteristic of much regulation has been to seek cross subsidies usually from long-haul markets to the benefit of short-haul markets. Since the possibility of cross subsidization essentially has disappeared under the competitive pressures unleashed by deregulation, some adjustment of fare levels also had to occur in order to bring fares into better alignment with costs. To a considerable extent, many of the observations of fare inequities after deregulation are really observations about the nature of this adjustment process.

Different markets have also differed in their competitive characteristics. For example, the new entrant jets with their emphasis on lower costs and lower fares have not instantaneously appeared in all major, let alone minor, U.S. intercity travel markets since deregulation; like most institutions, the new entrant jets required time to develop operations and scale.

Uneven patterns of competition since deregulation are also attributed in part to prior regulation. Because of CAB policies, the airlines were equipped with an excess of wide-bodied, long-range aircraft and a deficiency of aircraft suitable for short-haul, low-density operations when deregulation came. Consequently, under deregulation, rate wars have been particularly prevalent in long-haul, high-density markets suited to wide-bodied operations. By contrast, the scarcity of aircraft suitable for short-haul operations has permitted relatively high markups in many of those markets. Also, as noted, in some of these short-haul markets, higher markups were needed in order to bring fares into alignment with costs (although that need has been greatly attenuated by expansion of low-cost commuter operations). Thus, as discussed in chapters 5 and 7, the major and most dramatic fare wars since deregulation have generally occurred as much in long-haul markets without benefit of new entrant jet carriers as they have in short-haul or other markets where the new entrants have appeared.

To the extent that any fare wars represent an adjustment to the legacies of regulation, as many of them do, "solutions" should come with the passage of time. Airlines had indeed already begun the process in the early 1980s of adapting their fleets to the new realities by ordering more small short-haul jets and relatively fewer large long-haul jets. Similarly aircraft suitable for long-haul operations were being retired or mothballed relatively more quickly than those suitable for short-haul operations. In general, any market deliberately disequilibrated, as the airline market was under regulation, may require some time to establish a new market-determined equilibrium, especially since the new equilibrium requires some changes in equipment policies that, in turn, require two- to six-year planning lead times. In fact, from the standpoint of consumers, the whole adjustment process has proved to be relatively free of trauma, since in most instances the so-called inequities have been created because lower markups are charged in more markets than before deregulation rather than because of higher markups becoming a common phenomenon (see chapter 7).

Summary and Evaluation

The intercity passenger travel industry in the United States has responded well to the experience of moving from a roughly 80 to 90 percent deregulation status (the private automobile segment) to virtually complete deregulation. Most of the relevant markets and submarkets seem to be served at a lower real cost to both consumers and government than under prior regulatory regimes. And when new market niches have opened, the deregulated industry seems quite capable of responding promptly and effectively.

Deregulation may, though, have created problems as well. Financing the industry may be at least marginally more complex than before since, above all else, bankruptcy is now a possibility. On balance, though, financial markets and investors seem to have been little affected by deregulation.

The biggest losers from deregulation, in fact, are almost surely prior unionized labor forces. Specifically, their ability to extract rents, created either by regulatory distortions or technological gain, has been greatly diminished. In the longer run some of labor's losses under deregulation may in turn be diminished, at least to labor as a totality, since deregulation has also kept the growth rate of the industry above levels that otherwise would have been experienced.

In large measure most of the transitional problems of the deregulated airline and bus industries should disappear with the passage of time. Managements will eventually learn to cope with their new and more competitive environments as they learn and recruit the needed skills. In the same vein the various participants in the industry will determine their relative strengths and weaknesses, and develop relationships or arrangements that best capitalize on the strengths while minimizing the weaknesses. Finally, with the passage of time most of the legacies and disequilibria between equipment supplies and needs, fares and costs, and so forth, will be largely eliminated.

Adaptation to the new realities of deregulation was also greatly complicated in the early years by economic recession and sharply rising energy prices. The recessions and sharp increases in energy prices occurring between 1979 and 1982 created of course problems for virtually all industries. But these problems were perhaps more acute for intercity passenger travel in that the industry has always been somewhat more vulnerable to recessions than industry in general and also is relatively energy intensive in that a substantial percentage of total cost, particularly for the airlines, is for fuel.

The principal effect of deregulation has been to bring the workings of intercity passenger travel markets into alignment with those goals and premises that underlie the workings of the rest of the U.S. market economy. Specifically, for better or worse, consumers rule and their needs are to be served. By contrast, producer interests, whether they be labor or capital, are expected to adapt with those adapting best receiving appropriate rewards for their foresight and abilities.

That of course is the primitive law of the market. But the market, with all of its imperfections and problems, may nevertheless not be too bad an allocator of capital and director of economic development. Even professed social goals may be met as well by a market approach as by government controls and subsidies. Certainly in intercity passenger transportation—a sector with as much or more experience of government guidance as any in the U.S. economy—that seems to be the case.

Appendix A
Costs of the Various Intercity Modes

by José A. Gómez-Ibáñez

Common Costing Assumptions

The cost estimates for each mode incorporate common assumptions about the types of costs considered, the quality of service provided, and the characteristics of the travel markets.

Costs Considered

The principal costs are transportation operating expenses and capital outlays for right-of-way and vehicles. Operating expenses include the costs of fuel, crews, passenger reservations and marketing, maintenance of vehicles and right-of-way, and general administrative functions. Capital expenses for right-of-way include the costs of any land, roadbed, and other structures required. Capital expenditures for durable equipment or facilities, such as vehicles and right-of-way, are amortized over the relevant expected lifetimes using a 10 percent discount rate. All costs are reported in 1980 dollars and the relative prices of all inputs, including energy, are assumed to hold constant at 1980 levels.

Environmental costs of intercity transportation, such as air and noise pollution, are not included, largely because consistent estimates of these costs are not readily available for all modes. Inclusion of environmental costs would probably not affect the estimated costs of the modes greatly, since they appear to be relatively small compared to operating, right-of-way, and equipment expenses. For example, the private aûtomobile is widely regarded as the most environmentally offensive of the intercity modes, but careful estimates suggest that the inclusion of environmental damages would increase the costs associated with intercity automobile travel by only 5 percent or so.[1]

For the public modes (air, bus, and rail), the typical intercity trip can be divided into three distinct segments: travel from the passenger's origin to the intercity terminal, line-haul travel between intercity terminals, and travel from the second terminal to the ultimate destination. The cost estimates are generally for the line-haul segment only. The costs of access to and from intercity terminals are considered, though, in some of the simulations reported in chapter 11.

Quality of Service

Whenever practical, a similar quality of service is assumed on each mode so that the cost estimates are for nearly comparable services. The costs of on-board food and beverage service on airlines and railroads are excluded, for example, since this service is not provided in buses or automobiles.[2]

The estimates also assume that each public mode offers a minimum of three round trips per day between a pair of cities, regardless of the number of passengers carried, so that the frequencies and convenience of the schedules are similar. Even with this assumption, however, some modes still offer more convenient schedules than others. Travelers using a private automobile are often not constrained by a fixed schedule, for example, and can depart at a time convenient to them. Buses also often offer more frequent service than either airlines or trains since the smaller seating capacity of a bus permits more frequent departures when carrying comparable passenger volumes.

The ratio of passengers to seats, or the load factor, is constrained to be 65 percent on all modes so that the availability of a seat on short notice is approximately the same. Load factors on buses, trains, and airplanes in the 1970s typically averaged between 50 and 60 percent; unexpected fluctuations in travel demand and the peaking of demand at certain hours of the day, days of the week, or seasons make it difficult for transportation managers to achieve higher average load factors without turning away many travelers. The private automobile is also assumed to be 65 percent full, or an average of 2.6 persons in a four-passenger vehicle, which is not too far from the actual average of 2.34 passengers per auto in intercity travel.[3] Cost comparisons for automobiles carrying a single passenger and larger groups are also provided.

Average speeds and travel times vary considerably among the modes, particularly on longer-distance trips where air and high-speed rail services have a substantial advantage over conventional rail, bus, and auto. The fact that many long-distance travelers select higher-priced air service over other modes suggests that they value time savings. To test these advantages, a few of the cost comparisons include an estimate of the value passengers place on the time they spend traveling. In chapter 11 the relative travel times are also used together with operating and capital cost estimates to predict the future market shares for different modes.

Intercity Markets

The average cost per passenger mile on most modes is likely to decline, all else equal, with longer distances or increasing volumes of passengers. The costs of terminal operations—such as stations, passenger ticketing and reservations, and turnaround time for crews and vehicles—can be spread over more mileage as the length of haul increases. Similarly, requirements for right-of-way, vehicles, and other inputs may not increase proportionately with higher passenger volumes. These "scale" or "length-of-haul" effects may not be observable or very pronounced in practice, however, because of important offsets; for example, the complexity of terminal operations and baggage handling typically increases with length of haul, and achieving a specified load factor is obviously more difficult, all else equal, with a larger vehicle.

To test these effects on the relative costs of the modes, cost estimates were developed for lengths of haul ranging between 50 and 2,000 miles (one way) and for traffic volumes of between 10 thousand and 10 million trips per year in each direction between a pair of cities. Intercity travel volumes close to 10 million persons are observed only between very large cities that are relatively close to one another, such as New York–Washington, New York–Boston, or Los Angeles–San Diego. Even between such city-pairs, however, the traffic volumes are typically divided among several intercity modes so that no single mode carries more than a few million passengers per year.

On any mode the line-haul distance between a given city-pair is longer than the direct or geographic distance because of circuitous routings to avoid difficult terrain, congested cities, or other obstacles. As table A.1

Table A.1 Comparison of distances between selected city-pairs by train, highway, and airline, 1960

City-pairs	Distance in miles			
	Geographic distance[a]	Train route[b]	Highway route[b]	Air route[c]
Chicago–Oakland	1,850	2,390	2,136	1,917
Chicago–Los Angeles	1,745	2,240	2,054	1,810
Chicago–Miami	1,188	1,597	1,329	1,242
New York–Chicago	713	906	802	757
Chicago–New Orleans	833	923	912	880
Chicago–Dallas	803	987	917	849
Chicago–Houston	940	1,333	1,067	989
Dallas–Houston	225	346	243	260
Cincinnati–Chicago	252	299	287	287
New York–Washington	205	225	233	239
New York–Buffalo	292	439	372	328

a. U.S. Department of Commerce, *Air-Line Distances between Cities in the United States* (Washington: Government Printing Office, 1947).
b. William D. Warren, "Changes in American Intercity Rail Transportation: 1950–1980," *Transportation Quarterly* 36 (January 1982), pp. 148, 149, 155.
c. Airline distances were calculated using a formula of 1.02 times the geographic distance plus 30 miles.

illustrates, for all but the closest city-pairs train routes currently are the most circuitous, highway routes somewhat more direct, and air routes the most direct. Trains are more circuitous than highways, not only because they have more difficulty negotiating grades but also because of the current practice of routing long-distance trains (e.g., the Chicago–Los Angeles train) through other larger cities close to the direct route (e.g., Denver) in order to increase rail patronage.[4]

The cost estimates assume that the line-haul highway route between a given city-pair is 15 percent longer than the geographic distance, approximately the current situation today. The assumed relationship between air routes and geographic distances is slightly more complicated, because of the need to allow for maneuvering after takeoff and before landing as well as circuity added by en route navigation controls.[5] Generally, however, airline distances are similar to, or slightly longer than, highway routes for very close city-pairs but are substantially shorter than highways for long-distance travel. Train routes are assumed to be the same distance as highway routes to account for the possibility that future rail system improvements may reduce intermediate stops and indirect routings, although this assumption probably favors the rail mode unduly.

The cost estimates for only the line-haul portion of a passenger's journey probably understate the advantages of the automobile. Motorists often have relatively easy access to high-performance intercity highways throughout a metropolitan area, whereas the users of public carriers will usually have a trip of significant time and cost from their true origin point to the intercity terminal. The bias is probably not large, however, since buses and trains can sometimes stop to pick up or discharge passengers at one or two satellite terminals without greatly degrading line-haul travel times, thereby reducing access costs. Between city-pairs with high traffic volumes, moreover, direct air or bus service is sometimes offered from several terminals in the same metropolitan area, although at the cost of reducing the frequency available at any given terminal.

Costs for Individual Modes

Costs of Conventional Rail Passenger Service

Amtrak's estimates of its operating costs under early 1980s operating conditions are summarized in table A.2.[6] These include Amtrak's estimates of its short- and long-term avoidable costs (except those for on-board passenger service labor and supplies) plus part of the costs Amtrak regards as fixed (excluding depreciation and interest expenses). Some fixed costs are

Table A.2 Full operating costs for conventional rail passenger service, 1980 dollars

Cost element	Assumed to vary as a function of	Unit cost[a] Two self-propelled cars	Three-car Amfleet	Six-car Amfleet
Seating capacity		128	228	456
Short-term avoidable costs[b]				
Train and engine crew	Train miles	$4.26	$4.26	$4.26
Fuel and power	Train miles	1.31	0.93	1.43
Part of switching and dispatching	Train miles	1.91	2.34	2.34
Part of stations and marketing	Passengers	2.66[b]	2.66[b]	2.66[b]
Part of maintenance of locomotives, cars, and way	Train miles	2.90	3.12	4.23
Part of general support	Train miles	0.19	0.27	0.31
Long-term avoidable costs[c]	Train miles	2.28	2.35	2.71
	Passengers	0.57	0.57	.57
"Fixed" costs (excluding depreciation)[d]	Train miles	4.17	4.31	4.96
	Passengers	1.05	1.05	1.05
Total operating costs	Per train mile	17.02	17.58	20.24
	Per passenger	4.28	4.28	4.28

a. Derived from simulations supplied by Amtrak. Three different train configurations are evaluated: two diesel self-propelled cars operating as a train, a diesel locomotive pulling three standard Amfleet passenger coaches, and a locomotive pulling six standard Amfleet coaches. Labor and supplies for on-board passenger service are excluded. Short-term avoidable costs were allocated on a train mile or per passenger basis by examining how the individual cost elements varied in simulations supplied by Amtrak for routes with different lengths of haul and train frequencies.
b. Average of four Amtrak-supplied simulations.
c. Amtrak's simulation model estimates only the short-term avoidable costs in detail. Amtrak then assumes that long-term avoidable costs are 21.55 percent of short-term avoidable costs on the typical route.
d. Estimated as 39.47 percent of short-term avoidable costs. Short-term plus long-term avoidable costs accounted for 70.33 percent of off-Northeast Corridor total expenses in 1980. Depreciation accounted for 5.2 percent of Amtrak's total costs. Fixed costs (excluding depreciation) are estimated at 24.47 percent of total costs, or 39.47 percent of short-term avoidable costs.

included because most of these expenses—such as heavy repairs to locomotives, mainline switching and dispatching, and corporate overhead—seem ultimately a function of the number of routes and trains operated.[7]

Capital costs for rail passenger cars and locomotives are calculated using Amtrak's estimates of the numbers of locomotives and cars needed for different lengths of haul, frequencies, and trains and amortizing the initial purchase prices of these vehicles over their expected lifetimes.[8] The capital costs for right-of-way are based on early 1980s estimates prepared by Amtrak and the U.S. Department of Transportation of the incremental investments required to upgrade existing rail facilities to accommodate rail passenger service on 12 proposed additional routes. The expenditures include improvements in track, ties, grading, ballast, and signals to accommodate a 79 mph top speed and added signals, passing tracks, or sidings to reduce the interference and congestion that would otherwise be imposed on existing freight service. These incremental expenditures probably represent a lower bound for rail passenger right-of-way costs, since the current right-of-way is in good condition and underutilized on many of the routes for which the Amtrak/DOT analysis of incremental expenditures was based.[9]

Estimates of what costs might be if Amtrak could rationalize its operations are shown in table A.3. These "deregulated" cost estimates assume that if rail passenger service were operated along the lines of a small, efficient bus company or airline, it would be possible to achieve significant improvements in labor productivity, a large decrease in general overhead expenses, and higher utilization of locomotives and passenger cars. On net, especially at low passenger volumes, the potential deregulated costs average around 25 percent lower than full or conventional rail costs.

Rail costs per passenger mile are strongly affected by passenger volumes. The costs of rail right-of-way are substantial, and rail costs become reasonable only when right-of-way costs can be spread over high passenger volumes. Rail costs per passenger mile also fall with high volumes because daily utilization of rolling stock increases slightly, the extent depending on the scheduled frequency. For example, assuming a frequency of three trains per day in each direction, costs per passenger mile fall sharply with increasing passenger volumes and do not begin to level out until traffic reaches well over 200,000 passengers per year; this is more than four times higher than the traffic volume at which bus costs level out. If a minimum of only two trains per day is required, costs decline slightly more rapidly and level out at lower passenger volumes.

The optimal size of the train also depends strongly on passenger volumes

Table A.3 "Deregulated" operating costs for conventional rail passenger service, 1980 dollars

Cost element	Assumed to vary as a function of	Unit cost[a] Two self-propelled cars	Three-car Amfleet	Six-car Amfleet
Seating capacity		128	228	456
Short-term avoidable costs[a]				
Train and engine crew	Train miles	$1.29	$1.29	$1.72
Fuel and power	Train miles	1.31	0.93	1.43
Part of switching and dispatching	Train miles	1.91	2.34	2.34
Part of stations and marketing	Passengers	2.66[b]	2.66[b]	2.66[b]
Part of maintenance of locomotives, cars, and way	Train miles	2.90	3.12	4.23
Part of general support	Train miles	0.19	0.27	0.31
Long-term avoidable costs[c]	Train miles	1.64	1.71	2.16
	Passengers	0.57	0.57	0.57
"Fixed" costs (excluding depreciation)[d]	Train miles	2.09	2.16	2.48
	Passengers	0.53	0.53	0.53
Total operating costs	Train miles	11.33	11.82	14.67
	Passengers	3.76	3.76	3.76

a. Derived from simulations supplied by Amtrak. Three different train configurations are evaluated: two diesel self-propelled cars operating as a train, a diesel locomotive pulling three standard Amfleet passenger coaches, and a locomotive pulling six standard Amfleet coaches. Labor and supplies for on-board passenger service are excluded. Short-term avoidable costs were allocated on a train mile or per passenger basis by examining how the individual cost elements varied in simulations supplied by Amtrak for routes with different lengths of haul and train frequencies.

b. Average of four Amtrak-supplied simulations.

c. Estimated as 21.55 percent of short-term avoidable costs. According to Amtrak long-term avoidable costs are 21.55 percent of short-term avoidable costs on the typical route.

d. Assumed as 50 percent of fixed costs associated with current full costs.

and to a lesser degree on the minimum train frequency. For example, with a minimum of three trains per day the two-car train has the lowest cost for volumes below approximately 100,000 to 125,000 passengers per year, whereas a three-car train has least costs between approximately 125,000 and 200,000 passengers, and a six-car train for volumes in excess of around 200,000 passengers. If a minimum of two trains per day is required instead of three, larger trains become cost-competitive at slightly lower passenger volumes.

Rail costs also decline with length of haul because passenger ticketing, reservations, and station expenses are spread out over more mileage and because train utilization is improved with longer distances. But beyond 300 miles the economies of longer distances are relatively minor.

Even using the optimal size train and assuming relatively high traffic densities, however, conventional rail costs are usually substantially higher than bus and auto costs (estimates of which are presented later in this appendix). At one million passengers per year and a 200-mile geographic distance between cities, for example, full rail costs are 12.8 cents per passenger mile, and potential rationalized costs are 10.0 cents per passenger mile, both of which are above ordinary bus or low-cost airline operations at about 8 cents per passenger mile.

Costs of High-Speed Rail Service

The cost of high-speed rail depends heavily on whether existing rail right-of-way can be easily adapted to high-speed service. If a completely new rail right-of-way has to be built, as was the case of the Japanese bullet train, or Shinkansen, then the cost can average at least $20 to $40 million per mile, with the higher average for lines that pass through hilly terrain or dense urban areas.[10] If an existing rail right-of-way is available that is redundant, or can be otherwise released from freight service, and has sufficiently gentle grades, broad curves, and few at-grade crossings so as to allow easy adaptation to high-speed service, then the cost of constructing the right-of-way might be as low as $5 million per mile. Costs in that range were enjoyed by the French when they upgraded sections of their Paris to Lyon line for 170 mph service in relatively flat and sparsely populated rural areas and by the U.S. government when it upgraded selected sections of the Washington–New York corridor to 120 mph service.[11] There are probably very few corridors in the United States that have redundant rail track of sufficient quality to permit a low-cost upgrading to high-speed service, however, and most proposals for high-speed service between U.S. city-pairs call for entirely new rights-of-way.[12]

Cost estimates were developed in the early 1980s for a proposed 140 mph service over a 130-mile route between Los Angeles and San Diego using the Japanese Shinkansen technology. The Los Angeles–San Diego proposal calls for a right-of-way built on concrete piers in the median strip of an existing interstate highway with a maximum capacity of approximately 80 trains per day in each direction. Construction costs for the right-of-way were estimated by the project's backers at around $18 million per route mile, substantially lower than the reported costs of the new Shinkansen extensions then under construction in Japan.[13] Trains with 500 seats of capacity were estimated to have an initial cost of $9 million per train.

According to Amtrak, one of the potential participants in the proposed service, costs for power, crew wages, and equipment maintenance would amount to only $7.00 per train mile, far lower than comparable costs for smaller (though slower) conventional trains. All other operating expenses, including maintenance of way, station, and passenger reservations, would average $400,000 per route mile per year assuming 80 trains per day and load factors of 50 to 60 percent.[14]

Since these costs (as supplied by proponents of the Los Angeles–San Diego line) are probably understated, no additional economies seem probable for high-speed rail in a deregulated environment.[15] High-speed rail costs per passenger mile are more strongly affected by traffic density than conventional rail service because of the extraordinarily high costs of right-of-way, but much less affected by length of haul. For a 200-mile trip, for example, full costs for high-speed rail average around 53 cents per passenger mile when only 1 million passengers are carried each year but fall to 13 cents with 10 million passengers, costs close to existing conventional rail service but still well above the costs of a rationalized conventional service. Perhaps even more significant, 13 cents is about equal to conventional airline operations and about 50 percent higher than low-cost (e.g., new entrant) airline operations or ordinary bus services.

Bus Costs

Bus expenses can be divided into three categories: those that are a function primarily of the number of bus miles operated, those that are a function of the number of passengers carried, and those that vary according to the number of vehicles owned. Most expenses can be assumed to vary with mileage, including fuel, drivers' wages and fringes, maintenance, insurance, administrative overhead, taxes, and highway capacity costs. Station expenses and ticket commissions seem to be primarily a function of the

Table A.4 Costs of intercity bus service, 1980 dollars

	User-paid costs	Full costs	Potential deregulated costs
Costs that vary with bus mileage (in dollars per bus-mile)			
Fuel	$0.15	$0.15	$0.15
Driver's wages	0.39	0.39	0.25
Driver's fringes	0.11	0.11	0.07
Maintenance and tires	0.22	0.22	0.20
General and administrative	0.21	0.21	0.10
Insurance	0.06	0.06	0.06
Social Security taxes	0.06	0.06	0.06
Highway user taxes	0.04	—	—
Highway system capacity costs (rural-urban)	—	0.09–0.43	0.09–0.43
Subtotal	$1.24	$1.29–1.63	$0.98–1.32
Average for line-haul[a]	$1.24	$1.32	$1.01
Costs that vary with passengers carried (in dollars per passenger)			
Stations and commissions	$2.01	$2.01	$2.01
Costs that vary with buses owned (in dollars per bus year)			
Vehicle capital costs	$150,000	$150,000	$150,000
Maximum hours of bus utilization per day[b]	12	12	12
Average line-haul speed	45 mph	45 mph	45 mph

a. In calculating average line-haul bus costs, 10 percent of all mileage is assumed to take place on congested roads and 90 percent on uncongested facilities.
b. This includes turnaround time for vehicles but excludes vehicles used as maintenance spares. Maintenance spares are assumed to be an additional 10 percent of the fleet needed for operations.

number of passengers carried rather than mileage, whereas the capital costs and depreciation for buses vary according to the number of buses operated.

Estimates of bus costs are summarized in table A.4. The "user-paid" costs shown in the left-hand column represent the status quo or established practice and are based primarily on the average 1980 expenses of Class I motor bus carriers as reported by the Interstate Commerce Commission.[16] The full costs, in the middle column, differ from user-paid costs only in that highway user taxes are replaced by estimates of the actual highway system capacity costs due to congestion, pavement damage, and administrative expense of accommodating additional buses on the existing highway system.[17] As the broad range of these capacity costs suggests, bus highway capacity costs are substantially greater on highly congested urban highways than on less congested rural roads.

The potential deregulated cost estimates reported in the final column are based on actual reported expenses for several low-cost and very small (200 or fewer buses) carriers in 1980.[18] The major difference between these carriers and their Class I counterparts is that labor wage and fringe costs are about one-third lower per vehicle mile, probably due to a combination of lower wage rates and higher labor productivity. General and administrative expenses are also smaller and the low-cost carriers are able to use their vehicles about 10 to 15 percent more intensively. Suggestively, the differences in costs and productivity between the present Class I and low-cost motor carriers are similar to those between the old guard airlines and the new entrants (as reported in chapter 5).

Typical bus costs per passenger mile drop quickly as traffic volumes increase, but beyond 40,000 passengers per year (or about 110 per day) there are few additional economies of volume. At these volumes user-paid costs on buses average only 5.4 cents per passenger mile, whereas current full costs are only slightly higher (5.6 cents) and potential deregulated costs about 17 percent lower (4.6 cents). At these levels the bus is also cost-competitive with almost any mode, even the private automobile (depending on the level of auto occupancy and whether vehicle ownership costs are included); indeed, such costs put the bus at roughly one-half the level of the other public modes, rail and air.

Automobile Costs

Illustrative estimates of operating costs for a 1980 four-passenger compact car with an average highway fuel economy of 28 mpg are shown in table A.5. If the automobile is assumed to be owned primarily for commuting and other intracity trips, user-paid costs for intercity trips (at the margin) amount to 10.06 cents per vehicle mile and include only operating costs such as fuel (assumed to be $1.07 per gallon), oil, maintenance, tires, depreciation related to use (rather than time), and highway user taxes. If however, the car is owned primarily for intercity travel, such as a traveling sales representative's car, then the user-paid costs would include an additional 11.1 cents per vehicle mile in expenses associated with vehicle ownership, such as insurance, personal property taxes, registration fees, and depreciation related to time (rather than use).[19]

The full cost estimates exclude highway user taxes but include estimates of the costs of providing highway capacity to accommodate additional intercity automobile travel.[20] The specific highway capacity cost estimates in table A.5 are based on a 1982 government report of the costs of accommodating additional traffic.[21] On relatively uncongested rural high-

Table A.5 Costs of using a compact automobile for an intercity trip, 1980 (cents per vehicle mile)

	User-paid costs	Full costs (and potential deregulated costs)
Costs, excluding vehicle ownership		
Fuel (excludes taxes)[a]	3.82	3.82
Oil (excludes taxes)[b]	0.13	0.13
Scheduled maintenance[b]	1.51	1.51
Unscheduled maintenance[b]	3.10	3.10
Tires[b]	0.52	0.52
Depreciation with use (and not age)[c]	0.50	0.50
Highway user taxes (taxes on gasoline, oil, and tires only)[b]	0.48	—
Highway system capacity costs (rural-urban)[d]	—	0.60–11.90
Subtotal	10.06	10.18–21.48
Vehicle ownership costs		
Depreciation with time	7.70	7.70
Insurance and property tax	2.40	2.40
Subtotal	11.10	11.10
Average costs in line-haul uses[e]		
Without ownership	10.06	11.31
With ownership	21.17	22.41
Assumed average speed		
Intercity line haul	50 mph	50 mph
Urban access	30 mph	30 mph

a. Assumes 28 mpg and $1.07 per gallon of fuel.
b. These cost elements are based on government estimates for a 1979 compact car updated to 1980 using the relevant consumer price indexes; see U.S. Federal Highway Administration, Office of Highway Planning, *Costs of Owning and Operating Automobiles and Vans, 1979* (Washington: Federal Highway Administration, 1980).
c. Depreciation related to use was estimated by examining the decline in average used car prices with increased mileage for cars of the same age as reported in *Edmund's 1982 Used Car Prices.*
d. U.S. Department of Transportation, Final Report of the *Highway Cost Allocation Study* (Washington: Government Printing Office, 1982), app. E.
e. All access mileage is assumed to take place on congested urban highways at a full cost of 21.48 to 32.58 cents per vehicle mile, depending on whether ownership costs are included. Ten percent of line-haul intercity auto mileage is assumed to be on congested urban highways and the balance on rural highways.

ways these capacity costs are only 0.6 cents per vehicle mile so that user costs and full costs are little different. By contrast, on congested urban highways these capacity costs are estimated to average as much as 11.90 cents per vehicle mile so that full auto costs become substantially greater than user-paid costs.

When expressed in cents per passenger mile of travel, automobile line-haul costs depend strongly on the average passenger load as well as whether vehicle ownership costs are included.[22] At a 65 percent load factor (2.6 persons) automobile costs are around 4 to 5 cents per passenger mile, excluding ownership expenses and 9 to 10 cents including ownership.[23] If only one person is traveling in the automobile, however, costs per passenger are 160 percent higher (10 to 13 cents per passenger mile), and if four persons are traveling, they are 34 percent lower (2.6 to 3.25 cents per passenger mile). Obviously the competitiveness of the automobile with other modes depends on trip purpose. For the occasional family outing, where the car is owned for other purposes, the automobile's costs are almost unbeatable. On the other hand, an automobile used only for business trips involving one person can be relatively expensive. The popularity of the car for personal trips and of the public modes for business trips thus seems quite rational.

Air

All air costs assume a low-cost, high-efficiency operating philosophy similar to that of the new entrant airlines. A wide range of propeller and jet aircraft are evaluated in order to identify the least-cost aircraft sizes and technologies for different market densities and lengths of haul.

Cost estimates, summarized in tables A.6 and A.7, are based upon a variety of sources, including typical operating expenses by low-cost commuter and new entrant airlines as reported to the Civil Aeronautics Board, maintenance costs provided by the aircraft manufacturers and operators, and engineering data from aircraft performance charts. Fuel, crew, and miscellaneous operating expenses are assumed to vary with the number of block hours, which are hours spent taxiing to and from the gate, taking off, landing, and flying. Maintenance costs are charged to a combination of flight hours and departures, and aircraft servicing costs are charged according to departures. Promotion, sales, and station costs are charged per passenger. Capital costs for aircraft are amortized over useful lives appropriate to the individual models.

As with other modes, user-paid costs differ from full costs in that user-

Table A.6 Costs for propeller aircraft, 1980

	Chieftain, 1 pilot	Chieftain, 2 pilots	Metro IIA	Shorts SD-330-220	DHC-7
Seats	9	8	19	30	50
Operating costs[a]					
Crew and miscellaneous ($/block hour)	21.25	34.25	41.26	49.80	76.80
Fuel, less tax ($/block hour)[b]	32.99	32.99	107.14	129.04	242.32
Maintenance, part ($/flight hour)	31.33[c]	31.33[c]	43.27	59.62	69.83
Maintenance, part ($/departure)	0	0	47.80	61.26	100.28
Aircraft servicing and station ($/departure)	21.09	19.28	45.79	72.30	120.50
Promotion and sales ($/passenger)	2.50	2.50	2.50	2.50	2.50
General and administrative ($/seat mile)	0.0039	0.0039	0.0039	0.0039	0.0039
Capital costs for aircraft[d]					
($/airplane year)	65,992	65,992	225,324	367,858	884,964
User taxes and fees[e]					
Landing fees ($/departure)	1.95	1.95	3.90	6.60	11.70
Domestic passenger tax	8%	8%	8%	8%	8%
Aircraft registration ($/airplane year)	165.00	165.00	463.00	795.00	1,530.00
Airport and airway system costs[e]					
Locally financed airport ($/departure)	1.95	1.95	3.90	6.60	11.70
Federally financed airport ($/departure)	15.36	15.36	15.36	15.36	15.36
Federally financed terminal control ($/flight hour)	35.99	35.99	35.99	35.99	35.99
Federally financed enroute control ($/flight hour)	29.46	29.46	29.46	29.46	29.46

a. Derived by the authors from operating data supplied by airplane manufacturers.
b. Block fuel consumption for a typical 200-mile trip, derived from aircraft performance data. Fuel cost is set at typical 1980 values of $0.18 per pound (of aviation gas) and $0.16 per pound (jet fuel).
c. In $/block hour.
d. Assumes 7-year life for Chieftain and 10-year life for all other propeller aircraft. Aircraft are assumed to be available for a maximum of 16 hours per day (including turn around and block time). Minimum turn around time is assumed to be 0.25 hours. One spare aircraft is required for every 10 in service.
e. For sources, see note 24 to appendix A.

Table A.7 Costs for jet aircraft, 1980

	DC-9-30 (new)	DC-9-30 (used)	DC-9-80	DC-10-10
Seats	115	115	155	380
Operating costs[a]				
Crew and miscellaneous ($/block hour)	117.40	117.40	125.20	187.57
Fuel, less tax ($/block hour)	797.40	797.40	922.20	2,454.00
Maintenance, parts ($/flight hour)	97.40	97.40	121.74	387.35
Maintenance, parts ($/departure)	143.92	143.92	183.66	692.21
Aircraft servicing ($/departure)	277.15	277.15	373.55	915.80
Promotion and sales ($/passenger)	2.50	2.50	2.50	2.50
General and administrative ($/seat mile)	0.0039	0.0039	0.0039	0.0039
Capital costs for aircraft ($/airplane year)[b]	1,546,740	853,176	2,556,984	4,766,748
User taxes and fees[c]				
Landing fees ($/departure)	25.20	25.20	35.10	99.00
Domestic passenger tax (% of total costs)	8	8	8	8
Aircraft registration ($/airplane year)	4,260.00	4,260.00	5,415.00	15,950.00
Airport and airway system costs[c]				
Locally financed airport ($/departure)	25.20	25.20	35.10	99.00
Federally financed airport ($/departure)	30.71	30.71	30.71	30.71
Federally financed terminal control ($/departure)	35.99	35.99	35.99	35.99
Enroute control ($/flight hour)	58.91	58.91	58.91	58.91

a. Derived by the authors from operating data supplied by airplane manufacturers.
b. Assumes 7-year life for used DC-9-30 and a 12-year life for all other jet aircraft. DC-10-10 is assumed to be available for a maximum of 18.5 hours per day; all other aircraft are assumed to be available for a maximum of 16 hours per day (including turnaround and block time). Minimum turnaround is 0.5 hours for a DC-10-10 and 0.33 hours for all other jet aircraft. One spare is required for every 10 aircraft in service.
c. For source see note 24 of appendix A.

paid costs include the actual landing fees and fuel and ticket taxes paid by airlines and passengers to defray the costs of the airport and airway system, whereas full costs include approximate estimates of the actual costs of these systems. For federally financed airport development grants and FAA-operated terminal and enroute control systems, the actual system costs are based on studies that allocate federal airport and air traffic control outlays among different types of aviation users.[24] Since estimates of locally financed airport expenditures were not readily available, these expenditures were assumed to be approximately recovered through landing fees and station rentals, even though there are reasons for believing that airline passengers flying mainly between large airports probably should be assessed less and those using smaller airports extensively should be charged more.

Air costs decline with traffic volumes, but much less so than do rail costs. Airlines have fewer "right-of-way" expenses that must be spread over traffic volumes.[25] Airlines may also have a slight advantage over rail in that there is a somewhat greater variety of plane sizes and technologies (e.g., propeller vs. jet) from which to select for markets of different traffic density. Costs decline sharply with volume if only jets are considered, but if propeller aircraft can be substituted for jets at low traffic volumes, costs are far less affected by traffic volume.

However, air costs do decline more sharply with length of haul than do railroad costs. In a typical situation (250,000 passengers per year and full costs), average costs per passenger mile will decline from 35 cents to about 10 cents as the length of haul increases from 100 to 400 miles.

Comparative Costs of the Modes

Cost comparisons are made under three different sets of assumptions about government policies with regard to what costs travelers are required to pay and the degree of government regulation. The first of these would be that travelers pay the full costs of travel but that only the airlines are deregulated; a second would be that existing subsidy and regulatory practice as of 1980 is continued; third are the costs that should result from a comprehensive deregulation and rationalization of surface passenger transportation following, say, the precedent of airline deregulation.

Full Cost Comparisons

When the full costs of air, rail, bus, and automobile transportation are considered, the two highway modes, bus and auto, are generally the cheapest, and rail is usually the most expensive, with airlines somewhere in between (exactly where depending mainly on length of haul). Rail can be cost-competitive with at least air, however, in very short-haul, high-volume markets. In this type of market, though, both rail and air are roughly three times as costly as bus or auto. In long-haul, high-volume markets air travel costs decline to levels that are just above the bus and auto, while the full cost of passenger rail service remains far above. In low-volume markets air transportation is roughly twice the full cost of bus or auto, while the rail mode is, in turn, twice the cost of air.

The Effects of Density

The relative costs of the four modes vary with the density of the passenger markets that they serve. The cost per passenger mile of rail and (to a lesser extent) air declines in higher-volume markets, as it becomes easier to fill the larger vehicles used by these modes, as these vehicles can be utilized for more hours per day, and as overhead expenses are spread more thinly. The full costs of the different modes for a 200 mile trip are graphed against market size in figure A.1. The bus and auto costs are flat and consistently well below both air and rail, in the 0.07 to 0.10 dollars per revenue passenger mile range. The lower end of the market size range on the graph is set at the very small travel volume of 50,000 one-way trips per year (or about 140 per day) which is a market that can normally be expected to support unsubsidized common carrier service using either buses or small

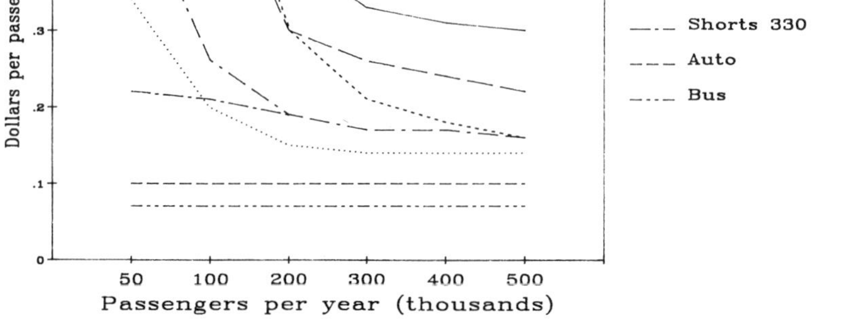

Figure A.1 Full costs for a 200-mile trip by conventional rail, air, bus, and auto.

propeller-driven aircraft. The upper end, a reasonably dense market of 500,000 one-way annual trips, is a volume that can easily support unsubsidized jet aircraft service. Trip distance, held constant in figure A.1 at 200 miles (geographic distance), is a relatively long haul compared with actual average trip lengths on intercity buses and propeller-driven aircraft. This distance is representative, however, of the lengths of some of the dense intercity corridors where rail service exists or is under consideration, whereas the typical jet aircraft trip is much longer than 200 miles.

At these medium distances of 200 miles or so, buses and automobiles are roughly cost competitive with each other in all market sizes, with the least expensive mode being determined by the size of the travel party and whether the cost of auto ownership enters into the traveler's mode choice for an intercity trip. Thus bus is always below auto in figure A.1 since full costs are considered and 2.6 passengers (a 65 percent load factor) is assumed for auto. Air transportation's cost is significantly greater than auto or bus, but conventional rail is even more expensive than air. The cost disadvantage of rail compared with air is especially pronounced in less dense markets.

Although not graphed, high-speed rail could become cost-competitive with air in extremely dense markets—for example, in markets where the rail mode's share is 10 million annual one-way passengers. At trip distances shorter than 200 miles, high-speed rail needs an even smaller passenger volume to cost less than air transportation.

Vehicle Size and Market Size

A perennially difficult problem in managing and planning resources for public carriers is matching vehicle or unit size with markets of different size. In general, the complexity of the problem increases, even disproportionately, with increases in the smallest basic efficient or effective unit of service; that is, indivisibilities in a carrier's technology complicate resource planning and scheduling. Specifically, standard Amfleet trains and narrow-body jet aircraft are unable to match efficiently the schedule convenience of buses and autos in thinly traveled markets, since the highway vehicles are smaller and consequently easier to fill.

The plots in figure A.1 illustrate the problem. Figure A.1 includes cost curves for three different types of conventional passenger trains, ranging in capacity from 128 for a two-car train to 456 seats for a six-car train (while still providing a minimum of three round trips per day). The least-cost curve for rail service is traced by the lower envelope of these three curves, showing efficiencies from matching train size to market size; for example, at volumes greater than 200,000 passengers per year, a six-car train is markedly superior to two- or three-car trains.

The aircraft types plotted in figure A.1 demonstrate that the envelope of airline passenger mile costs is relatively flat when aircraft size is matched to the size of the market. The 30-seat Shorts turboprop is able to operate efficiently in markets that are too small to be served by the DC-9-30 narrow-body jet, but the two aircraft have similar costs when each is operated in its own market niche.

The Effects of Distance

There are large changes in the relative costs of the modes when trip distances vary, as figure A.2 demonstrates. With a moderate volume of 250,000 passengers per year, passenger rail transportation is less costly than air at distances of less than 100 miles. But the cost of air travel declines below rail for trips of more than 100 miles, and by 500 miles aircraft are even cost-competitive with autos.

The shifts in the rankings of modes with trip distance result largely from the high terminal cost inherent in air transportation, which induces the sharp decline in the airline cost curve with trip distance. Terminal costs are higher for air than for the surface modes because of the large amounts of fuel and time that are required to get an aircraft up to cruising altitude and back down to the ground. Longer-hauls also facilitate somewhat higher utilization of aircraft by increasing average block speed and requiring fewer

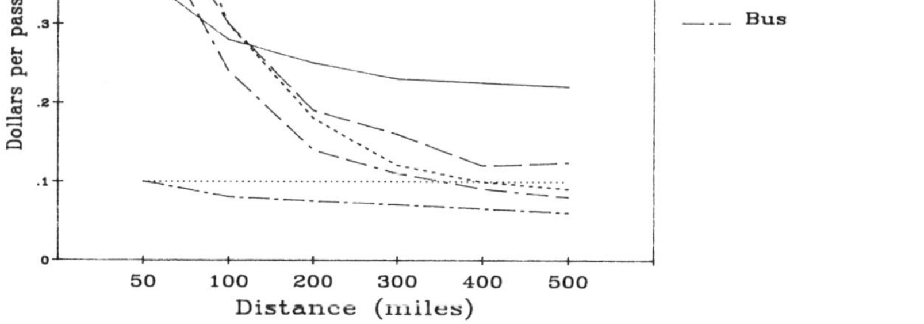

Figure A.2 Air, auto, bus, and rail full costs at 250,000 passengers per year.

unproductive turnarounds per day. The surface modes do not experience a similar increase in average speed with longer trip distances, nor must they overcome gravity in the departure portions of their trips. The small declines in cost per passenger mile that are obtained by buses and trains on longer hauls are derived primarily from improved vehicle utilization and only secondarily from spreading terminal expenses over longer distances.

Figure A.2 also indicates that, holding the passenger volume constant at 250,000 annual one-way trips, the decline of costs with distance for a turboprop Dash-7 is very similar to that for a much larger DC-9-30 jet. Both aircraft types exhibit much the same relationship between terminal and line-haul expenses. Thus the relatively flat envelope for airline costs over varying market sizes (shown for a 200-mile trip length in figure A.1) remains essentially flat for other trip distances as well.

The Effects of Travel Time

One of the most important quality differences between the modes is the time required to make a trip. These differences can be taken into account by attributing a dollar value to the traveler's time and adding a charge for time to the fully allocated operating cost of the mode. Cost curves for rail, air, bus, and auto are plotted in figure A.3 with travel time valued at $10.00 per hour.

The $10 per hour figure for the value of travel time is slightly lower than the average hourly wage of a typical air traveler and slightly higher than the

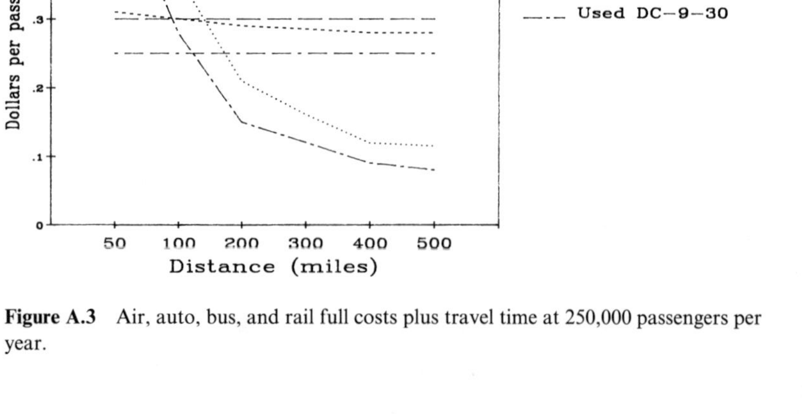

Figure A.3 Air, auto, bus, and rail full costs plus travel time at 250,000 passengers per year.

typical average wage of a bus traveler. Most studies show that intercity business travelers value travel time savings at about their wage rate, whereas intercity leisure travelers value travel time savings at below their wage rate.[26] The $10 figure is thus probably a reasonable approximation for air travelers, assuming a mix of business and leisure travel, but high for bus travelers. A lower value of time, more consonant with the earnings of bus passengers, would show a less extreme effect on the modes' relative costs.

Lacking any marked speed advantage over alternative surface transportation options, conventional rail is never the least costly mode, even when the value of travel time is taken into account. However, with travel time costs incorporated, air becomes the least costly mode at trip distances greater than 100 or 175 miles, depending on the type of aircraft and on how the issue of automobile ownership costs is resolved. Auto and bus, the modes with the lowest operating costs, are shifted sharply upward when time costs are included due to their slow speed relative to aircraft.

Current User-Paid Costs

Figure A.4 displays cost curves for user-paid costs in 1980 (including user taxes, and excluding costs which are covered by federal subsidies out of general funds). When these costs are compared with the full costs for an identical market of 250,000 annual one-way passengers on each mode (figure A.2), it is apparent that the only significant effect of subsidy is on the

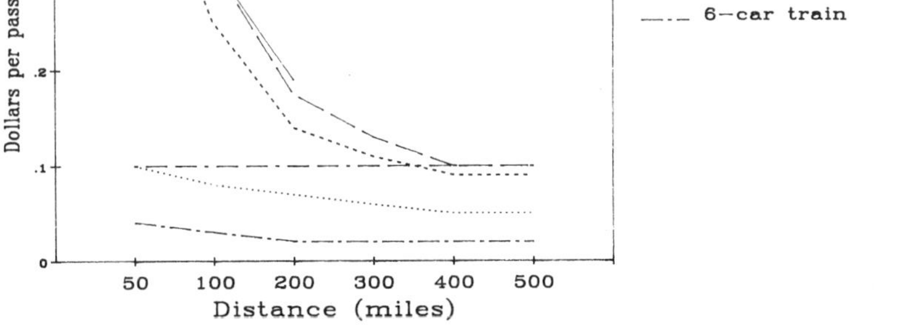

Figure A.4 Air, auto, rail, and bus user-paid costs at 250,000 passengers per year.

passenger rail mode. Current subsidies for passenger trains allow Amtrak to price below bus fares, even though the full costs of rail are much higher than those of the bus (figure A.2).[27]

Potential Deregulated Costs

Aside from the issue of passenger rail subsidies, deregulation should not result in any large shifts in rankings, distance, or market size breakpoints among the four modes. Cost curves estimated for a completely deregulated environment are shown in figure A.5 and may be compared with the modes' current full costs in figure A.2. In an identical market of 250,000 annual one-way passengers, deregulated (and unsubsidized) conventional rail can still undercut air costs on extremely short trips (due to potential cost economies of about 20 percent from rationalization), but in turn rail is also still substantially undercut by the cost advantages of deregulated bus and the automobile. Air transportation remains much less expensive than rail for trip distances above 150 miles. The cost of bus travel declines slightly, relative to the automobile, under favorable cost reduction assumptions about the long-term effects of bus deregulation. But overall, there are no large shifts in the mileage or market size breakpoints differentiating the modes' cost characteristics and advantages.

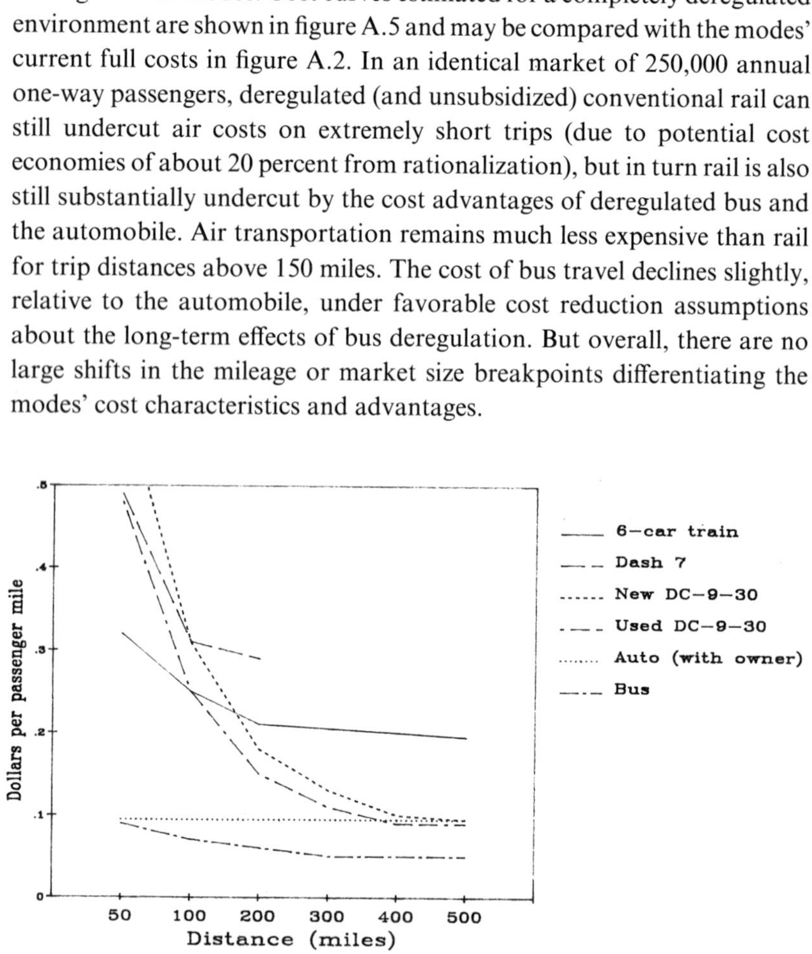

Figure A.5 Air, auto, bus, and rail potential deregulated costs at 250,000 passengers per year.

Conclusions

In summary, several key regularities of intercity passenger costs are largely unaffected by either the type of market considered or policies to subsidize or deregulate the modes. Automobiles and buses are the least-cost modes at many passenger volumes and distances, especially if the value of travel time is not included as one of the components of cost. Air travel is typically more expensive than either auto or bus, although it can be competitive at distances in excess of 500 miles and with moderate traffic volumes or if the value of travel time is included as a cost. Intercity rail service is almost always more costly than other modes, the only exceptions being when government subsidies to rail are subtracted from costs or when travel volumes are extraordinarily high and trip distances quite short.

Appendix B
Models of Intercity Travel Demand

by Don H. Pickrell

Two different types of econometric models of intercity travel demand were employed in these analyses. The first is a conventional regression analysis of the *total* demand for air travel *only*; this analysis was designed to separate the effects on total air travel of recession, fuel price increases, the PATCO strike, deregulation's fare and route freedoms, and so on. The second type of analysis is based on a *modal share* model aimed at predicting the different market shares the various modes might achieve under different circumstances, *given* a total volume of demand for *all* intercity travel. In short, the first type of model is concerned with estimating the potential scale of the market for one particular mode, airlines, whereas the other is concerned with how a specified total demand for all intercity travel might be divided among the different modes.

Air Travel Demand

Econometric models of the demand for air travel were estimated using quarterly data for the period 1970 through 1982.[1] With 1970 as the starting date, recessions that occurred prior to deregulation were included in the analysis, thus enabling the modeling and estimation process to better differentiate between the impacts of recession and deregulation. On the other hand, earlier periods were not included because they were not readily comparable to the late 1970s and early 1980s, mainly because of the dramatically different mix of aircraft in the carriers' fleets; prior to 1970 the airlines' domestic operations used virtually no wide-bodied aircraft (with the exception of a few B-747s) while wide-bodies became quite common in the 1970s.

The dependent variable was total U.S. domestic revenue passenger miles (including both scheduled and nonscheduled service).[2] Ten factors were used as independent or explanatory variables. These included measures of fares and airline route structures, as well as a range of macroeconomic and seasonal variables. Unfortunately no direct measures of service quality were included, as construction of systemwide quality measures is difficult. Moreover service quality measures are generally not exogenous and are thus likely to be collinear with the fare variables included in the model. This was particularly true during the regulated period, where administered prices induced frequency and other service rivalries.[3]

Total domestic revenue passenger miles was chosen as the dependent variable because it represented the most accurate overall demand measure for the entire period. Prior to deregulation some carriers used nonscheduled (primarily charter) service as a means of utilizing aircraft during periods of slack demand on their regular scheduled routes and as a means of targeting low fares at price-sensitive leisure travelers. Following deregulation, the airlines could accomplish the same goals by simply redeploying aircraft from charter to scheduled service and using capacity-controlled discount fares to stimulate travel. Consequently, if nonscheduled service were not included in the analysis, an observed increase in scheduled rpms following deregulation might be misinterpreted as totally new business in response to deregulation's fare and route freedoms rather than simply a transfer of passengers from nonscheduled to scheduled service. For the major carriers, nonscheduled RPMs are quite small compared to scheduled RPMs, so it is unlikely that this distinction is vital in practice.

Two functional forms of the RPM model were estimated. The results of a linear additive functional form are reported in table B.1. In addition a logarithmic (multiplicative) functional form was estimated. Both forms gave remarkably similar results, suggesting that the conclusions of the

Table B.1 Airline demand model

Dependent variable: domestic revenue passenger miles
Period: 1970:2 to 1982:3, quarterly

Independent variable	Coefficient	Standard error	*t*-Statistic
Constant	38,266,435.0	27,041,101.0	1.415
JACKCN	43,156,763.0	7,316,526.4	5.899
INCOME	24,136.3	18,199.8	1.326
GAS	147,987.0	114,647.8	1.291
QRTER2	3,364,869.0	320,158.7	10.510
QRTER3	7,592,691.3	494,315.0	15.360
QRTER4	287,847.2	339,411.9	0.848
FARE	−2,359,938.0	1,598,182.7	−1.477
DSCNT	− 82,914.4	91,102.6	−0.910
DISCNT JK	− 518,721.3	89,603.4	−5.789
PATCO	−5,025,209.1	1,616,052.5	−3.110
ROUTE	1,047,975.7	1,381,230.6	0.759
AR(1)[a]	0.9448	0.0571	16.536
R^2	0.9912		
Adjusted R^2	0.9883		
Standard error of regression	1,152,389		
Durbin-Watson statistic	2.131		
F-statistic	346.289		

a. Given the presence of autocorrelation in economic time-series data, the two-stage Cochran-Orcutt procedure was used to generate estimates of the first-order serial correlation coefficient. The model presented here is based on this generalized differencing transformation process.

analysis are not highly sensitive to functional form. A Cochrane-Orcutt procedure was used to correct for first-order serial correlation.[4]

Real (inflation-adjusted) disposable personal income (designated in the table as INCOME) was used to capture the effects of general economic conditions on airline travel.[5] As expected, the effect of income on revenue passenger miles is positive.

The real (inflation-adjusted) price of gasoline (designated in the table as GAS) was used to gauge the cost competitiveness of the private automobile, the principal alternative to intercity travel by air.[6] Under this interpretation an increase in the price of gasoline, all else equal, would be expected to increase travel by air. However, increased energy prices in the late 1970s and early 1980s had two separate effects on the amount of airline travel—on the one hand, decreasing airline travel through increasing airline costs while, on the other hand, stimulating a partially offsetting increase in airline travel by raising the price of gasoline and thus the cost of private auto. Rising prices of crude oil increased the cost of both jet fuel and gasoline in roughly the same manner, making it difficult for an econometric model to obtain reliable separate estimates of the two effects. Fortunately separating these effects is not critical for present purposes; because the concern is with the net effect of rising oil prices on airline travel and airline employment, it is sufficient to capture the combined effects of rising oil prices so as to guard against improper attribution to deregulation. It is the combined effect of the GAS and FARE variables (discussed later) that control for rising oil prices.

The next three independent variables listed in table B.1 (QRTER2, QRTER3, and QRTER4) are dummy variables for the second, third, and fourth quarters. These variables control for the distinct seasonality in airline output. The coefficients can be interpreted as the average difference in RPMs between the quarter in question and the first quarter, after controlling for the other explanatory effects incorporated into the model.

The next factor, the real (inflation-adjusted) standard airline fare per mile (designated as FARE), was calculated by applying the average passenger trip length to the CAB fare formula in effect during the quarter. Throughout the period 1970 to 1982 the CAB adjusted the standard fare formulas to reflect changes in airline costs; particularly frequent adjustments were made during the period of rapidly rising fuel costs beginning in mid-1979. Thus the standard fare per mile serves as a readily available index of inflation-adjusted costs of providing airline services. The CAB adjustments were based on changes in costs per available seat mile and therefore reflect both the increases in the price of fuel and the steps taken by the airlines to mitigate those price increases. As expected, the effect of this variable on RPMs is negative.

DISCNT represents the extent of discounting by the airlines below the standard fare, defined as the ratio of yield to standard fare.[7] Yield is the airline industry term for the actual average fare received per revenue passenger mile. Thus a negative relationship would be expected with RPMs; the greater the discounts, the lower the value of this variable, and the higher the amount of travel.

Deregulation allowed the carriers to make more extensive use of discount fares and to offer deeper discounts. With better targeting, the same amount of aggregate discounting should have had a larger impact on revenue passenger miles after deregulation. To allow for this possibility, jacknife regression techniques were used. A dummy variable was included for the period corresponding to fare deregulation (JACKCN) as a second constant, and a second fare discounting variable (DISCJK) was added; DISCJK is the product of the jacknife dummy variable (JACKCN) and the fare discount variable (DISCNT).[8] The effect is to allow different impacts of fare discounting before and after deregulation. For the purposes of this analysis, fare deregulation was considered to have begun in the first quarter of 1978. Although formal deregulation did not begin until the fourth quarter of 1978, the CAB had loosened its controls on the use of discount fares sufficiently through administrative action by the first quarter of 1978 to allow the airlines to begin targeting discount fares quite effectively.

The total effect of a level of discounting after deregulation is the sum of the DISCNT and DISCJK coefficients. The coefficient of the fare-discounting variable (DISCNT) is negative but small in magnitude and not statistically significant, indicating that before deregulation, what little discounting that did exist (night coach, military discounts, youth discounts, etc.) had little effect on airline traffic. The coefficient on the jacknife discounting variable (DISCJK) is much larger and highly significant statistically. With the targeting of discounts permitted under deregulation, the discounts were more effective at stimulating traffic. In addition, of course, the discounting was more widespread and the discounts were deeper after deregulation.

The PATCO variable measures the degree to which the air traffic controllers' strike restricted flight availability and capacity at the nation's 22 major airports (taken as a whole and as reported by the FAA). Structured somewhat like a dummy variable, the variable takes on a value of zero from 1970:1 through 1981:2, then assumes a value of 0.62 in 1981:3 (since only two of the three months in the quarter were impacted by the strike).

The variable rises to 1.0 in the fourth quarter of 1981 and declines steadily to a value of 0.22 in the second quarter of 1983. This specification was selected over a conventional dummy variable because of the diminishing influence of the PATCO action on air service beginning in 1982.

The final variable (ROUTE) is a dummy variable to represent the impacts of route entry and exit freedoms under deregulation and has a value of zero for 1970 through 1978 and a value of one for 1979 through 1982. Although the deregulation act became effective in October 1978 (and fare freedoms began earlier under CAB administrative action), the airlines did not really have an opportunity to respond to the freedom to enter new markets or leave existing ones until after the beginning of 1979. No strong prior expectations were held about the direction of the route freedom effect. On the one hand, since airlines were better able to tailor their route networks to the demands of the market, route freedom might be expected to result in more RPMs for most carriers. Conversely, some carriers could use route freedom primarily to withdraw from unprofitable markets, resulting in fewer RPMs. The estimated coefficient on the ROUTE variable is positive, indicating that on net route freedoms resulted in increased RPMs for the major carriers.

The financial simulations conducted in chapter 3 were based on the RPM estimates generated by the preceding demand model under varying assumptions about the values of the independent variables. The estimated RPMs were combined with assumptions about yields, operating expenses, and load factors to calculate hypothetical earnings or losses for the major airlines, as explained in the chapter.

Modal Shares

Characteristics that commonly influence individuals' choices of travel mode include the cost or fare charged for a trip; the time required to complete the trip, including traveling to and from terminals used by common carriers; and the difference between the desired departure time and the closest available scheduled departure. In addition a range of more subtle attributes are likely to enter travelers' decisions, such as seating comfort aboard vehicles, perceptions of the safety of individual modes or specific common carriers, and reliability or adherence to published schedules.

To analyze more systematically the influence of these traveler and modal characteristics on the choices among modes for domestic intercity travel, a sample of nearly 2,700 person-trips was drawn from the 1977 National Travel Survey. The sample is composed of trips over 46 routes on which travel was most frequently reported in the National Travel Survey, including most of the nation's most heavily traveled corridors.[9] The decision-making unit was hypothesized to be a traveling party ranging in size from one to six members.

Specific variables were employed to describe each mode's characteristics. For the automobile these were the estimated cost and time entailed in traveling by car over each route in the sample. For the common carriers the published fare, scheduled travel time, and frequency of departures were used. In addition an estimate was made of the distance from each traveler's residence to the airport, bus station, or rail terminal that would logically be used in traveling by these modes.[10] Because the distribution of travelers' desired departure times cannot be determined, the frequency of scheduled departures is used as an index of how closely actual departure times match ideal ones. Of course a single scheduled departure might exactly match the ideal schedule of some travelers, so overall frequency is not a perfect index of schedule disruption or delay; nevertheless, more frequent service should raise the probability that any traveler will find a suitably scheduled departure.

These data were used to estimate the parameters of a conventional multinomial logit model of travelers' choices among the modes available; such a model will predict the choices of individual travelers for specific trips as a function of comparative costs and service levels offered by the available modes. The effect of trip purpose on the relative importance travelers might attach to travel time was examined by estimating separate models for business trips and other trips. The influence of traveler income on the valuation of travel time was tested by combining income and travel time variables into a single index that allows the monetary equivalent of travel time to increase with income. Finally, the effect of group size on modal choice was controlled by making the common carrier fare for any particular trip equal to the travel party size multiplied by the individual fare.

Empirical Results

Table B.2 reports the estimated coefficients, their standard errors, sample sizes, and a measure of goodness-of-fit (rho^2) for various specifications of separate mode choice models for business and other trip purposes. These coefficients represent the weights attached to the corresponding variables in calculating a utility index for each of the modes. Each mode's utility value for an individual trip is the sum of the coefficients on travel time, cost, frequency, and access multiplied by that mode's values of these variables

Table B.2 Coefficient estimates, sample sizes, and goodness-of-fit measures for intercity travel mode choice models (standard errors of coefficient estimates in parentheses)

Trip purpose	One-way line-haul time × income[a]	One-way travel cost[b]	Weekly departures[c]	Access distance[d]	Constant terms			N	$\overline{\text{Rho}}^2$
					Auto	Air	Bus		
Business	−0.03163 (0.01156)	−0.02017 (0.00276)	0.00513 (0.00065)		−2.9629	0.4529	−2.2684	1102	0.3031
Business	−0.03146 (0.01137)	−0.02076 (0.00273)	0.00525 (0.00066)	−0.02632 (0.00484)	−2.6569	0.3892	−2.1176	1102	0.3161
All other	−0.01195 (0.00806)	−0.06217 (0.01383)	0.00201 (0.00045)		1.4893	0.5200	0.5477	1571	0.3169
All other	−0.01194 (0.00806)	−0.06248 (0.01383)	0.00203 (0.00045)	−0.00437 (0.00338)	1.5322	0.5031	0.5594	1571	0.3174

a. Time in hours multiplied by hourly equivalent of annual income in 1977 dollars.
b. In 1977 dollars.
c. Scheduled common carrier departures providing direct service, arbitrarily set at 1,080 for automoble.
d. Miles from point of trip origin (residence or workplace) to common carrier terminal, arbitrarily set at 0.05 for autombile.

for that trip, plus the mode's specific constant term. These utility indices are then transformed into mode choice probabilities for specific trips by the general logit model:

$$P_{ij} = \frac{e^{U_{ij}}}{\sum_{j=1}^{J} e^{U_{ij}}}$$

where P_{ij} is the probability that individual i will choose mode j, U_{ij} is the utility supplied to individual i by the characteristics of mode j, and there are $j = 1, 2, \ldots, J$, separate modes (four in this case). Rho^2 is a measure of the improvement in explanatory power over a naive model (specifically, one that assigns all travelers to the mode with the highest market share) offered by the combination of variables included in each specification.

At 1977 prices and income levels, typical business travelers appear to value travel time at 150 to 160 percent of their equivalent hourly wage rates or \$19 to \$20 per hour, whereas nonbusiness travelers seem to value traveling time at 20 to 25 percent of their somewhat lower average hourly wage rates, or at about \$1.50 to \$2.00 per hour. That business travel time appears to be *more* highly valued than working time may reflect that the employer is the travel decision maker. For the typical employer the cost of the employees' time (fringes, support activities, etc.) may substantially exceed the *aftertax* wage rate, on which these comparisons were based. Business travel time could also be valued more highly than the wage if most business travelers found time spent working more enjoyable than time spent traveling.[11]

The estimates reported in table B.2 also suggest that nonbusiness travelers are considerably more responsive to the costs of traveling than their counterparts traveling for business purposes, although this no doubt partly arises because nonbusiness travel is typically done in larger parties (and common carrier fares in the model are charged per person). The frequency of scheduled departures also seems to have a pronounced effect on travelers' choices among modes, and as hypothesized, business travelers appear to be considerably more sensitive to frequency than are nonbusiness travelers. Finally, access distance from travelers' homes to common carrier terminals apparently also influences choices among modes, although there remains considerable uncertainty about the exact magnitude of this effect; the standard errors associated with the estimates of access distance coefficients are fairly large in relation to the coefficients themselves.

Table B.3 reports so-called direct elasticities; these show the proportional change in the probability that a specific mode will be chosen in response to change in one of the mode's own characteristics, such as cost

Table B.3 Direct elasticities of individual mode choice probabilities implied by model coefficient estimates

			Choice probability elasticities					
	Initial choice probabilities		Travel time		Travel cost		Frequency	
Mode	Business	Other	Business	Other	Business	Other	Business	Other
Auto	0.320	0.656	−0.69	−0.13	−0.81	−0.70	3.63[a]	0.75[a]
Air	0.598	0.226	−0.05	−0.02	−0.68	−1.98	0.44	0.18
Bus	0.015	0.086	−0.96	−0.34	−0.85	−1.19	0.92	0.33
Rail	0.066	0.033	−0.97	−0.38	−1.18	−1.84	0.11	0.05

Source: Computed from model coefficient estimates reported in table B.2 and data used in coefficient estimation.
a. Affected by arbitrary assumption regarding auto departure frequency.

or departure frequency. A negative sign indicates that the probability will decline, and a positive sign indicates an increase. For example, an elasticity with respect to a mode's own fare of −1.0 means that a 20 percent increase in the fare will produce an identical decline of 20 percent in the probability that some typical traveler will choose to travel by that mode for the specific trip in question. The elasticity values shown in table B.3 are computed from the coefficients in table B.2 and apply to individual business and nonbusiness travelers having characteristics typical of the sample used to estimate the models.

The elasticity values in table B.3 indicate that all travelers' choices among the four modes are fairly sensitive to their costs or fares. Business travelers' probabilities of choosing auto, bus, and rail travel would be changed approximately in proportion to changes in the costs or fares of using them; that is, any given percent change in the cost of using one of those modes would produce approximately the same percent change in the probability that it would be chosen for a typical business trip (with higher costs reducing that probability, and cost or fare declines increasing it). Business travelers' use of air service appears to be slightly less sensitive to variation in fares than for the other modes; for example, a 10 percent increase in air fares would only reduce the probability of flying by about 7 percent.

Generally, the mode choices of those traveling for nonbusiness purposes appear to be more sensitive to costs or fares than travel for business. For air and rail service the computed elasticity values suggest that percent changes in the probabilities of these modes being chosen would be nearly twice as large as the corresponding percent changes in fares. On the other hand, nonbusiness travelers appear relatively insensitive to variation in the costs of making automobile trips.

Travel time elasticities for business travelers are considerably larger than for other travelers, reflecting the much higher values evidently attached to travel time by those making business-related intercity trips than by those traveling for other purposes. Within each travel group, however, the modal pattern of these elasticities is similar: bus and rail choices are much more sensitive to travel time than auto driving. The choice of air service is very insensitive to scheduled flying times, probably because air travel times are so much shorter than for the competing modes that the relative time savings from air travel are not substantially altered when scheduled flying times change.

The estimated elasticities for scheduled departure frequencies are slightly more difficult to interpret. To start, the auto travel elasticities are not directly comparable because their estimated values depend on the arbitrary assumption that auto departures are available with nearly infinite frequency. For all modes, but particularly rail, business travelers' choices appear to be much more sensitive to departure frequencies than do those of nonbusiness travelers. The common carrier departure elasticities are generally lower than those for fare and travel time, suggesting that increases in the frequency of service provided by individual modes would only modestly increase the probability that travelers would choose them. For air and bus service the particular sample of markets may partly explain these low departure elasticity estimates; the markets in the sample already have relatively frequent service so that more frequencies may not allow travelers to achieve significant reductions in delay.

Of course the probability that an individual traveler will choose any mode depends not only on its own travel time, fare, and service level but also on how these compare to similar measures for the competing modes. To illustrate the sensitivity of mode choices to changing prices and travel times for competing modes, individual travelers' mode choices were predicted and aggregated to market share estimates at different hypothetical levels of costs and travel times for each mode. The changes in aggregate mode shares predicted in response to hypothetical 25 percent cost increases are shown in table B.4 and are relatively minor. Only for the bus and rail modes, those currently used least frequently for intercity travel, would the predicted mode shifts translate into significant changes in the amounts of traffic carried and resulting revenues. (Of course some *individual* carriers might experience very large passenger and revenue changes, but this analysis focuses on industrywide effects rather than those for individual firms.) In

Table B.4 Predicted mode shifts in response to cost/fare increases

	Initial mode shares		Predicted mode shares after 25 percent increase in cost			
Travel purpose	Mode	Percentage of trips	Auto	Air	Bus	Rail
Business	Auto	32.1	30.1	36.1	32.1	32.2
	Air	59.8	61.5	54.7	59.9	60.2
	Bus	1.5	1.6	1.7	1.3	1.6
	Rail	6.6	6.8	7.5	6.6	5.9
Other (social, recreation, entertainment)	Auto	65.6	60.7	71.4	67.2	66.1
	Air	22.6	25.8	15.8	22.8	22.8
	Bus	8.6	9.8	9.4	6.4	8.7
	Rail	3.3	3.7	3.6	3.6	2.4

Source: Estimated from travel mode choice models reported in table B.1.

absolute terms the most important predicted shifts are between auto and air travel, especially as the cost of flying increases relative to that of driving. Generally, business trips appear less responsive to cost and fare changes than travel for other purposes—exactly as expected if business trips have higher direct monetary values or if their costs are borne only partially or indirectly by travelers themselves.

Table B.5 reports predicted mode shifts in response to hypothetical 20 percent reductions in the travel times offered by each mode on a route representative of the city pairs included in the sample. Travel time reductions of this magnitude are about the largest likely to result from forseeable nontechnological innovations (e.g., higher speed limits for interstate highway travel, upgrading of rail rights-of-way, or reductions in air traffic congestion levels at major airports). Again, none of the predicted mode shifts is very large. The most significant predicted shifts take place between air and automobile travel, although in this case the shares of those modes for nonbusiness trips seem to be more sensitive to changing travel time comparisons than business trips. For example, the largest predicted change reported in table B.5 is the shift of nonbusiness travel from the various common carrier modes (principally air) to automobile resulting from a hypothetical 20 percent reduction in typical driving times. This result is probably largely explained by business trips being, on average, considerably longer than those for other purposes, so that modest reductions in auto times are unlikely to significantly narrow the gap between flying and driving times. However, for shorter nonbusiness trips improvements in driving times of the magnitude considered may be sufficient to alter critically the comparison between air and surface travel.

Table B.5 Predicted mode shifts in response to travel time reductions

	Initial mode shares		Predicted mode shares after 20 percent reduction in travel time			
Travel purpose	Mode	Percentage of trips	Auto	Air	Bus	Rail
Business	Auto	32.0	34.4	31.0	32.0	31.9
	Air	59.8	57.7	61.1	59.7	59.7
	Bus	1.5	1.4	1.4	1.6	1.5
	Rail	6.6	6.4	6.4	6.6	6.8
Other (social, recreation, entertainment)	Auto	65.6	76.3	64.8	65.0	65.5
	Air	22.6	15.6	23.5	22.4	22.6
	Bus	8.6	6.1	8.5	9.4	8.6
	Rail	3.3	2.0	3.3	3.2	3.4

Source: Estimated from travel mode choice models reported in table B.1.

Notes

Preface

1. John R. Meyer and Clinton V. Oster, Jr., eds., *Airline Deregulation: The Early Experience* (Boston: Auburn House, 1981).

2. John R. Meyer and Clinton V. Oster, Jr., *Deregulation and the New Airline Entrepreneurs* (Cambridge: The MIT Press, 1984).

Chapter 1

1. John R. Meyer, M. J. Peck, C. Zwick, and J. Stenason, *The Economics of Competition in the Transportation Industries* (Cambridge: Harvard University Press, 1959).

2. Ibid., p. vi.

3. The imposition of mandated corporate average fuel economy standards was delayed subsequently by the government due to continued declines in oil prices and purchases of larger, less fuel-efficient cars by consumers. In 1986 the standard was reduced to 26.0 miles per gallon.

4. *Bus Regulatory Reform Act of 1982*, Conference Report 97-780, p. 2.

5. *Transportation Facts and Trends* (Washington: Transportation Association of America, December 1981), p. 7.

6. *Statistical Abstract of the United States*, (U.S. Department of Commerce, Bureau of the Census, 1985), p. 589.

Chapter 2

1. T. E. Keeler, "Airline Regulation and Market Performance," *Bell Journal of Economics* 3 (Autumn 1972), pp. 399–424; General Accounting Office, "Report to the Congress, Lower Airline Costs per Passenger Are Possible in the United States and Could Result in Lower Fares," February 1977; George Douglas and James C. Miller III, *Economic Regulation of Domestic Air Transport* (Washington: The Brookings Institution, 1974).

2. Good analyses of these issues can be found in Elizabeth E. Bailey, David R. Graham, and Daniel P. Kaplan, *Deregulating the Airlines* (Cambridge: The MIT Press, 1985); Steven Morrison and Clifford Winston, *The Economic Effects of Airline Deregulation* (Washington: The Brookings Institution, 1986); and Melvin A. Brenner, James O. Leet, and Elihu Schott, *Airline Deregulation* (Westport, Conn.: Eno Foundation for Transportation, Inc., 1985).

3. However, almost 125 small towns lost all service between 1978 and 1984. Virtually all of these towns were served only by unregulated commuter carriers prior to deregulation, and these carriers were always free to exit, even prior to deregulation since they were *not* subsidized by government. Deregulation, though, might be blamed, at least temporarily, for this total loss of service because (as explained in chapter 4) deregulation opened up larger and more lucrative markets to the commuters when these larger markets were abandoned by the local service carriers (who in turn were pursuing larger and better market opportunities opened up to them by deregulation).

4. See Robert A. Leone, *Who Profits: Winners, Losers, and Government Regulation* (New York: Basic Books, 1986).

5. Clinton V. Oster, Jr., and C. Kurt Zorn, "Deregulation and Commuter Airline Safety," *Journal of Air Law and Commerce*, 49 (1983).

6. Commuter airlines are found to have a worse safety record than certificated jet carriers, and commuter airlines account for a larger share of total airline traffic since deregulation. Safety performance varies widely and systematically within the commuter industry, with carrier size being an important determinant of this record. For example, the top 20 commuter carriers that carry about 58 percent of U.S. commuter passengers, have a safety record much the same as the excellent safety record of the certificated jet carriers. An expected consolidation of the commuter industry into fewer and bigger firms, as described in chapter 4, therefore might be expected to improve the industry's safety record.

Chapter 3

1. Civil Aeronautics Board, *Air Carrier Financial Statistics*, various years. The data cover domestic and international operations.

2. "Debt is Still Growing—But Only Half as Fast as Assets" *Business Week*, June 25, 1984, pp. 68–101.

3. The subsequent decline in fuel prices that began in 1982 has helped the airlines, in part by extending the economic lives of older flight equipment. Still, fuel prices in 1985 remain substantially above pre-1979 levels.

4. Alexander Stuart, "Boeing's New Beauties are a Tough Sell," *Fortune*, October 18, 1982, pp. 114–120.

5. It should be noted that in many cases the sale of used planes and other equipment and assets represented a means of rapid adjustment to the excess capacity of some aircraft types that characterized the early years of deregulation, as well as a means to generate cash and strengthen reported earnings.

6. Calculated from air carrier financial statements for 1980.

7. Calculated from airline annual reports for 1981 and 1983.

8. Calculated from airline annual reports for 1981, 1982 and 1983.

9. Although the 1982 tax law revisions sharply curtailed the use of safe harbor leasing, several airlines were able to sell tax benefits under the program in 1983 because such arrangements were contracted prior to the legislative revisions.

10. Calculated from airline annual reports. A substantial portion of this new borrowing was undertaken to finance aggressive equipment acquisition programs; the question of whether these investment programs should have been reduced in the wake of unprecedented interest rate increases has been raised by many industry analysts.

11. Although Pan Am's losses were attributable to some degree to its 1979–1980 acquisition of National Airlines, the direct merger-related costs were small relative to the losses resulting from operations of the airline (due in part to the problems in restructuring the merged company).

12. Entry into long-haul markets was mainly by established carriers aggressively seeking outlets for their surfeit of wide-bodied aircraft—a surfeit largely brought on by the incentives under CAB rate regulation that awarded higher fare markups to long-haul than to short-haul trips.

13. Part of the reason for the better performance of the short-haul carriers may have been that they served markets subject to less fare discounting.

14. The assumption of a 20 percent addition to capacity closely approximates historical carrier responses to traffic increases.

15. Several more complex models and specifications were tried, with less satisfactory results than the model presented.

16. A 60 percent "target" load factor was indicated by several industry analysts, and was corroborated by an examination of historical responses to increased traffic volumes.

17. "Air Transport Basic Analysis," *Standard and Poor's Industry Survey*, March 10, 1983, p. A47. The $1.02 gallon price used in table 3.5 for 1981 reflects the average price for the year.

18. The effect of this assumption is to place actual performance in a more favorable position relative to the simulation under the no fuel price increase scenario, because the financial estimates in the simulation do not include any such efficiency savings.

19. The structure of the model used in the simulation includes separate measures for standard and discount fares, so that a restrictive single fare elasticity is not assumed. See the appendix for a more detailed discussion.

20. These estimated operating cost savings using the simulation model are larger for the major airlines because these carriers have longer stage lengths and thus a greater portion of operating costs is for fuel.

21. The coach fare was calculated by applying the CAB's fare-setting formulas to determine the Standard Industry Fare Level or SIFL.

22. In the densest markets, however, the extension of discounting appears to have reduced standard coach fares, so that the SIFL index was becoming an increasingly unreliable measure of standard fares.

23. A similar conclusion was reached using a different methodology by Steven Morrison and Clifford Winston, *The Economic Effects of Airline Deregulation* (Washington: The Brookings Institution, 1986), p. 40.

24. For a discussion of this technique, see R. S. Hamada, "The Effect of the Firm's Capital Structure on the Systematic Risk of Common Stocks," *Journal of Finance* 27 (May 1972). Similar conclusions were reached by Lawrence Cunningham, Myron Slovin, Wallace Wood, and Janis Zaima, "Systematic Risk in the Deregulated Airline Industry," unpublished manuscript, University of Colorado, 1986.

25. Calculated from air carrier annual reports.

26. Calculated from air carrier annual reports, various years.

27. Calculated from airline financial statements.

28. "Air Transport Basic Analysis," p. A79.

29. McDonnell-Douglas estimates that the arrangements with American and TWA will require an investment of $700 million through 1985.

30. Alexander Stuart, "Boeing's New Beauties Are a Tough Sell," *Fortune*, October 18, 1982, pp. 114–120.

31. Calculated from 1982 airline annual reports.

32. "Air Transport Basic Analysis," p. A79.

33. Ibid.

Chapter 4

1. Committee on the Judiciary, U.S. Senate, "CAB Practices and Procedures," Hearings before the Subcommittee on Administrative Practice and Procedure (Washington: Government Printing Office, 1975).

2. Pan American had acquired National; Texas Air included in its holding company not only its original or prederegulation position in Texas Air but Continental Airlines and newly created New York Air as well; Republic Airlines was created by consolidating three local service airlines (North Central, Southern, and Hughes Airwest). In 1986 Northwest acquired Republic, and proposals emerged for Texas Air acquiring People Express, Frontier, and Eastern, TWA buying Ozark, and Delta acquiring Western. If all these mergers were consummated, the industry structure would be roughly like that outlined in most prederegulation speculations, although Texas Air's large role was not expected. In addition USAir, Piedmont, and several other smaller airlines remain competitive and of some size.

3. The gain in market share by the former intrastate and new entrant jet carriers and by the commuters was particularly impressive, coming on top of 1976 shares of only 3.3 and 0.5 percent, respectively. A change in CAB data collection and reporting procedures prevents updating the figure to 1986 in precisely the same form. Nevertheless, between 1982 and 1984 total RPMs increased for each group of carriers, but the trunks continued to lose market share while the market share of the local service airlines remained about the same and the market shares of new entrant jet carriers and commuters continued to increase.

4. These developments are documented in a series of CAB Staff Studies, *Report on Airline Service, Fares, Traffic, Load Factors, and Market Share* (Washington: Government Printing Office, various years beginning in 1978).

5. These entrepreneurial possibilities, to the extent they were anticipated, were mainly noted by a few academics and consultants outside or peripheral to the industry. These exceptions moreover mainly focused on the potential impact of unleashing intrastate carriers.

6. For a brief overview of the legislative movement toward deregulation, see James P. Rakowski and James C. Johnson, "Airline Deregulation: Problems and Prospects," *Quarterly Review of Economics and Business* 19 (Winter 1979), pp. 71–76.

7. John R. Meyer and Clinton V. Oster, Jr., eds., *Airline Deregulation: The Early Experience* (Boston: Auburn House, 1981), pp. 7–8, 44–52.

8. Ibid., pp. 27–31.

9. John R. Meyer and Clinton V. Oster, Jr., *Deregulation and the New Airline Entrepreneurs* (Cambridge: The MIT Press, 1984), chap. 10, p. 194.

10. For a detailed discussion of the small community subsidy system see: *Deregulation and the New Airline Entrepreneurs*, chap. 10.

11. Ibid., p. 76.

12. Ibid., p. 75.

13. *Airline Deregulation: The Early Experience*, pp. 128–138.

14. These figures are based on General Accounting Office, *The Changing Airline Industry: A Status Report through 1982*, July 6, 1982, app. III.

15. These figures are based on data contained in table 5 of Civil Aeronautics Board, *Report on Airline Service, Fares, Traffic, Load Factors, and Market Shares*, issue 31, December 1984.

16. Of the communities that have lost all of their service by September 1984, only one had been receiving certificated service and therefore might have expected to have retained that service under continued regulation. That community, Winona, Minnesota, was eligible for guaranteed essential air service but requested that such service be allowed to lapse. See Civil Aeronautics Board, *Report on Airline Service, Fares, Traffic, Load Factors, and Market Shares*, issue 29, March 1984, p. 17. Among the remaining communities, recession may have also played a major role in their service losses. Of the communities that lost all service between 1978 and 1983, over 75 percent had received their 1978 service from a carrier no longer operating by the end of 1983.

17. *Deregulation and the New Airline Entrepreneurs*, p. 199.

18. Regional Airline Association, *1985 Annual Report*, p. 21.

19. For a more detailed analysis of commuter airline safety, see *Deregulation and the New Airline Entrepreneurs*, chap. 5.

20. Clinton V. Oster, Jr., and C. Kurt Zorn, "Airline Deregulation, Commuter Safety, and Regional Air Transportation," *Growth and Change*, 14 (July 1983), pp. 3–11. *Deregulation and the New Airline Entrepreneurs*, chap. 8.

21. Meyer and Oster, *Deregulation and the New Airline Entrepreneurs*, tables 5.3, 5.4.

22. For a more detailed discussion see: Clinton V. Oster, Jr., and C. Kurt Zorn, "Deregulation and Commuter Airline Safety," *Journal of Air Law and Commerce*, 49 (1983), pp. 315–335.

23. Civil Aeronautics Board, *Report on Airline Service, Fares, Traffic, Load Factors, and Market Shares*, issue 30, June 1984, pp. 5–16. Note that these figures slightly overstate the turnover in the commuter industry by excluding the more stable Allegheny Commuter System. Moreover, since turnover was highest among the smallest carriers, fewer passengers were affected by the turnover than these figures might suggest at first glance.

24. *Deregulation and the New Airline Entrepreneurs*, chapter 4. Also see appendix A, particularly figure A.1.

25. *Airline Deregulation: The Early Experience*, pp. 20–22. and George C. Eads, *The Local Service Airline Experiment*, (Washington: The Brookings Institution, 1972).

26. As consequence of this unevenness in the presence of new entrant competition, some disparities in the fare structure opened up that many travelers considered inequitable or unfair. An appearance of inequity may have been further heightened by some markets becoming much more competitive since deregulation even *without* the entrance of new carriers, the most conspicuous examples being long-haul markets where regulation created excessive capacity prior to 1978 (e.g., the transcontinental and Florida markets).

27. These figures and those in the next sentence were derived from Civil Aeronautics Board, *Report on Airline Service, Fares, Traffic, Load Factors, and Market Share*, issue 30, June 1984, table 5, pp. 69–70, and issue 31, September 1984, table 5, pp. 22–24.

28. The concept of "workable competition" has a long history in the industrial economics literature. See Joe S. Bain, *Barriers to New Competition* (Cambridge: Harvard University Press, 1956); E. S. Mason, *Economic Concentration and the Monopoly Problem* (Cambridge: Harvard University Press, 1957); Darius Gaskins, Jr., "Dynamic Limit Pricing: Optimal Pricing under Threat of Entry," *Journal of Economic Theory* 3 (September 1971), pp. 306–322.

29. See, for example, E. E. Bailey and J. Panzar, "The Contestability of Airline Markets During the Transition to Deregulation," *Law and Contemporary Problems* 44 (1981); and E. E. Bailey, D. R. Graham, and D. P. Kaplan, *Deregulating the Airlines* (Cambridge: The MIT Press, 1985), chap. 6.

Chapter 5

1. Two other provisions of the act also eased route restrictions. The "Dormant Authority" provision allowed a carrier to be granted authority to serve a route if another carrier already holding a certificate for that route had not been providing at least five round trips per week for thirteen weeks. The "Automatic Entry" provision allowed a carrier to initiate nonstop service between any single pair of points it wished to select in each of the calendar years 1979, 1980, and 1981, subject to the restriction that each carrier was also allowed to "protect" one pair of points from entry under this program. The speed with which the CAB processed

normal route applications, however, removed the need for carriers to rely on either of these provisions.

2. See John R. Meyer and Clinton V. Oster, Jr., *Deregulation and the New Airline Entrepreneurs* (Cambridge: The MIT Press, 1984), chapter 10.

3. For a more detailed description of each of these options, see Meyer and Oster, eds., *Airline Deregulation: The Early Experience* (Boston: Auburn House, 1981), pp. 93–96.

4. To help determine the hub strategies the trunk and local service airlines adopted following deregulation, the carriers' route networks were examined in July 1976, July 1981, and July 1984. July 1976 was chosen for the beginning of the comparison because it was clearly before any substantial route liberalization under administrative deregulation and because comparing July with July eliminated the effects of any seasonal adjustments. July 1981 was chosen as an intermediate point in the comparison because it was the last month before the PATCO strike and thus before any modifications to airline strategies stemming from subsequent air traffic control capacity reductions. Finally, July 1984 represents a point by which the major effects of the PATCO strike were over and the airlines were once again developing their route networks.

5. The choice of 50 is admittedly arbitrary, but the general conclusions of the analysis are not sensitive to the specific choice.

6. The comparisons involving Pan Am included the National Airlines route network in both 1976 and 1981.

7. The inclusion of international flights, including those to Canada, Mexico, and the Caribbean, would further reinforce this finding of pervasive hub strengthening since these international flights depart from a relatively small number of international gateways that are typically supported by domestic feeder networks. For example, the inclusion of international flights would reinforce New York–Kennedy's role as a hub for Pan American and TWA, and Miami's role as a hub for Eastern.

8. See Meyer and Oster, *Airline Deregulation: The Early Experience*, chapter 8.

9. Civil Aeronautics Board, *Report on Airline Service, Fares, Load Factors, and Market Shares*, issue 18, p. 6, and issue 29, p. 36.

10. Lower fares may also be instituted on some parallel routes to prevent diversion of traffic.

11. For a discussion of the impact of Braniff's pricing on American's revenues, see American Airlines 1982 annual report, and Standard and Poor's, "Industry Survey: Air Transport," March 1983.

Chapter 6

1. Committee on the Judiciary, U.S. Senate, "CAB Practices and Procedures," Report of the Subcommittee on Administrative Practice and Procedure (Washington: Government Printing Office, 1975). For a more complete discussion of early experiences with deregulation see John R. Meyer and Clinton V. Oster, Jr., eds., *Airline Deregulation: The Early Experience* (Boston: Auburn House, 1981), chap. 3.

2. See John W. Kendrick, *Productivity Trends in the United States* (Princeton: Princeton University Press, 1961), table G-X.

3. See John W. Kendrick, *Postwar Productivity Trends in the United States, 1948–1969* (New York: National Bureau of Economic Research, 1973), table 5.1.

4. For a discussion of aggregate productivity growth in the airline industry both before and after deregulation see Elizabeth E. Bailey, David R. Graham, and Daniel P. Kaplan, *Deregulating the Airlines* (Cambridge: The MIT Press, 1985), chap. 8.

5. Douglas W. Caves, Laurits R. Christensen, and Michael W. Tretheway, "Airline Productivity under Deregulation," *Regulation*, November–December 1982.

6. Bernard Sobin, "An Index of Input Costs for Domestic Trunk and Local Carriers," Office of Economic Analysis, Civil Aeronautics Board, 1981.

7. Meyer and Oster, eds., *Airline Deregulation: The Early Experience*, chap. 8.

8. Because some essential information on input quantities for domestic operations is not separately available for the trunk airlines, controls must be established for potential differences in productivity between international and domestic operations. For those carriers involved in mergers during the 1978 to 1980 period, operations of the merged carriers have been consolidated. Three airlines also had significant strike periods in either 1978 or 1980 (Continental and Ozark in 1980 and Northwest in 1978) and because of irregularities in the reporting of outputs, inputs, or both during the strikes, these airlines could not be fully analyzed.

9. If the output definition had included a component reflecting passenger volume (e.g., revenue passenger miles), then productivity gains under that definition would stem not only from improvements in the technical efficiency of producing the industry's basic output but also improvements in the industry's ability to market that output. Meyer and Oster, eds., *Airline Deregulation: The Early Experience*, chap. 5.

10. Although these adjustments control for the route and fleet characteristics that seem to have the greatest influences on measured productivity, by no means are they all-inclusive. Other route characteristics, such as the extent and precise nature of hub connecting operations, almost certainly influence productivity. There are also unquantifiable differences among airlines in the quality of their output, which may in turn require different amounts of inputs to produce. Thus "high quality" carriers may appear in the analysis to have achieved lower productivity than was in fact the case.

11. For a detailed discussion of the airlines' adaptation see Meyer and Oster, eds., *Airline Deregulation: The Early Experience*, chap. 8.

12. The measurement of labor productivity could also be distorted for some airlines if these carriers were to subcontract significant amounts of other labor-intensive functions, such as baggage handling.

13. See Meyer and Oster, eds., *Airline Deregulation: The Early Experience*, chap. 5.

14. Meyer and Oster, eds., *Airline Deregulation: The Early Experience*, pp. 177–185.

15. A study by Douglas W. Caves, Laurits R. Christensen, and Michael W. Tretheway ("Productivity Performance of U.S. Trunk and Local Service Airlines in the Era of Deregulation," University of Wisconsin, Social Systems Research Institute, Number 8205, February 1982) estimated total factor productivity levels and changes among the individual airlines using expenditure shares and a translog production function. They found large increases in total factor productivity for the industry as a whole between 1976 and 1979, no influence of stage length on total factor productivity, and strong indications of scale economies. By contrast, though the analysis summarized in table 6.3 found generally improved aggregate productivity, stage length was found to affect some components of productivity, and in other analyses (not reported) no evidence was found of scale economies. Nevertheless, for the one year common to both studies (1978) the relative productivities of the different carriers were similar.

16. For more detail of the origins of the local service airlines and their evolution following deregulation see: George Eads, *The Local Service Airline Experiment* (Washington: Brookings Institution, 1972); Meyer and Oster, eds., *Airline Deregulation: The Early Experience*; and Meyer and Oster, *Deregulation and the New Airline Entrepreneurs*.

17. Meyer and Oster, eds., *Airline Deregulation: The Early Experience*, chap. 5.

18. Because of strikes, it was not possible to include United, Continental, or Ozark.

19. The same adjustment equations were used for Southwest as for the established carriers so that Southwest's numbers are also adjusted for their route and fleet characteristics.

20. For a more detailed analysis of the sources of cost advantage of carriers such as Southwest over the former trunk and local service airlines, see Meyer and Oster, *Deregulation and the New Airline Entrepreneurs*, pp. 64–68.

21. American Airlines 1983 Annual Report, p. 13.

22. *Business Week*, July 2, 1984, pp. 26–27.

23. *Aviation Week and Space Technology*, November 21, 1983, pp. 27–30.

24. *Aviation Week and Space Technology*, August 29, 1983, pp. 30–31.

25. Interestingly, relatively low wages coupled with partial employee ownership was also the approach taken by a rapidly growing new entrant, People Express.

26. *Business Week*, June 4, 1984, pp. 60–68, and *Aviation Week and Space Technology*, March 28, 1983, p. 29.

27. *Aviation Week and Space Technology*, March 28, 1983, p. 26.

28. Eastern Airlines 1983 Annual Report, p. 3.

29. Western Airlines 1983 Annual Report, pp. 4–6.

30. Republic Airlines 1983 Annual Report, pp. 1, 2, 8, 11; and *Wall Street Journal*, May 24, 1984.

31. Because of a tender offer from Northwest Airlines, Republic's common stock achieved quotations in the $16 range in early 1986.

32. *Aviation Week and Space Technology*, August 15, 1983, p. 33.

33. *Aviation Week and Space Technology*, January 30, 1984.

34. On May 18, 1984, the U.S. District Court for the District of Columbia held the labor protection provisions unconstitutional on the grounds that they involved the use of a congressional veto and that the congressional veto was not severable from the remainder of the labor protection provisions [*Alaska Airlines, Inc.* v. *Donovan*, 594 F. Supp. 92, 94 (D.D.C. 1984)]. On July 16, 1985, however, the U.S. Court of Appeals for the District of Columbia Circuit ruled that the congressional veto provision was severable from the remaining labor protection provisions and reinstituted these remaining sections [*Alaska Airlines, Inc.* v. *Donovan*, 766 F. 2d 1550 (1985)].

35. The twelve carriers were American, Braniff, Continental, Delta, Eastern, Northwest, Pan Am, Republic, TWA, United, USAir, and Western.

36. Alternative models were also tested using different assumptions about the changes in traffic and changes in employment. The fundamental conclusions of the analyses were the same for each form of the model tested. For further details see Clinton V. Oster, Jr., *The Effect of Deregulation on Airline Industry Employment*, Final Report to the U.S. Department of Transportation, March 1984.

37. Deregulation-induced changes in productivity were not explicitly modeled in these employment equations. As indicated earlier in the chapter, there almost certainly were productivity improvements during the 1979 to 1982 period. The effect of these productivity gains would have been to reduce the amount of labor needed to produce a given amount of RPMs, and such gains are probably most highly correlated with the deregulation route freedom variable and, to a lesser extent, with the PATCO variable. The likely effect on the deregulation route freedom variable is to bias it downward; in other words, deregulation's route freedoms probably had a slightly greater positive impact on employment than the coefficient indicates. The likely effect on the PATCO variable is that the coefficient may indicate a very slightly

more negative effect on employment than actually was the case. The effect of this specification on the employment simulations is to assume implicitly that there would have been no productivity gains in the 1979 through 1982 period in the absence of deregulation. To the extent that there would have been productivity gains without deregulation, the expected employment under continued regulation would have been even lower, and thus the employment gains from deregulation even higher, than indicated in figure 6.3 and table 6.6.

38. Of course after 1982 two of the carriers, Continental and Braniff, entered bankruptcy with resulting changes in both the level and terms of their employment.

Chapter 7

1. CAB Rule SPR-110.

2. CAB Orders 77-2-133 and 77-3-80.

3. For a more detailed discussion of the transition to deregulation see, John R. Meyer and Clinton V. Oster, Jr., eds., *Airline Deregulation: The Early Experience* (Boston: Auburn House, 1981), chap. 3.

4. There are some minor exceptions to free exit if a carrier's exit would leave a community with less than "essential air service." See John R. Meyer and Clinton V. Oster, Jr., *Deregulation and the New Airline Entrepreneurs*, (Cambridge: The MIT Press, 1984), chap. 10.

5. General Accounting Office, *The Changing Airline Industry: A Status Report through 1982*, July 6, 1983, table 1, p. 7. Between 1978 and 1982 average airline fares increased 46.4 percent (in nominal terms), but at the same time the consumer price index rose 59.2 percent and the CAB index of airline costs rose 87.4 percent.

6. Melvin A. Brenner, James O. Leet, and Elihu Schott, *Airline Deregulation* (Westport, Conn.: Eno Foundation for Transportation, Inc., 1985), chap. 4, especially table 9.

7. For a more detailed discussion of airlines' use of discount fares, see Meyer and Oster, eds., *Airline Deregulation: The Early Experience*, chap. 4.

8. The data presented in figure 7.1 were derived from tables 1, 2, and 3 in Joseph P. Schwieterman, "Fare is Fair in Airline Deregulation—The Decline of Price Discrimination," *Regulation* (July–August 1985), although the data were used in this article to investigate trends in price discrimination rather than the impact of varying degrees of competition. The data were taken from random samples of 25 markets served by a single carrier, 25 markets served by two carriers, and 25 markets served by multiple carriers. The specific markets in each sample are listed in the article.

9. The survey is reported quarterly on the basis of a continuous 10 percent ticket sample. The detail recorded for each trip shows the complete routing from origin to destination, carriers used, and fare basis code for each stage of the itinerary. The sample information becomes more reliable as market density increases.

10. For earlier examples of airline fare studies, see T. E. Keeler, "Airline Regulation and Market Performance," *Bell Journal of Economics* 3 (Autumn 1972), pp. 399–424; General Accounting Office, "Report to the Congress, Lower Airline Costs per Passenger Are Possible in the United States and Could Result in Lower Fares," February 1977.

11. See, for example, M. A. Brenner et al., *Airline Deregulation*, chap. 4.

12. See Meyer and Oster, *Deregulation and the New Airline Entrepreneurs*, chapter 8, pp. 149–162.

13. The May 1 date may not fully eliminate seasonal considerations, because airlines may have put summer fares into effect in some years earlier than others. In 1981, however, the

choice of May 1 avoids complications introduced by the air traffic controllers' strike beginning in August 1981.

14. This is important because fuel can account for one-third of airline costs compared with only 10 percent for the economy as a whole.

15. The SIFL is adjusted based on average airline costs and thus reflects any productivity gains made by the airlines. To the extent productivity gains were induced by deregulation, the increase in SIFL understates the expected price rise under continued regulation.

16. None of the smaller markets in the sample were served by local service carriers receiving Section 406 subsidy in exchange for provision of service. Fare increases since deregulation are more likely to have occurred in these previously subsidized markets, in the wake of subsidy reductions since 1978. See Meyer and Oster, *Deregulation and the New Airline Entrepreneurs*, chapter 10.

17. As of mid-1978, the slot-constrained airports were Kennedy and La Guardia in New York City, O'Hare in Chicago, and Washington-National. Subsequently capacity problems and resultant delays have strongly affected air service in Atlanta, Dallas, Denver, and Newark.

18. See Meyer and Oster, eds., *Airline Deregulation: The Early Experience*, chap. 4.

19. Data on the extent and nature of capacity-controlled fares are not available. Although data can be found on unrestricted discount fares, such data are not very useful because many discount fares have "restrictions" that are not effective or enforced.

20. There is a growing literature in economics over the efficacy of pricing differentials based on differential elasticities of demand. See William B. Tye and Herman B. Leonard, "On the Problems of Applying Ramsey Pricing to the Railroad Industry with Uncertain Demand Elasticities," *Transportation Research* (November 1983), pp. 439–450; Martin L. Weitzman, "Contestable Markets: An Uprising in the Theory of Industry Structure: Comment," *American Economic Review* (June 1983), pp. 486–487.

21. For a detailed discussion of cross subsidies in joint fare arrangements see Meyer and Oster, *Deregulation and the New Airline Entrepreneurs*, chap. 8, pp. 156–162.

22. For a discussion of the determinants of the value of commuter feed traffic, see Meyer and Oster, *Deregulation and the New Airline Entrepreneurs*, chapter 11, p. 213–217.

23. For a good discussion of these effects, see Elizabeth E. Bailey, David R. Graham, and Daniel P. Kaplan, *Deregulating the Airlines* (Cambridge: The MIT Press, 1985), chapter 3.

24. William M. Carley, "Big Airlines Alter Scheduling Strategies as Costly Delays Increase 50 Percent in a Year," *The Wall Street Journal*, July 19, 1984, p. 6.

25. Such arguments are frequently accompanied by stories of individual cities where a major carrier has terminated operations. A more useful perspective, however, can be gained by analyzing trends in service patterns for a larger sample including a variety of markets. Many of the anecdotes of severe service losses are also misleading because they reflect a transition from one carrier to another. The level of service shortly after one carrier has pulled out but before the replacement carrier has fully adjusted service to the new market is obviously not a good indication of long-term service trends, yet those are frequently the situations cited by deregulation's critics.

26. The market classification was based on the results of a travel survey conducted by the Air Transport Association in 1982.

27. The apparent higher markups in business markets may also be due in part to the higher proportion of business flights involving slot-constrained airports.

28. See "Hidden Cities," *OAG Frequent Flyer*, July 1985, pp. 74–76.

29. John W. Olcott, "Crystal Ball Gazing," *Business and Commercial Aviation*, May 1981, p. 13.

30. Where low-fare carriers such as People Express or Southwest Airlines have entered, unrestricted fares have fallen sharply with fares frequently only 50 to 60 percent of SIFL in peak periods and still lower for evening and weekened travel. Meyer and Oster, *Deregulation and The New Airline Entrepreneurs*, chap. 7, pp. 125–127.

31. Steven A. Morrison and Clifford Winston, *The Economic Effects of Airline Deregulation* (Washington: Brookings Institution, 1986).

Chapter 8

1. Cited by David Martindale, "A Fairer Fare," *OAG Frequent Flyer* (September 1983), p. 42.

2. Data from *Air Transport World*, various issues and the Air Transport Association.

3. Ibid.

4. *Investigation into the Competitive Marketing of Air Transportation*, Docket 36595, Order 79-9-64, p. 44.

5. ATC Resolution 90.3, Section IV.A.8.

6. The abolition of fixed commissions was very similar to the termination of fixed stock brokerage commissions on the New York Stock Exchange, which had been put into effect in 1975.

7. Elizabeth E. Bailey, David R. Graham, and Daniel P. Kaplan, *Deregulating the Airlines* (Cambridge: The MIT Press, 1985), p. 185.

8. Data from *Aviation Week and Space Technology*, June 14, 1982, and from the Air Transport Association.

9. Data provided by the Air Transport Association.

10. *Business Week*, August 23, 1982, and "Reservations Systems Likely to be Disciplined," *Air Transport World* (September 1983), p. 24.

11. *Business Week*, April 7, 1980.

12. *Business Week*, August 23, 1982.

13. "A Bid to End Bias," *OAG Frequent Flyer* (November 1984), p. 36.

14. Eastern's SYSTEM ONE and Delta's DATAS systems, later entrants, attempted to collect subscribers from the rapidly shrinking group of still unautomated agents but apparently met with only limited success.

15. For a more detailed discussion of these issues, see "Special Report: Computers," *Air Transport World* (September 1983), pp. 24–30.

16. "A Bid to End Bias," p. 40.

17. *Third-Party Complaint of Delta Airlines before the U.S. Department of Transportation*, Docket 44094, June 16, 1986, p. 10.

18. Ibid., pp. 5, 12–33.

19. Cited in David Martindale, "New Reservations about Airline Computers," *OAG Frequent Flyer* (December 1982), p. 45.

20. Some of these ideas were initially set forth by Donald Evans, unpublished paper on the travel agent industry, Harvard Business School, May 1984.

21. For an extended discussion of the nature of competition in a variety of industries, see Michael E. Porter, *Competitive Strategy* (New York: Free Press, 1980).

Chapter 9

1. Albert W. Stoffel, "American Bilaterial Air Transport Agreements on the Threshold of the Jet Transport Age," *Journal of Air Law and Commerce* 26 (1959), pp. 120–123, for a description of the dispute at the Chicago conference and the subsequent Bermuda I agreement.

2. "Cabotage" is a French term for coastal trade. Cabotage laws restrict the movement of people or goods between two points within a nation to carriers of that nation.

3. J. G. Gazdik, "Rate Making and the IATA Traffic Conferences," *Journal of Air Law and Commerce* 16 (1949), p. 298 et seq. The acceptance of the IATA conference machinery was not an easy one. The CAB was empowered by the 1938 Civil Aeronautics Act to approve or disapprove of rate agreements "with each other or with foreign air carriers." The initial acceptance of the IATA rate machinery was for one year only.

4. P. McGoldrik, "Regulation of Service Competition in International Air Travel," *Harvard International Law Journal* 8 (1967), pp. 101–102. Also "Sandwich Settlement," *The New York Times*, April 27, 1958, p. 11, which demonstrates the extent such standardization reached for limiting cold sandwiches provided on board aircraft.

5. Fears that IATA regulation would lead to inefficient operations was always mitigated to some extent by the existence of competitive alternatives. It was only in the mid-1950s, for example, that aviation volumes measured in passengers began to exceed maritime volumes for travel across the North Atlantic. But the largest competitive force outside of the IATA system was that of the nonscheduled (charter) operations. These were of two types, one dedicated to charter service and the other being the nonscheduled operation of a major scheduled carrier. Many IATA members were therefore also providing competition to the IATA system. Charter operations, though, had always been held in check by rules that curbed their market penetration; relaxation of the rules during the 1970s brought increasing market share to these operations. See R. M. Smithies, "The Changing Demand for Air Transport: The North Atlantic Case," *Journal of Transport Economics and Policy* 7 (September 1973), p. 251 et seq.; J. Mutti and Y. Murai, "Airline Travel in the North Atlantic," *Journal of Transport Economics and Policy* 11 (January 1977), pp. 45–51; K. Hammarskjold, "Trends in International Aviation since World War II and Government Policies with Respect to Routes, Rates, Charters, Capacity and Deregulation," *Proceedings of the International Aviation Symposium held at Kingston, Jamaica*, 1979, pp. 23–25.

6. Data extracted from International Civil Aviation Organization statistics.

7. A Provisional International Civil Aviation Organization (PICAO) was formed at the 1944 Chicago Convention to oversee operational safety and other such matters as they arose during the development of international commercial aviation. This became the International Civil Aviation Organization (ICAO) on April 4, 1947. In October 1947 ICAO developed a relationship agreement with the newly formed United Nations.

8. M. Straszheim, *The International Airline Industry* (Washington: Brookings Institution, 1969), pp. 15–16.

9. John R. Meyer and Clinton V. Oster, Jr., eds., *Airline Deregulation: The Early Experience* (Boston: Auburn House, 1981), chapter 2, pp. 33–37.

10. Agreement on International Aviation, July 23, 1977, U.S.-Great Britain, TIAS No. 8641.

11. Senator Howard Cannon, Opening Statement to the Hearings before the Senate Subcommittee on Aviation of the Committee on Commerce, Science, and Transportation, 95th Congress, November 29 and December 1, 1977, p. 2 (hence referred to as Hearings).

12. See Alan Boyd, Special Ambassador to the United States-United Kingdom Bilateral Air Transport Negotiations in *Hearings*, pp. 72–74, for a description of the events surrounding the Bermuda II negotiations.

13. Bermuda II contained a formula for allowing capacity additions related to the market growth. Capacity additions beyond those allowed by the formula required prior approval.

14. Alfred Kahn in *Hearings*, pp. 4–11.

15. The liberal agreement with Belgium was done in two stages. The general form was stated in November 1977, and it was completed in its full form in December 1978. (TIAS No. 8923).

16. Public Law 96-192. 94 Sat 35 (49 USC 1301).

17. The statements here are contractions and simplifications of the goals stated in the International Air Transportation Act of 1979, Section 17.

18. The first use of the term "open skies" goes back to the Roosevelt administration. The subject became the focus of hearings and reports from Congress, the CAB, the Army, and the Navy. The substance of the views held then formulated the views put forward by the United States at the 1944 Chicago Convention.

19. See Federal Aviation Act of 1958, Section 101 72 Stat. 737 as amended, which limits non-U.S. citizen ownership or control of a U.S. carrier to a maximum of 25 percent.

20. See M. Straszheim, *The International Airline Industry*, pp. 46–47. There has been some evidence of a shift within Europe for a weakening of such pooling agreements. See, for example, Wall Street Journal, "Soon to Lose Subsidy, British Airways Seeks to Increase Efficiency," February 28, 1985, p. 1.

21. In referring to a 1973 Department of State report on the North Atlantic, the CAB had commented:

No European government, because of its air transport interests and national interests in tourism, would risk the possibility that its agreement with us might be less advantageous than a bilateral agreement we might subsequently enter into with another European government.

The fear of traffic diversion embodied in this statement would appear to be greater where connections between competing bilateral gateways are cheap and result in a small time penalty. For example, the airports of Paris face a greater likelihood of traffic diversion to Brussels which is only two hours away by surface transportation, then those of London, which require connection by air at high internal European air fares or by an extremely time-consuming land/sea link. The likelihood of a diversion also depends on the origin of the traveler. On a journey from the United States to Europe, for example, the dominant part of the route in terms of price and time would normally be the trans-Atlantic portion of the journey, and many European gateways would be considered regardless of final destination. In journeys with shorter origin/destinations, the traveler is much less likely to consider indirect routes; a traveler from Zurich to Paris, for example, is unlikely to consider traveling over London. In bilateral negotiation, the likelihood of diversion will play a more important role therefore between distant bilateral partners than it will between those who are geographically close. Over shorter distances the question may be more the use of air over some surface mode rather than diversion between air routes.

22. One action by the CAB that crucially affected the atmosphere for conducting bilateral negotiations was the CAB Show Cause Order 78-6-78 of June 9, 1978. This CAB Show Cause Order effectively withdrew the antitrust immunity enjoyed by the IATA tariff agreements since their first exemption in 1946. The Show Cause Order potentially made U.S. airline participation in IATA traffic conferences illegal; non-U.S. airlines flying to the U.S. gateways were also potentially subject to U.S. antitrust action. The attempt by the CAB to ensure that international tariffs were arrived at in a competitive manner was clearly in keeping with its

stated objectives and the future IATCA. But many IATA airline members considered the Show Cause Order as a unilateral imposition of U.S. antitrust laws to international aviation. The CAB order was modified over time to apply only in the first instance to airline activities on the North Atlantic, a region where the competitive forces were so strong that it seems doubtful that any comprehensive agreement on rates would be possible with or without the Show Cause Order. The Show Cause Order coincided with the announcement of a reorganization within IATA.

23. Citizenship statistics are considered more reliable for arrivals than for departures.

24. The geographical position of Japan is such that there are no easy alternatives for intermediate stops for travelers in the U.S.–Japan market. Most likely alternatives require Japan to be overflown from the United States thereby adding time and cost to alternative routes.

25. It is at least conceivable that the economics of direct operation could be such that higher prices would result. All other things being equal, a reduction in the landings and takeoffs involved in a direct flight should lead to reduced costs and travel times—and therefore the more gateways, the lower costs should be. But passenger demand may be so low as to lead to uneconomic load factors or excessive overhead for gateway infrastructure. The probability of such a cost increase occurring at present volume levels for U.S. gateways (assuming sensible management) would seem minimal.

26. Interpretation of these data is conditioned by the role of individual carriers in particular regions; Pan Am in Europe, for example, is heavily involved in domestic West German markets, and TWA also has considerable traffic within Europe.

Chapter 10

1. For descriptions of the development of turnpikes, canals, and railroads during the nineteenth century, see Elliott James, *Principles of Railway Transportation* (New York: Macmillan, 1924), pp. 36–70, or John F. Stover, *American Railroads* (Chicago: University of Chicago Press, 1961).

2. Some typical canal and packet journeys are described in Clyde H. Freed, *The Story of Railroad Passenger Fares* (no publisher given, 1942), pp. 3–6, 16–21.

3. John F. Stover, for example, cites only 48 hours to travel between New York and St. Louis, a distance of more than 1,000 miles, in the late 1850s; *Iron Road to the West: American Railroads in the 1850s* (New York: Columbia University Press, 1978), p. 186.

4. For a description of the extensive network of limited trains in the decades around the turn of the century, see William W. Kratville, *Steam, Steel, and Limiteds*, 2d ed. (Omaha: Kratville Publications, 1983).

5. Freed, *The Story of Railroad Passenger Fares*, p. 6.

6. Freed, *The Story of Railroad Passenger Fares*, pp. 8–10, and Lewis C. Sorrell and Harry A. Wheeler, *Passenger Transport in the United States: 1920–1950* (Chicago: Railway Business Association, 1944), p. 2.

7. The ICC would allow fares higher than 3 cents on lines with low traffic density or which were unusually difficult to construct. Freed, *The Story of Railroad Passenger Fares*, pp. 26–27, 245–295.

8. Freed, *The Story of Railroad Passenger Fares*, p. 33.

9. For a brief description of the circumstances leading to the Transportation Act of 1920, see Dudley F. Pegrum, *Transportation Economics and Public Policy*, 3d ed. (Homewood, Ill.:

Richard D. Irwin, 1973), pp. 290–298. For an account of the immediate impact of the act on interstate and intrastate passenger fares, see Freed, *The Story of Railroad Passenger Fares*, pp. 34–38.

10. Contemporaries regarded intercity buses as close competitors to the railroads and bus industry associations were very active in lobbying the ICC against contemplated 1.5 or 2 cent railroad fares during the 1930s; see Freed, *The Story of Railroad Passenger Fares*, pp. 46, 47, 53, and Sorrell and Wheeler, *Passenger Transport in the United States: 1920–1950*, p. 5.

11. Some of the early streamlined equipment was designed to reduce air resistance, but railroads soon realized that the principal advantages lay in lightweight construction; see John H. White, Jr., *The American Railroad Passenger Car* (Baltimore: Johns Hopkins University Press, 1978), pp. 158–163, 612–625.

12. The engineering firm of Cloverdale and Colpits was hired by the railroad industry to evaluate the results of streamlining, and their reports were uniformly enthusiastic. For the last and most detailed report, see Cloverdale and Colpits, *Report on Streamline, Light-Weight, High Speed Passenger Trains*, 1950.

13. White, *The American Railroad Passenger Car*, pp. 193–200, 625–630.

14. For a good overview of the cost allocation controversy, see James C. Nelson, *Railroad Transportation and Public Policy* (Washington: Brookings Institution, 1959), pp. 286–301. Also see John R. Meyer et al., *Avoidable Costs of Passenger Train Service*, report prepared for the Association of American Railroads by the Research Committee of the Aeronautical Research Foundation, 1957.

15. George W. Hilton, *The Transportation Act of 1958: A Decade of Experience* (Bloomington: Indiana University Press, 1969), pp. 35–38, 97–154, 193–198.

16. Although Amtrak was not initially subject to ICC fare and service regulation, the original legislation stipulated that once the "basic system" was established, it was to function at the same level of service until June of 1973. After that time Amtrak would be allowed to withdraw service from unprofitable routes, subject to ICC approval. With the passage of the Amtrak Improvement Act of 1973, the ICC was required to establish a set of service quality standards governing the behavior of Amtrak and any railroad providing 500 passenger train miles a day (commuter trains were exempt). These rules included a toll-free phone reservation system, maximum permissible delay times, and requirements concerning food and beverage service, baggage handling, handicap access, sleeping car availability, seating specifications, lounge space, and smoking regulations.

17. Amtrak supporters have traditionally defended intercity rail passenger subsidies as a means to promote energy conservation, reduce highway and airport congestion and pollution, or help low-income travelers. For a critical evaluation of these arguments, see Sally A. Ferris, *Federal Subsidies for Rail Passenger Service: An Assessment of Amtrak* (Washington: U.S. Congressional Budget Office, 1982), or George W. Hilton, *Amtrak: The National Railroad Passenger Corporation* (Washington: American Enterprise Institute, 1980).

More recently Amtrak supporters have defended rail subsidies by arguing that they are no larger than airline subsidies. The principal airline subsidy, they contend, is the deductability of airline fares for business travel as a business expense in the calculation of the corporate profit tax. If perhaps half the travelers are on business, and the corporate tax rate is around 50 percent, the argument continues, then approximately one quarter of all airline fares is paid for by this indirect tax subsidy. See W. Graham Claytor, Jr., "Testimony of W. Graham Claytor, Jr., President and Chairman of the Board [of the] National Railroad Passenger Corporation, before the Subcommittee on Commerce, Transportation and Tourism, Committee on Energy and Commerce, U.S. House of Representatives, Thursday, March 14, 1985," photocopied.

The business travel deduction argument is fallacious for at least two reasons. First, rail fares can be deducted as business expenses, as there is no distinction between the rail and air modes in the corporate tax code. The fact that business travelers tend not to use the rail mode, despite identical tax deductability (and heavier direct subsidies), reflects the inferior service offered by rail rather than any tax differences. Second, and most important, the corporate income tax is not a rebate for the specific use of one input (e.g., air fares) or another but rather a tax on profits. The income tax therefore should have *no* impact on the choice of the mix of inputs a firm uses, since it applies equally to every one.

18. For a review of high-speed passenger rail technologies, see U.S. Congress, Office of Technology Assessment, *U.S. Passenger Rail Technologies*, Report OTA-STI-222 (Washington: Government Printing Office, 1983), pp. 15–26.

19. By the mid-1980s, however, none of these proposals had managed to raise the required capital, and there were serious doubts whether patronage would be high enough to make the trains self-supporting. For a summary of recent proposals for high-speed rail service in the United States, see U.S. Congress, Office of Technology Assessment, *U.S. Passenger Rail Technologies*, pp. 57–68.

20. For an excellent overview of the early growth and regulation of the intercity bus industry, see Carlton Jackson, *Hounds of the Road: A History of the Greyhound Bus Company* (Bowling Green, Ohio: Bowling Green University Popular Press, 1984).

21. In 1972, for example, 27.7 percent of bus travelers had incomes below $5,000, and 47.9 percent were either under 18 or 65 and older. For all intercity modes the comparable statistics are 8.7 percent with incomes under $5,000 and 30.0 percent under 18 or 65 and older. See Interstate Commerce Commission, *The Intercity Bus Industry* (Washington: Government Printing Office, 1978), pp. 29–30.

22. American Bus Association (formerly National Association of Motor Bus Owners) *Bus Facts*, 1981 ed. (Washington: American Bus Association, 1981), p. iii.

23. American Bus Association, *Bus Facts*, 1971 and 1981 eds.

24. American Bus Association, *Bus Facts*, 1981 ed., pp. ii, 3.

25. For evidence on the extent of cross-subsidies among charter, package, and regularly scheduled services, see Interstate Commerce Commission, *The Intercity Bus Industry*, pp. 93–100, and Elizabeth A. Pinkston, "The Intercity Bus Transportation Industry," Ph.D. dissertation, Yale University, 1975, pp. 29–33.

26. Interstate Commerce Commission, *The Intercity Bus Industry*, pp. 101–104.

27. The best known example, which Greyhound cited in explaining its need to reduce bus driver wages, was the trip from Newark, New Jersey, to Norfolk, Virginia, for which People Express Airlines charged $23.00 while Greyhound charged $56.15. For more details, see James H. Miller, "The New Competitive Order in the Intercity Bus Industry," paper presented before the Transportation and Public Utilities Group of the American Economic Association, San Francisco, 1983, p. 17.

28. For excellent summaries of the early effects of the 1982 act, see Miller, "The New Competitive Order," and Elizabeth A. Pinkston, "The Rise and Fall of Bus Regulation," *Regulation* 8 (September–December 1984), pp. 45–52. For a more complete description of the 1982 act, see Martin T. Ferris and Norman E. Daniel, "Bus Regulatory Reform Act of 1982," *Transportation Journal* 23 (1983), pp. 4–15.

29. Clinton V. Oster, Jr., and C. Kurt Zorn, "Impact of Regulatory Reform on Intercity Bus Service in the United States," *Transportation Journal* 25 (Spring 1986).

30. Miller, "The New Competitive Order," p. 14.

31. Draft versions of the 1982 Bus Regulatory Reform Act included essential service guarantees, but those provisions were dropped from the final law.

32. See the comparisons between Class I and small bus carriers in chapter 11 and the figures cited in Miller, "The New Competitive Order," pp. 16–17.

33. Miller, "The New Competitive Order," p. 17.

34. Clinton V. Oster, Jr., and C. Kurt Zorn, "Franchising as a Response to Increased Competition in the Intercity Bus Industry," *Transportation Research Forum* 27 (1986).

35. Motor Vehicle Manufacturers Association, *Motor Vehicle Facts and Figures 1981* (Detroit: Motor Vehicle Manufacturers Association, 1981), p. 16.

36. The 1927 figure is from a survey of 4.1 million families conducted by the General Federation of Women's Clubs and cited in James J. Flink, *The Car Culture* (Cambridge: The MIT Press, 1975), p. 142.

37. John B. Rae, *The American Automobile: A Brief History*, The Chicago History of American Civilization, Daniel J. Boorstin, ed. (Chicago: University of Chicago Press, 1965), pp. 45–48, 74–75, 90, and Flink, *The Car Culture*, p. 173.

38. The retail prices are for the touring version of the Model T; see Rae, *The American Automobile*, p. 61.

39. John B. Rae, *The Road and the Car in American Life* (Cambridge: The MIT Press, 1971), p. 69.

40. Flink, *The Car Culture*, p. 150.

41. Rae, *The Road and the Car*, pp. 74–75.

42. These estimates are from John F. Stover who, unfortunately, does not cite his sources; see John F. Stover, *American Railroads*, The Chicago History of American Civilization, Daniel J. Boorstin, ed. (Chicago: University of Chicago Press, 1961), p. 212.

43. Transportation Association of America, *Transport Facts and Trends*, 6th ed., 1969 as cited by Rae, *The Road and the Car*, p. 92.

44. Rae, *The Road and the Car*, pp. 79–81, 173.

45. Ibid.

46. Mark H. Rose, *Interstate: Express Highway Politics, 1941–1956* (Lawrence: The Regents Press of Kansas, 1979), pp. 15–19.

47. For a map of the eastern toll road system, see Rae, *The American Automobile*, p. 183. The system is described in more detail in Rae, *The Road and the Car*, pp. 173–183.

48. Rae, *The Road and the Car*, pp. 183–187.

49. Rose, *Interstate*, esp. pp. 18, 74, 85–87. In 1954 the President's Advisory Committee on a National Highway Program, chaired by Lucius D. Clay, recommended against a toll system because 10 to 20 percent of the proposed system could not be so financed.

50. For a detailed description of the 1956 act and its provisions, see U.S. Congressional Budget Office, *Highway Assistance Programs: A Historical Perspective* (Washington: U.S. Congressional Budget Office, 1978), pp. 12–29.

51. Approximately $40 billion of the $104 billion 1977 estimate is the cost of sections uncompleted. See U.S. Congressional Budget Office, *Highway Assistance Programs*, p. xiii.

52. *Statistical Abstract of the United States* (Washington: U.S. Bureau of the Census, 1985), p. 591.

53. For a more complete description of federal regulations and programs to promote more balanced transportation in urban areas, see John R. Meyer and José A. Gómez-Ibáñez, *Autos, Transit and Cities* (Cambridge: Harvard University Press, 1981).

54. For a more complete analysis of the achievements of the federal air pollution control program, see Lawrence J. White, *The Regulation of Air Pollution Emissions from Motor Vehicles* (Washington: American Enterprise Institute, 1982).

55. Meyer and Gómez-Ibáñez, *Autos, Transit and Cities*, pp. 90–91.

Chapter 11

1. User-paid costs thus include the various fuel and ticket taxes and airport landing fees that users pay to help finance the highway, airport, and airway systems but exclude any such costs not covered in these fees. In the case of rail service the user-paid costs assume the continuation of the recent policy of charging rail fares that cover only about 34 percent of rail passenger operating costs.

2. Some of the policies examined would change the cost of intercity travel and thus the volume. However, since the two major modes, auto and air, are assumed to be deregulated throughout and receive virtually no subsidy, these modes will not have significant cost changes.

3. Since the relative costs of each mode depend on the volumes of passengers they are carrying, and vice versa, it is important to ensure that the mode share projections are consistent with the cost estimates on which they are based. Thus the demand projections are developed through an iterative procedure wherein mode share is initially projected using cost estimates that assume that travelers are divided equally among the modes. If these initial projections are not consistent with the shares assumed in the cost estimates, demand is reestimated using cost estimates based on the previous round of demand projections. This process is repeated until the demand and cost estimates are roughly consistent with one another. Thus volume changes on a route, regardless of source, can influence modal shares.

4. As explained in appendix B, the lack of reliable data on access time or cost in the National Travel Survey made it impossible to estimate a reliable access variable in the demand model. As a result the assumptions about access distance or cost are those implicit in the data from the 1977 travel survey in most of the simulations, but as noted in the text, a few simulations make alternative access assumptions.

5. U.S. Bureau of the Census, *Current Population Reports*, Series P-60, No. 122, *Illustrative Projections of Money Income Size Distributions for Households, 1980–1985* (Washington: Government Printing Office, 1980), p. 100.

6. This assumption is highly speculative. Although average household size probably strongly influences the size of the travel party for nonbusiness trips, for example, it may not have any effect on the size of the travel party for business trips. Moreover, even if party size is proportional to household size, forecasts of household size are uncertain. The median census projection of household size were used for the projections; see U.S. Bureau of the Census, *Current Population Reports*, Series P-25, No. 805, *Projections of the Number of Households and Families: 1979–1995* (Washington: Government Printing Office, 1979), p. 17. These projections have been criticized, however; see George S. Masnick and John R. Pitkin, "The Baby Boom and the Squeeze on Multigenerational Households," working paper of the Joint Center for Urban Studies of MIT and Harvard, presented at the annual meetings of the Population Association of America, Pittsburgh, April 14–16, 1983.

7. The traffic densities on routes connecting cities of various sizes were estimated by tabulating actual travel volumes for city-pairs in various population categories from the 1977 National Travel Survey, and then expanding those sample volumes to estimates of actual travel based on the proportion of households that were interviewed in each urban area as part of the survey.

8. See chapter 4 and John R. Meyer and Clinton V. Oster, Jr., *Deregulation and the New Airline Entrepreneurs* (Cambridge: The MIT Press, 1984), chapter 11. In 1977–78 the effects of low-cost carriers were still largely confined to intrastate markets in Texas and California.

9. The elimination of subsidies actually reduces long-haul air fares slightly (since the federal air ticket tax "overcharged" long-haul air travel relative to short-haul air travel in 1980).

10. For a detailed discussion of the effects of incomes and other factors on auto ownership, see John F. Kain and Gary R. Fauth, *The Effects of Urban Spatial Structure on Household Auto Ownership Decisions and Journey to Work Mode Choices*, Report DOT-OS-30099-11 to the U.S. Department of Transportation, 1976.

11. Though including both an auto ownership and an income variable might exaggerate the effects of income on auto availability and use, excluding auto ownership entirely and entering income only in the travel time variable may underestimate its effects. Modal split models are extremely sensitive to the manner in which income and auto ownership variables are included, and there is little theoretical reason to prefer one specification over another. For a discussion of these problems in the context of urban travel modes, see José A. Gómez-Ibáñez and Gary R. Fauth, "Using Demand Elasticities From Disaggregate Mode Split Models," *Transportation* 9 (1980), pp. 105–124.

12. Japan, Britain, France, and West Germany operate rail passenger trains with speeds of 125 mph or more. For descriptions of foreign high-speed rail systems, see John W. Fisher and Lenore Sek, *High Speed Passenger Trains: Foreign Experience and U.S. Prospects* (Washington: U.S. Congress, Congressional Research Service, Report 82-157E, 1982); and U.S. Congress, Office of Technology Assessment, *U.S. Passenger Rail Technologies*, Report OTA-ST1-222 (Washington: Government Printing Office, 1983). The Japanese Shinkansen serves as the model for the high-speed rail cost estimates in the simulations and is designed to operate at speeds up to 160 mph, although public concern about noise and vibration has largely limited operations to 130 mph or less. The original line from Tokyo to Osaka was opened in 1964 and later extended south of Osaka to Okayama and Hakata (in 1972 and 1975, respectively) and from a suburb north of Tokyo to Marioka and Niigata (in 1981). Two new branches from the Omiga suburb of Tokyo to Marioka and Niigata opened in 1982. A connection between the Omiga station and the main station in Tokyo is under construction. The French TGV has operated between Paris and Lyon since 1982 with maximum speeds of 170 mph. The French National Railway plans to extend the original line to Marseilles and to build a second high-speed rail line between Paris and Bordeaux if the government will agree to subsidize the capital costs. British and West German high-speed trains operate on conventional rather than specially constructed tracks and thus can reach top speeds of only 125 mph. The British have operated several high-speed routes out of London since the mid 1970s, whereas the West Germans operated an experimental service between Munich and Hamburg for a brief period during the 1970s.

In addition to the high-speed rail systems in operation, several foreign countries have research programs to investigate potential improvements that would allow even faster trains. The most widely publicized are the Japanese and German research into the use of electromagnetic forces to provide support, lateral guidance, and propulsion for trains without direct physical contact between the vehicle and the guideway. By reducing vehicle-guideway friction, trains can reach safe speeds of 250 mph or more. Although several test cars have been demonstrated, so many serious questions remain about both the technical feasibility and the economic costs of magnetic levitation that it will be a decade or more before it can be known whether the technology is practical. For a description of the promises and problems of magnetic levitation technologies, see U.S. Congress, Office of Technology Assessment, *U.S. Passenger Rail Technologies*, pp. 71–79.

A less glamorous but potentially more important area of current research is the British and

Canadian efforts to develop a train that will tilt on curves to permit speeds of 150 to 200 mph on conventional track. Technical problems with the tilting mechanism had not been resolved as of the mid-1980s. See U.S. Congress, Office of Technology Assessment, *U.S. Passenger Rail Technologies*, p. 20, and Stig Noldqvist and John Rosen, *Faster Trains—Technology, Prospects, and Impact* (Stockholm: National Swedish Board for Technical Development, 1984), pp. 33–36.

13. Fisher and Sek, *High Speed Passenger Trains*, p. 9.

14. The JNR's bullet train may capture as much as 80 percent of the market for 200 to 300 mile trips in the corridors where it operates; these estimates were developed by Arthur D. Little, Inc., as part of a confidential report for the American High Speed Rail Corportation on the possible market for a bullet train from Los Angeles to San Diego; interview with P. Ranganath Nayak of Arthur D. Little, June 1982.

15. Amtrak carried 21 million passengers in 1980; for Japanese and U.S. statistics, see U.S. Congress, Office of Technology Assessment, *U.S. Passenger Rail Technologies*, p. 21; and National Railroad Passenger Corporation, *Annual Report, 1980* (Washington, 1981).

16. For a comparison of the populations and densities of major U.S. and foreign cities, see U.S. Congress, Office of Technology Assessment, *U.S. Passenger Rail Technologies*, p. 31.

17. United Nations, *Yearbook of National Statistics, 1980*, Vol. 2, p. 17.

18. Japan, Prime Minister's Office, Statistics Bureau, *Japan Statistical Yearbook, 1982*, p. 122.

19. Japanese regular coach fares appear to be about the same as U.S. coach fares for trips under 400 miles, based on a small sample of fares from the March 1980 international and U.S. editions of the *Official Airline Guide*. Fewer discount fares are available in Japan, however, and thus the average fare actually paid is probably lower in the United States than Japan. The deregulated fares assumed in most of the simulations in this chapter are about half the level of regular Japanese economy fares.

20. Tokyo has two airports, for example, an older one close to the center of town and a newer one further from the center. Several of the scheduled flights from Tokyo to Osaka originate from the more distant airport.

21. U.S. Congress, Office of Technology Assessment, *U.S. Passenger Rail Technologies*, p. 24.

22. According to Mr. Ichiroh Mitsui, director of the Washington Office of the Japanese National Railway, in 1980 the Shinkansen operating and capital expenses amounted to $1.9 billion while passenger revenues were $3.2 billion (telephone interview, July 13, 1983). Other estimates place the Shinkansen closer to break-even, however, and predict substantial losses for both the Shinkansen extensions and for the French TGV; see "No Way to Run a Japanese Railway," *The Economist* 283, April 17, 1982, pp. 96–97; "Faster than Flying," *The Economist* 280, September 26, 1981, p. 75; and U.S. Congress, Office of Technology Assessment, *U.S. Passenger Rail Technologies*, pp. 22, 24, 25.

23. This approach was used because of the lack of a separate access variable in the demand equation used to predict modal split.

24. Although some of the promoters of high-speed rail systems in the United States have prepared analyses that claim that the rail systems would be self-supporting, few independent assessments generally concur with these findings. For an excellent independent assessment of high-speed rail proposals in the midwest, see Herbert Baer and Donna Vandenbrink, "High Speed Rail in the Midwest," *Economic Perspectives* 8 (September–October 1984), pp. 3–12; and Herbert Baer, William Testa, Donna Vandenbrink, and Bruce Williams, *High Speed Rail in the Midwest: An Economic Analysis* (Chicago: Federal Reserve Bank of Chicago, 1984). For a critique of the economic feasibility study prepared by promoters of the Los Angeles–San Diego bullet train, see Jonathan Richmond, *Slicing the Cake: The Case for a*

Los Angeles–San Diego Bullet Train Service, report prepared for the City of Tustin, Calif., October 1983.

25. Fuel economy measured in miles per gallon by federal test procedures; see John R. Meyer and José A. Gómez-Ibáñez, *Autos, Transit, and Cities* (Cambridge: Harvard University Press, 1981), pp. 138–139, 90–93.

26. John R. Meyer and Clinton V. Oster, Jr., eds., *Airline Deregulation: The Early Experience* (Boston: Auburn House, 1981), chap. 8.

27. Meyer and Oster, *Deregulation and the New Airline Entrepreneurs*, chapter 9.

28. See, for example, National Academy of Sciences, *Jamaica Bay and Kennedy Airport* (Washington: National Academy of Sciences, 1971); and U.S. Department of Transportation, *Recommendations for Northeast Corridor Transportation*, report to the U.S. Congress (Washington: U.S. Department of Transportation, 1971).

29. See, for example, Richard de Neufville, *Airport Systems Planning* (Cambridge: The MIT Press, 1976), pp. 50–51.

30. For example, new microwave landing systems may reduce congestion; see U.S. Congressional Budget Office, *Improving the Air Traffic Control System: An Assessment of the National Airspace System Plan* (Washington: Government Printing Office, 1983), p. 17.

31. As of the summer of 1985, for example, off-peak seats from Boston to New York were available for slightly more than half the peak fare. Similarly a round trip from Boston to National Airport in Washington, D.C., cost around $230 on an unrestricted coach ticket and $149 on the least expensive restricted fare, while round trips from Boston to Dulles Airport in Washington were available for only $99 for unrestricted coach service.

32. There are many studies of the advantages of landing fees; for example, see Ross D. Eckert, *Airports and Congestion: A Problem of Misplaced Subsidies* (Washington: American Enterprise Institute, 1972).

33. Meyer and Oster, *Deregulation and the New Airline Entrepreneurs*, chap. 9.

34. The bus contribution, however, will be somewhat greater by many measures than these numbers would suggest: buses will continue to carry more passengers (but on relatively short hauls) than any other public mode and will disproportionately serve the young, the poor, the aged and those living in very small communities (e.g., less than 2,500 population), all groups that often have been targeted as special concerns of public policy.

Chapter 12

1. Alfred E. Kahn, "The Macroeconomics of Microeconomic Policy," paper presented at American Economic Association conference, Dallas, December 1984.

2. John R. Meyer, "Toward a Better Understanding of Deregulation: Some Hypotheses and Observations," *International Journal of Transport Economics* 10 (April–August 1983). pp. 35–53.

3. John R. Meyer and A. L. Morton, "A Better Way to Run the Railroads," *Harvard Business Review* (July–August 1974), pp. 141–148.

4. William E. Fruhan, *The Fight for Competitive Advantage: A Study of the U.S. Domestic Trunk Air Carriers* (Boston: Division of Research, Harvard Business School, 1972).

5. Michael E. Porter, *Competitive Strategy: Techniques for Analyzing Industries and Competitors* (New York: The Free Press, 1980), chap. 2.

6. Porter, *Competitive Strategy*, p. 39.

7. John R. Meyer and Clinton V. Oster, Jr., *Deregulation and the New Airline Entrepreneurs* (Cambridge: The MIT Press, 1984), chap. 10.

8. Clinton V. Oster, Jr., and C. Kurt Zorn, "Impact of Regulatory Reform on Intercity Bus Service in the United States," *Transportation Journal* 25 (Spring 1986).

9. Meyer and Oster, *Deregulation and the New Airline Entrepreneurs*, chap. 10.

Appendix A

1. A recent government study estimated that air and noise pollution costs amounted to 1.6 cents per automobile mile in urban areas and negligible amounts in rural areas. Since most of the mileage on intercity trips is through rural areas, the average air and noise pollution costs are probably less than 0.5 cents per auto mile. Vehicle ownership and operating costs, by comparison, amount to around 20 cents per vehicle mile. See U.S. Department of Transportation, Federal Highway Administration, *Final Report on the Federal Highway Cost Allocation Project* (Washington: Government Printing Office, 1982), p. E-12.

2. One aspect of service quality that is not comparable for all the modes, depending on the preferences of individual travelers, is the cost of a hotel room that may be required on a long automobile trip.

3. The average vehicle occupancy on trips of over 40 miles highway distance was 2.34 in 1977. See J. Richard Kuzmyak, *Vehicle Occupancy*, Report No. 6 of the *1977 Nationwide Personal Transportation Study* (Washington: U.S. Department of Transportation, Federal Highway Administration, 1981), p. 16.

4. William D. Warren, "Changes in American Intercity Rail Transportation: 1950–1980," *Transportation Quarterly* 36 (January 1982), p. 155.

5. The cost estimates provided here assume that highway and train routes are 15 percent greater than the geographic distance. Air routes for jet aircraft are 2 percent greater than the geographic distance plus added maneuvering distance of 30 miles for takeoff and landing. Air routes propeller aircraft are 5 percent greater than the geographic distance plus 15 miles for maneuvering.

6. The Amtrak cost model estimates only those expenses that Amtrak regards as avoidable within one or two years by adding or deleting a train route from its national rail system. These short-term avoidable expenses—which consist mainly of fuel, engine and train crew wages, on-board passenger service, and some switching and dispatching costs—account for only 58 percent of Amtrak's total systemwide costs, including depreciation. Over a period of several years Amtrak estimates that additional costs amounting to 21.25 percent of short-term avoidable costs (or 12.33 percent of total systemwide costs) are also affected by changing routes; these so-called long-term avoidable costs include most light locomotive and passenger car maintenance and a portion of right-of-way maintenance. Approximately 29.67 percent of total Amtrak system costs are regarded by the company as fixed, or unaffected, if a single route is added or deleted. Fixed expenses include corporate overhead expenses, heavy repair expenses, some costs of stations used by several routes, maintenance of mainline right-of-way, and most depreciation of equipment and facilities. For a full explanation of Amtrak's cost accounting see U.S. Congressional Budget Office, *Federal Subsidies for Rail Passenger Service: An Assessment of Amtrak* (Washington: Government Printing Office, 1982), pp. 45–46, 72–77.

7. These "fixed" operating costs account for only about 15 percent of total rail operating and capital costs in most of the cost simulations reported here. In most cases the exclusion of these costs would not be sufficient to make rail cost competitive with other intercity modes.

8. Each self-propelled and Amfleet car is assumed to last for 20 years and have an initial purchase price of $1 million and $800,000 respectively. A 3000 hp diesel locomotive is assumed to cost $900,000 and last 15 years.

9. Incremental right-of-way capital expenditures varied from $23,529 to $500,000 per mile to accommodate between one and six additional passenger trains per day in each direction. A representative estimate of $200,000 per mile is used here and this expense is amortized over an expected 20-year life. These improvements are assumed to accommodate up to 12 trains per day in each direction. See U.S. Department of Transportation and National Rail Passenger Corporation, "Rail Passenger Corridors: Analysis of Potential Improvements" (Washington: February 1980).

10. Construction of the initial lines of the Shinkansen between Tokyo and Hakata is estimated to have cost an average of $20 million per mile in 1979 dollars. The two latest lines connecting Omiya with Marioka and Nigata were constructed through relatively hilly terrain at an estimated cost of $35 to $40 million per mile in early 1980s dollars. See U.S. Congress, Office of Technology Assessment, *U.S. Passenger Rail Technologies*, p. 22.

11. The French costs averaged $4 million per mile, while the U.S. costs were $4.5 to $6 million per mile, all in late 1970s or early 1980s dollars. The French costs include the construction of a few segments of entirely new right-of-way to reduce curves and grades, but it is not clear that land acquisition expenses of the new segments or delays and other interferences to freight trains on the upgraded segments were included in the reported French costs. Interference to freight trains was probably also not included in the U.S. cost estimates. See U.S. Congress, Office of Technology Assessment, *U.S. Passenger Rail Technologies*, pp. 24, 40, 60; and John W. Fischer and Lenore Sek, *High Speed Passenger Trains: Foreign Experience and U.S. Prospects* (Washington: Congressional Research Service, Report No. 82-157E, 1982), pp. 19–29.

12. Of the proposals that are the farthest developed, only the advocates of the Chicago–Detroit route and the Ohio system contend that they could significantly improve speeds on upgraded existing rail right-of-ways (at projected costs of $2.5 and $11 million per mile). The backers of the Los Angeles-San Diego, Los Angeles–Las Vegas, Tampa–Orlando–Miami, and Chicago–Milwaukee lines call for construction of entirely new right-of-ways. See U.S. Congress, Office of Technology Assessment, *U.S. Passenger Rail Technologies*, pp. 61–68.

13. The Japanese costs are for a higher-capacity rail line in hilly terrain, however, and may also include costs for land acquisition; telephone conversation with Tom Quade of the U.S. Federal Railroad Administration, May 18, 1982, and U.S. Congress, Office of Technology Assessment, *U.S. Passenger Rail Technologies*, pp. 21–23.

14. Telephone conversation with Nick Brand of Amtrak, June 28, 1982. The analyses reported in chapter 11 assumed that 40 percent of the reported average $400,000 operating cost per route mile is actually a function of route mileage, 50 percent is a function of train mileage, and 10 percent a function of passengers carried.

15. The specific annual costs used here include operating expenses of $13.85 per train mile, $160,000 per route mile, and $.59 per passenger carried. Capital expenses of $1,815,464 per route mile and $1,033,566 per train year were estimated by amortizing right-of-way investment over an expected life of 50 years and amortizing the $9 million investment per train over 20 years.

16. The Class I carriers are dominated by Greyhound and Trailways and account for approximately 36 percent of all passengers and 62 percent of all passenger miles carried by intercity buses in scheduled service. National Association of Motor Bus Operators, *Bus Facts, 1981 Edition* (Washington: 1981). The only expense not based on Class I averages is the annual capital cost and depreciation per bus; this cost is calculated directly by assuming a standard

47-passenger intercity bus with an initial price of $150,000, a useful life of 15 years, and no scrap value. The buses are assumed to be available for a maximum of 12 hours per day of service (including turnaround time at terminals but excluding maintenance spares). Average operating speed is assumed to be 45 mph (not including time spent in terminals).

17. Additional traffic can be accommodated on an intercity highway in one of two ways: by tolerating higher levels of congestion, pavement damage, and administrative expenses on the existing highway system or by building and maintaining additional highway capacity so that added traffic will not increase congestion levels. Given economically efficient levels of investment in the highway system, over the long run the costs of these two ways of accommodating additional traffic should be equivalent. The specific highway capacity cost estimates used here for buses are based on a recent government study of the costs of accommodating additional traffic by tolerating added congestion, pavement damage, and administrative costs. For buses these costs vary from 0.60 cents per bus mile on an uncongested rural highway to 11.90 cents per bus mile on a congested urban expressway. Ten percent of all intercity bus mileage is assumed to take place on congested urban roads and 90 percent on relatively uncongested rural roads. See U.S. Department of Transportation, Federal Highway Administration, *Final Report of the Highway Cost Allocation Study* (Washington: Government Printing Office, 1982), app. E.

18. See Elizabeth A. Pinkston, "The Rise and Fall of Bus Regulation," *Regulation* 8 (September–December 1984), pp. 45–52; and James H. Miller, "The New Competitive Order in the Intercity Bus Industry," paper presented before the Transportation and Public Utilities Group of the American Economic Association, San Francisco, 1983.

19. Depreciation related to the passage of time (as opposed to use) was estimated by the authors to be around 7.7 cents per mile. Insurance, property taxes, and registration fees were estimated to add an additional 3.4 cents per mile on the basis of inflation adjusted cost estimates reported in U.S. Federal Highway Administration, *Costs of Owning and Operating Automobiles and Vans*, 1979 (Washington: Government Printing Office, 1980).

20. For a discussion of the criteria for optimal highway investment, see John R. Meyer and José A. Gómez-Ibáñez, *Autos, Transit and Cities* (Cambridge: Harvard University Press, 1981), pp. 189–192.

21. The costs for auto highway capacity were calculated in the same mode as those for bus highway capacity, except that all access mileage as well as 10 percent of intercity line haul mileage is assumed to be on congested urban highways. See note 17 and U.S. Department of Transportation, Federal Highway Administration, *Final Report of the Highway Cost Allocation Study.*

22. As formulated here, auto costs per passenger mile do not vary with the distance or the travel volume between the city-pair in question.

23. Excluding vehicle ownership costs, user-paid costs per line-haul passenger mile amount to 4.45 cents, and full costs are 5.00 cents. Including ownership costs, user-paid costs are 9.36 cents per passenger mile, and full costs are 9.92 cents.

24. The estimates used here are what the Federal Aviation Administration terms the "separable" costs of commercial air carrier users of the federally financed portions of the airport and airway system. These costs conform closely to what economists would regard as marginal costs and charges based on separable costs would cover approximately two-thirds of total federally financed costs. See U.S. Department of Transportation, *Airport and Airway Cost Allocation Study Part I Report: Determination, Allocation and Recovery of System Costs* (Washington: U.S. Department of Transportation, 1973); and Paul F. Dienemann and Armando M. Lago, "User Taxes and Allocations of the United States Airport and Airway System Costs," *Journal of Transport Economics and Policy* 10 (January 1976), esp. p. 36.

Estimates have been prepared for the average separable cost per jet air carrier departure and flight hour. For propeller-driven aircraft, the airport paving/land costs and the enroute air traffic control costs have been assumed at 50 percent of the jet air carrier levels. Terminal air traffic control charges are assumed the same for jets and propeller-driven aircraft.

25. For airlines, airports and terminal and airway navigation systems play the role of "right-of-way," and their costs might be economized by spreading them over high traffic volumes. However, this model calculates airport and airway costs on a per departure and per flight basis so that these components exhibit no economies of traffic volumes.

26. For a brief review of research on the value of travel time, see Herbert Mohring, *Transportation Economics* (Cambridge, Mass.: Ballinger, 1976), pp. 25–36.

27. Although Amtrak's current revenues from passenger fares are less than the full costs of intercity buses systemwide, the levels of fares and subsidies vary in the individual rail markets. Fares in some rail markets come closer to covering their full costs than in others; likewise, Amtrak's pricing strategy is apparently to meet its bus competition in many, but not all, markets.

Appendix B

1. Models were estimated for the 12 major carriers as a group and for each of the 12 carriers individually. The 12 carriers were American, Braniff, Continental, Delta, Eastern, Northwest, Pan American, Republic, TWA, United, USAir, and Western.

2. The source of these data was CAB Form 41, Schedule T-2.

3. See S. Morrison and C. Winston, *The Economic Effects of Airline Deregulation* (Washington: The Brookings Institution, 1986). Using disaggregate data, Morrison and Winston have found that flight frequencies and service quality have improved markedly since deregulation. Thus it appears that the effect of service quality factors would have increased traffic volumes after deregulation, thereby understating the effects on increased profitability.

4. For a discussion of serial correlation and the Cochrane-Orcutt technique, see Robert S. Pindyck and Daniel Rubinfeld, *Econometric Models and Economic Forecasts*, 2nd ed. (New York: McGraw-Hill, 1981), sec. 6.2.

5. The sources of these data were the *Economic Report of the President* for the years 1973 (table C-18), 1974 (table C-18), 1977 (table B-22), 1980 (table B-22), and 1983 (table B-24).

6. The source of these data for 1970, 1971, and 1972 was *Platt's Oil Price Handbook*, and for 1973 through 1982 the source was *The Monthly Energy Review*. These figures were adjusted for inflation using the consumer price index obtained from the *Monthly Labor Review*.

It might be argued that an index of personal transportation costs that included more than just gasoline would be preferred to the price of gasoline as a variable to capture the costs of alternatives to air transportation. Since auto fuel costs are an important component in these indexes, the price of gasoline is highly correlated with most formulations of the cost index for personal transportation and the two alternatives behave similarly in the RPM equations. There are several problems, however, with such an index that make it inferior to the real price of gasoline for the purposes of this analysis. First is that personal transportation indexes typically include the cost of air travel (usually weighted by the relative mode share of air travel). It is preferable not to include the cost of air travel in a variable intended to reflect the cost of the principal alternative to air travel.

The second problem is that the auto cost component includes not only the variable cost of operating the automobile but also fixed costs such as depreciation, insurance, sales tax, and so forth. The decision the RPM model is implicitly trying to capture is whether to make a trip and whether to use air or auto as the primary mode for that trip. A comparison of the variable cost would seem to have the greatest bearing on that decision rather than the fully allocated costs. Put another way, it seems unlikely that decisions to use auto or air for a trip will be a major influence on the level of auto ownership in most households.

7. Using the variable DISCNT may appear less direct than simply using yield (average actual fare per mile) but offers the important advantage of straightforward interpretation of the most important aspect of postderegulation pricing—the increased use of targeted discount fares. The conclusions drawn from the results of a multiplicative (logarithmic) specification, which has the effect of using yield directly, are essentially the same as those drawn from the linear specification using DISCNT presented in the table.

8. For a desciption of the jacknife technique see Potluri Rao and Roger Miller, *Applied Econometrics* (Belmont, Calif.: Wadsworth, 1971), pp. 98–99.

9. The estimating sample includes 2,673 trips made over the 46 most heavily traveled city-pair routes within the continental United States during 1977. The average distance between the 46 city-pairs in the sample was approximately 450 miles. Direct rail service was available on 39 of the routes connecting them, while air and bus service were available on all 46.

10. These data were painstakingly assembled by Alan Grayson for the preparation of his paper, "A Disaggregate Model of Mode Choice in Intercity Travel," *Transportation Research Record* 835 (1981), pp. 36–42. Auto costs are evaluated at $.06 per mile of driving distance plus tolls en route (which average $3.50 per route), measured in 1977 dollars. Income is measured in 1977 dollars, and the income figure applied is that for the household of which the individual reporting data concerning the trip is a member. Household, travel party, and mode characteristics are drawn from the 1977 National Travel Survey, whereas modal travel times, costs, and frequencies were assembled from common carrier schedules, together with highway distances and driving times estimated by hand using assumed routings. Auto departures are arbitrarily assumed to be available every 10 minutes, which amounts to a cumulative frequency of 1,080 per week. Access distances to common carrier terminals were estimated as straight-line distances in miles, whereas auto access distance was arbitrarily set at 0.05 miles for all trips.

11. For a discussion of the relationships among the value of travel time, work enjoyment, and the wage rate, see M. Bruce Johnson, "Travel Time and the Price of Leisure," *Western Economic Journal* 4 (1966), pp. 135–145.

Index